What People Are Saying About
How to Be Like Jesus . . .

"Every so often a book comes along that is an essential read. *How to Be Like Jesus* is one of those rare books. If ever there was a blueprint for successful living, it is this well-researched and compassionately written book. As authors Pat Williams and Jim Denney are quick to point out, the book's title is actually a paradox: No one can really be like Jesus, but it would certainly be to our benefit if we could be. I highly recommend *How to Be Like Jesus* to all who wish to live a life that is an inspiration to their family, friends and coworkers."

—Tim LaHaye
educator, minister and coauthor, *Left Behind* series

"A memorable look at the greatest hero of all—Jesus Christ! No question, Pat Williams' book is destined to be a smash hit."

—Karen Kingsbury
author, *Gideon's Gift* and *One Tuesday Morning*

"Pat Williams has done those inside and outside God's church a favor with his book, *How to Be Like Jesus.* The title itself describes life lived the way it ought to be and the way God meant it to be. The chapter on integrity alone is worth the price of the book. The book is practical in its application, motivational in its message and inspirational page after page. Regardless of your spiritual—or nonspiritual—background, if you want to read a book that will positively and permanently change your life, get it and read it immediately!"

—James Merritt
former president, Southern Baptist Convention

"It is inspiring to see Pat Williams, who is admired by so many, turn our focus on the living, powerful Son of God, at whose name one day every knee shall bow."

—Bill Gothard
president, Institute in Basic Life Principles,
author and international seminar speaker

"A splendidly written, smooth-flowing book, starting with a clear premise based on knowing Jesus, to a triumphant conclusion that, knowing him, we can be like him. With a dramatic telling of the main events of Jesus' life—amplified and illuminated by an intelligent collection of quotes from a host of authorities—*How to Be Like Jesus* is a remarkable and compelling read for Christians and non-Christians alike."

—D. James Kennedy, Ph.D.
senior minister, Coral Ridge Presbyterian Church

"Drawing from the eternal truths of God's Word, Pat Williams, one of the most inspiring and motivational writers of our time, presents the life of Jesus—the perfect man, and a perfect example to everyone who wants to know how to live life in its fullness. You will be greatly blessed!"

—Dr. Bill Bright
founder, Campus Crusade for Christ

"Jesus said it again and again: 'Follow me!' He called ordinary people like you and me to learn from him, follow his example, and pattern our lives after his. In *How to Be Like Jesus,* Pat Williams and Jim Denney explore the life of Jesus in a fresh and compelling way. Some books change the way you think; this book could change the way you live."

—Josh McDowell
author, *More Than a Carpenter* and
Evidence That Demands a Verdict

"Don't miss Pat Williams' newest book, *How to Be Like Jesus.* Kids are looking for positive role models these days, and there is no greater role model than Jesus Christ. He is the ultimate example of what we all wish ourselves to be in our most serious moments."

—Dr. Jerry Falwell
founder and chancellor, Liberty University

"In this exceptional book on history's greatest leader, Pat Williams gives us insight on how to move beyond status, style and symbols into a life of substance and significance. As one of our nation's leading motivational speakers and authors, Pat shares with us his personal secret to success: a connection with the dynamic life and teachings of Jesus. Whether you are building your life, a company or your family, these truths will fortify you to be 'built to last.'"

—Dr. Jay Strack
founder and president, *studentleadership.net*

"If I wanted to be the best basketball player in the world, I would consult with Michael Jordan. If I wanted to be the best golfer in the world, I would consult with Tiger Woods. Because I want to live the most fulfilling life possible, I always consult Jesus Christ. That's what got me excited about this book. My friend Pat shares insights on how to be like the only perfect man ever to walk on Earth—Jesus Christ. In his thorough yet practical style, Pat walks us through the life of Jesus Christ, revealing in each chapter how he handled various situations in life. It is a must-read book."

—Dr. Tony Evans
president, The Urban Alternative and
senior pastor, Oak Cliff Bible Fellowship

"Dramatic, engaging and captivating! Pat Williams puts Jesus of Nazareth into real life, wrapped in readable and doable twenty-first century how-to principles. *How to Be Like Jesus*—savor it, live it and pass it along."

—Howard G. Hendricks
distinguished professor and chairman, Center for Christian
Leadership, Dallas Theological Seminary

"*How to Be Like Jesus* is accurate, informative, inspirational and life changing. I predict it will hit the bestseller lists, but more important, it will hit your heart and impact you forever."

—Dr. Wendell Kempton
missionary statesman and former president,
Association of Baptists for World Evangelism (ABWE)

How to Be Like

Jesus

LESSONS ON FOLLOWING IN HIS FOOTSTEPS

Pat Williams
with Jim Denney

Foreword by Jerry B. Jenkins, coauthor, *Left Behind* series

Faith Communications
Communications
A Division of Health Communications, Inc.®

Deerfield Beach, Florida

www.hci-online.com

Library of Congress Cataloging-in-Publication Data

Cataloging-in-Publication Data is on file with the Library of Congress.

©2003 Pat Williams
ISBN 0-7573-0069-3

Publisher: Health Communications, Inc.
            3201 S.W. 15th Street
            Deerfield Beach, FL 33442-8190

Cover design by Larissa Hise Henoch
Inside book design by Lawna Patterson Oldfield
Inside book formatting by Dawn Von Strolley Grove

To Mr. R. E. Littlejohn, Paul Anderson,
Bobby Malkmus and Bobby Richardson—
four men who invested in my life
when I needed it most.

All Scripture passages have been
paraphrased by the authors.
In some cases, dialogue has
been amplified or invented for the
sake of clarity or dramatic purposes.

CONTENTS

FOREWORD

There has never been a life like that of Jesus.

In *How to Be Like Jesus,* Pat Williams and Jim Denney tell the story of Jesus in a way that will reach your emotions and grip your soul. The authors don't merely *tell* the story. They tell what that story *means.*

In these pages, you will walk alongside Jesus and see him mentoring his disciples, communicating to crowds, reaching out to hurting people, opposing evil and attracting followers. You'll feel the suspense as his footsteps lead him toward the crisis of the cross.

Learn from the Master what it truly means to love and forgive—and to be forgiven. Find out how Jesus conquered temptation and attacks on his integrity.

Want to be a more effective leader? Learn from the greatest leader who ever lived—the leader who assembled a twelve-man team that changed the world. Learn how the key to effective leadership lies not in being a boss, but in being a humble servant.

Do you struggle with grief and loss? Learn from the Man of Sorrows how to grow through trials.

Fill these margins with notes, underline favorite passages and highlight powerful truths.

There is no more significant goal in life than becoming more like Jesus. Here's a book that will speed up your journey.

—Jerry B. Jenkins

CHAPTER ONE

WHO IS JESUS?

It was just before dawn in Jerusalem.

Inside a stone-walled house, in the pre-dawn darkness, a man and a woman lay together. The man was married, but not to this woman. What they did was a violation of the Law. If anyone caught them together . . .

There was a soft sound at the door.

The woman gasped and froze with fear. "There's someone at the door!" she whispered to the man.

The door burst open. The woman screamed. Men entered the room, some old, some young. She knew some of the men. They were pillars of the Jerusalem community, men of power and influence, religious men.

"In the act!" one of the younger men said. "In the very act!" He picked up the woman's cloak and threw it at her.

"Cover yourself," a bearded scribe said disgustedly. "You're coming with us."

A short distance from that scene, a man walked through the narrow streets of Jerusalem toward the Temple Mount. The Temple towered over Jerusalem like a man-made mountain of snow-white marble. The first rays of the sun slanted through the double rows of Corinthian pillars that lined its porches. The looming walls of the House of God shone in the early morning light like molten gold.

The man's name, in his own Aramaic tongue, was Y'shua. But the world would someday know him by the English transliteration of his name—Jesus.

He had spent the night alone on the Mount of Olives, east of the city, praying and gathering his strength after weeks of tiring, relentless opposition from his foes. He had slept beneath the olive trees and arose early, entering the city by the beautiful eastern gate. He climbed the white marble steps and paused to look out over the city of Jerusalem, its earth-colored houses and tidy green gardens spread out before him like an intricate map. Then, he turned his face toward the Temple Mount and felt the warm, golden sun on his back as he crossed the stone pavement toward Solomon's Porch.

Even at this early hour, there were people in the Temple porches. Some had come to worship God. Some had come to hear Jesus speak, for he had been teaching in the Temple courtyard for days. He sat down at the base of a great pillar. People gathered around him, first a few, then a dozen, then several dozen. Jesus began to speak.

He had only been teaching for a few minutes when he was interrupted by shouts at the back of the crowd. The crowd parted. The group of angry men pushed its way forward. They dragged a disheveled, dark-haired woman and shoved her in front of the crowd.

Jesus looked at the woman. She averted her eyes and

pulled her unbound cloak more tightly around her body. Her cheeks burned.

Jesus looked inquiringly at the men.

"Master," said an aging scribe, one of the men who copied and studied the Law of Moses. His brittle voice dripped with sarcasm and loathing. "Master, this woman has been caught in adultery."

"In the very act!" said a younger man, a member of the strict religious sect called the Pharisees.

"According to the Law," the old scribe continued, "Moses commands us to stone such women to death. What do you say should be done with her?"

> *In Jesus we have the holiest man who ever lived, and yet it was the prostitutes and lepers and thieves who adored him.*
> Rebecca Manley Pippert,
> AUTHOR AND SPEAKER

The woman's shoulders shook. She made no attempt to deny the accusation.

Written in the Dust

Jesus looked around at each of the men, as if reading each one's thoughts. His eyes conveyed the probing questions on his mind. *You've brought to me this woman who was caught in the very act of adultery? If that is so, you must have caught the man, too. Where is the man? Under the Law, he is as guilty as she. Why did you bring one and not the other? And how did you happen to catch her in the act? What were you doing at this woman's window?*

And why bring her to me, a traveling preacher? Why not take her to the religious authorities to be judged?

It was obvious what had happened. These scribes and Pharisees had plotted to lay a trap for this woman, and more importantly, for Jesus himself. Jesus understood the trap they had set for him. Under the Law of Moses, the penalty for adultery was death. Yet, Israel was under the boot of Rome, and the Romans had stripped the Jewish religious leaders of the right to impose the death penalty. If Jesus said that the woman should be spared, then the scribes and Pharisees would accuse him of violating the Law of Moses. If Jesus, however, said the woman should be stoned, then he would be in violation of Roman law.

The scribes and Pharisees waited impatiently for his answer.

Jesus stooped down on one knee and began moving his finger in the thin film of dust at his feet. The trembling woman looked at what he was writing, and so did the men.

Centuries later, scholars would ponder the meaning of that moment, wondering what Jesus wrote in the dust. It is a paradox: This is the only recorded instance in which Jesus wrote anything—but the words he wrote were never recorded and remain a mystery to this day.

"Well?" said one of the scribes.

"We asked you a question," snapped a gray-bearded Pharisee.

"What do you say?" demanded the aged scribe who first accused the woman. "Should she be stoned according to the Law?"

Jesus straightened and looked the old scribe in the eye. "Let the one among you who is without sin," he said, "throw the first stone at her." He eyed the scribe for a few moments, then swept the rest of the men with his gaze. Some looked away.

Jesus bent down again and wrote with his finger. He stayed like that for ten seconds, thirty seconds, a minute, just writing, writing, writing in the dust.

He heard the sound of sandal steps on stone. He glanced up. The older men had turned their backs and were walking away. Jesus glanced at some of the younger men who stood watching him, their eyes smoldering, their hands clenching and unclenching at their sides. Soon, they, too, turned and departed.

Finally, there was no one left but Jesus, the woman and the crowd that had been listening before the interruption. Still trembling with fear and flushed with shame, the woman stood with her face in her hands, weeping softly.

Jesus stood. "Woman," he said, "where are your accusers?"

She lifted her eyes and looked around—and she gasped. "They . . . they're all gone!"

"Isn't there anyone left to condemn you?" Jesus asked.

The woman looked at him with wide eyes. In a small voice, she said, "No one, sir."

> No other figure— spiritual, philosophical, political or intellectual— has had a greater impact on human history. To belong to a people that produced Jesus is to share in a distinction of vast dimension and meaning.
> Norman Cousins
> AUTHOR AND MAGAZINE EDITOR

There was a faint smile on the lips of Jesus. "Then I don't condemn you either," he said. "Go on your way."

The woman nodded, clutching her robes tightly about her. "But . . ."

The woman looked up at Jesus with questioning eyes.

"From now on," he said, "do not sin anymore."

The woman nodded, then turned and raced down the Temple steps.

How Can *Anyone* Be Like Jesus?

That story, from the Gospel of John, captures the essence of the man named Jesus. In it we see the full range of his character traits—his love for people, his forgiveness and compassion, his contempt for lies and hypocrisy, his capacity to think and focus, and his ability to outmaneuver his foes. He maintained a perfect balance of gracious forgiveness and absolute righteousness. He offered forgiveness to the woman, a sign of his Deity, but he also commanded her to leave her life of sin.

My goal in this book is to present a clear, accurate and balanced portrait of the flesh-and-blood man named Jesus. Together, you and I will rediscover his story in a new way by blending the accounts of the four gospels into one dramatic narrative. We'll explore the themes of his teachings and the issues of his life. We'll watch him as he taught, ministered, helped, healed, led, suffered, grieved, died and conquered as he rose from the grave. My aim is for Jesus to come alive in our minds and our imaginations so that he becomes real in our lives. Put these words in the mouth of any other man who ever lived, and they sound ludicrous.

Imagine how this world would change if every one of us was a little more like Jesus. Imagine how much more love and forgiveness there would be. Imagine how much more compassion and encouragement there would be. Imagine how many people would be lifted and empowered. Imagine how much evil and oppression would be stopped in its tracks.

As we begin this journey together, there is something we should be clear about: The theme of this book is a logical impossibility. It's a paradox. The title of this book is *How to Be Like Jesus*. Yet, at the same time, we have to acknowledge that *no one can be like Jesus!*

In all of history, there has never been anyone like Jesus. There will never be another like him. No human being— no king, statesman, general, author, scientist, preacher or philosopher—has ever had the impact on society and history that Jesus had. Jesus is unique.

Yet we can *all* be like Jesus. And we all *should* be like Jesus.

He is the most admired man who ever lived. His teachings are the most profound and life-altering words ever spoken. Of all the billions of lives that have ever been lived, his is the most admired, celebrated and worthy of emulation.

Jesus himself called us to imitate his life, to follow in his footsteps. "I am the light of the world," he said. "Whoever follows me will never walk in the dark but will live in the light of life."

You can't be like Jesus, nor can I—yet we all should be like Jesus. It is a paradox—a deep truth wrapped in a contradiction.

Before I started researching this book, I thought I knew Jesus fairly well. But in the process of studying his life and writing this book, I came to understand him in ways I never previously imagined. In these pages, I have tried to clear away preconceptions, misconceptions and stereotypes about Jesus. I have gone to the original source documents, the Gospels of Matthew, Mark, Luke and John, and I have based these insights and observations of Jesus purely on his recorded words and deeds.

In these pages, I don't want anything to come between us and Jesus. I want the purity of his story and his words to come through, so we can learn from his life, understand his words, and build the traits and character qualities of Jesus into our lives. I want the thinking, wisdom, love, humility, courage and goodness of Jesus to drench every page.

> *I know men and I tell you that Jesus Christ is no mere man.*
>
> *Between him and every other person in the world there is no possible term of comparison. Alexander, Caesar, Charlemagne and I have founded empires. But on what did we rest the creations of our genius? Upon force. Jesus Christ founded his empire upon love; and at this hour millions of men would die for him.*
>
> Napoleon Bonaparte
> EMPEROR OF FRANCE

No one can be like Jesus, yet we *all* should be like Jesus.
First, though, we must discover who he really is.
Let's go meet him together.

Meeting Jesus

The Bible does not give us a physical description of Jesus, and perhaps you don't need a detailed description in order to picture him. But it might be helpful for you to know in a general sense what he was like and the first impressions he made on those he met.

First, *Jesus was Jewish.* His features were probably dark—dark brown hair and dark brown eyes. Following the custom of his time, he was bearded and wore shoulder-length hair. Having spent most of his life as a hard-working carpenter in Nazareth, he was probably a physically strong and hard-muscled man. His facial features were most likely strong and lean. In the Gospels, we see that he walked all over Palestine during his three-year ministry, so he was physically fit and accustomed to steady exercise.

Perhaps it is significant that the writers of the Gospels never described the physical appearance of Jesus. It may well be that, in their wisdom, they chose to leave a blank slate in our minds, so that we could sketch in any image of Jesus with which we might identify, regardless of our ethnic, cultural or racial background. Clearly, his physical appearance is not nearly as important and relevant to our lives as his character.

That brings us to the next important feature we notice as we meet Jesus for the first time: Jesus made a powerful first impression. There was something intensely compelling about Jesus, something that impacted people at first glance.

When he began forming his twelve-man team of disciples, he walked along the Lake of Galilee near Capernaum. He came upon two fishermen, Simon (later called Peter) and Andrew. He said, "Follow me, and I will teach you to be fishers of men." They immediately left their boats and nets, and they followed him. A little farther down the shore, Jesus met two more fishermen, James and John. "Follow me," he said. They, too, dropped everything and followed him. A little later, he met a man named Philip from the village of Bethsaida, and he said, "Follow me." Philip followed.

There was something about Jesus that compelled people to believe in him and follow him. Whatever that quality was, it probably had more to do with his personality than with his physical appearance.

One of the fisherman who followed him, John, was so deeply impacted by Jesus that he later wrote that Jesus was the living Word of God—God's personal communication and expression of himself to humanity. Jesus, John said, existed with God from the beginning and became a human being and lived among us, God's expression to us of his own grace and his own truth. You may agree or disagree with John's assessment of Jesus, but one thing is clear: There was something about Jesus that made a profound impact on everyone who met him. Those who knew Jesus best were the most deeply impacted.

The next important feature we should notice when we meet Jesus for the first time is his culture and religious background. Not only was Jesus ethnically and genetically Jewish, he was culturally and religiously Jewish. He was steeped in the Scriptures of the Jewish faith.

In the very next moment, however, we notice something paradoxical about Jesus: He easily transcended his own Jewishness. He was a truly universal human being, and his appeal crosses all lines of culture, race and ethnicity. For example, if you visit the Convent of Santa Maria delle Grazie, in Milan, you can see a magnificent fresco by Leonardo da Vinci, *The Last Supper,* in which Jesus and his disciples are depicted as twelve white Europeans sitting at a long table. If you visit the pastor's office at the Sixth Avenue Baptist Church in Birmingham, Alabama, you'll see a different painting also called *The Last Supper.* It is a virtual duplicate of da Vinci's fresco, only Jesus and his disciples are depicted as black Africans.

Which is the more accurate depiction? Neither! They are equally fitting and accurate representations of the person of Jesus of Nazareth. Jesus and his disciples were neither black nor white, but Jewish, yet Jesus himself transcended racial and cultural barriers. Whether we

> *The charm of his personality has sent its rays all over the world, and infused countless human hearts with the spirit of love and self-sacrifice. . . .*
>
> *Yet the roots of the life and thought of Jesus lie entirely in Jewish soil.*
> Paul Goodman
> AUTHOR

are black or white or brown or any other shade, Jesus identifies with us, and we can identify with him.

Strong in Body, Wise in Mind

Jesus was born in humble circumstances. Though his birthplace is usually depicted as a stable in Bethlehem, the gospel accounts do not mention a stable. Some houses in those days were built with an upper room over a stable-like lower room, where animals were sheltered to prevent their theft. So Jesus may have been born in one of these lower rooms where the animals were kept. It is also possible that he was born out in the street, and the manger where Mary placed him was outside, under the sky.

All we know for sure is that Jesus was born under humble circumstances in the town of Bethlehem and he was raised in the Galilean village of Nazareth, in the northern part of Israel.

Joseph and Mary took the infant Jesus to Jerusalem and presented him to the Lord in a ceremony at the Temple. There was a godly man named Simeon who lived in Jerusalem, and God had revealed to this man that he would not die until he saw the Messiah, the savior of Israel, with his own eyes. When Joseph and Mary brought the infant Jesus into the Temple, Simeon was there, having been led there by the Spirit of God. When Simeon saw the infant Jesus, he took the baby in his arms and praised God, saying, "At last, Lord, you can let me die in peace! With my own eyes I have seen your salvation!"

Then Simeon turned to Mary and said, "This child will make many fall and many rise in Israel. He will raise a standard that many will attack, and he will reveal the secret thoughts of many hearts. And as for you, his mother, a sword will pierce your own soul." This was a shocking, troubling statement for Mary to hear, and thirty-three years later, when she stood at the foot of a Roman cross and watched her son suffer and die, those words were proven true.

When the purification ritual was complete, Joseph and Mary took the infant Jesus back to Nazareth. We are told little about the childhood of Jesus, though we do know that as he grew up, he became physically strong and full of wisdom. His adoptive father, Joseph, was a tradesman—a carpenter, which included stonemasonry—and Jesus learned the same trade.

At the age of twelve, Jesus went with Mary and Joseph to Jerusalem for the annual Passover festival. When the celebration was over, Mary and Joseph started back home to Nazareth. They assumed that the boy Jesus was somewhere among the group of friends and relatives who were on the same road, headed for home. But Jesus wasn't with them. When Joseph and Mary realized this, they were frantic. They looked for him among their friends and relatives, but no one had seen Jesus. So Mary and Joseph turned back and searched for him in Jerusalem.

After three days of worry and frustration, they went to the Temple to pray that God would bring him safely to them. Then, as they walked through the Temple courtyard, they saw Jesus. He was sitting among the scribes and teachers of the Law, listening to them and asking questions. The learned scholars were astonished at the boy's ability to understand the Jewish Scriptures. He not only asked insightful questions, but he also gave answers that showed an incredible depth of knowledge.

When Mary and Joseph saw the boy Jesus sitting among the great religious scholars in the Temple, they were astonished. "Son," Mary said sharply, "why have you treated us this way? Your father and I have been frantic with worry! We've been searching everywhere for you!"

"Why were you searching for me?" Jesus asked. "Don't you know that I must be in my Father's house?"

It was not a rebellious or flippant reply. The boy was honestly surprised that Joseph and Mary didn't know where to find him. He was saying, in effect, "You shouldn't have had to search for me. You should have known all along that the Temple, the House of God my Father, is where I would be."

Jesus obediently returned home to Nazareth with Mary and Joseph. His mother pondered and treasured this incident in her heart, no doubt along with many other astonishing incidents involving her exceptional son.

We know very little about Jesus' life from the time he was twelve until he began his public ministry at age thirty. What we do know about those eighteen years is contained in a single verse of the Gospel of Luke: "And Jesus increased in wisdom, in stature and in a favorable relationship with God and with other people."

In other words, Jesus grew in wisdom—in his mental

capacity, in learning and in his knowledge of the Jewish Scriptures. He grew in *stature*—he grew tall, physically strong and sinewy because of hard work, exercise, good nutrition and play. He grew in *favorable relationships with people*—he developed his social skills and people skills, and he had many friends. And he grew in a *favorable relationship with God*—he developed his spiritual life through prayer and faith.

> *I am a Jew, but I am enthralled by the luminous figure of the Nazarene. . . .*
> *No one can read the Gospels without feeling the actual presence of Jesus. His personality pulsates in every word. No myth is filled with such life.*
>
> Albert Einstein
> PHYSICIST

So while little is known of those early years of his life, we do know that they were crucial years of growth and preparation for what was to come. In all, Jesus invested three decades preparing himself for three years that would change the world.

I . . . Miss . . . Him

Throughout the Gospels, Jesus is referred to as "the Son of God." Jesus also referred to himself as "the Son of Man." People often assume that he used this term, "the Son of Man," as a way of identifying with the humanity of everyone around him.

To understand what he meant, though, we have to understand the Jewishness of Jesus and realize that he was borrowing a phrase from the Book of Daniel in the Old Testament. There, the prophet Daniel described the coming Messiah with these words: "In my vision at night I looked, and there before me was one like a Son of Man, coming with the clouds of heaven." When Jesus used that phrase, "the Son of Man," everyone around him knew that he was identifying himself as the long-awaited Messiah.

The purpose of this book is *not* to argue for a particular theological viewpoint. Instead, I have attempted to present Jesus exactly as he is presented in the New Testament source documents, the Gospels of Matthew, Mark, Luke and John. Even if you do not believe the claims of Jesus, I think you will still find this journey through the life of Jesus to be worthwhile and satisfying.

Let me tell you about a man who concluded that Jesus was *not* the Son of God—yet he still believed that everyone should be like Jesus. This man's name was Charles Templeton.

Charles Templeton was one of the most engaging, articulate and multitalented people who ever lived. He had a profound spiritual experience while he was living in Toronto, Canada, working as a cartoonist for *The Globe.* It happened at three in the morning. "Involuntarily, I began to pray," he later recalled. "My face upturned, tears streaming. The only words I could find were, 'Lord, come down. Come down. Come down. . . .' An ineffable warmth began to suffuse every corpuscle. It seemed that a light had turned on in my chest, and its fire had cleansed me."

Soon after, Charles Templeton became a preacher in the

Nazarene denomination. He used his skills as a cartoonist to illustrate his talks, drawing with chalk on a large easel in front of crowds at testimony meetings and youth rallies. Soon, he was preaching before huge crowds of as many as fifty thousand people. He became a close friend of Billy Graham, and he, Graham and Torrey Johnson cofounded an organization called Youth for Christ. Templeton, an eloquent and dramatic speaker, toured and spoke before great crowds throughout North America and Europe.

In time, however, Charles Templeton began to doubt his own experience with God. He read Thomas Paine's *The Age of Reason,* which challenged his belief in Jesus. He decided to study theology at Princeton University, and he graduated and became an ordained Presbyterian minister. However, he was a minister without a faith to believe in. "My mind," he later recalled, "was at war with my spirit."

He soon left the ministry and turned to writing, hosting network television interview shows, acting and even inventing. He eventually became an editor with the *Toronto Star* and the Canadian news magazine *Maclean's.* In 1996, Charles Templeton published a memoir on the death of his faith, *Farewell to God: My Reasons for Rejecting the Christian Faith.*

Soon after that book was published, Christian writer Lee Strobel met Templeton in his apartment for an interview. That interview became the centerpiece of Strobel's book, *The Case for Faith.* During their conversation, Strobel asked his questions, listened to the answers and took notes. Templeton, who was eighty years old by this time, made a strong case for his atheist views. Finally, Strobel asked Templeton, "What is your opinion of Jesus at this stage of your life?"

Strobel noted that upon hearing the name of Jesus, Templeton's "body language softened" and his voice became "melancholy and reflective." Templeton then began to describe his view of the man Jesus. "He was the greatest human being who has ever lived," Templeton said. "He was a moral genius. His ethical sense was unique. He was the intrinsically wisest person that I've ever encountered in my life or in my reading. His commitment was total and led to his own death, much to the detriment of the world."

Moved by Templeton's change of tone, Strobel quietly said, "You sound like you really care about him."

"Well, yes," Templeton said. "He's the most important thing in my life. I . . . I . . . I adore him. . . . Everything good I know, everything decent I know, everything pure I know, I learned from Jesus."

And then, Templeton's voice began to waver. "I . . . miss . . . him!" he said. With that, he began to cry. Seconds later, the old man regained control of his emotions, brushed away the tears and said with a wave of his hand, "Enough of that." It wasn't clear to Strobel if he was saying enough tears or enough questions about Jesus.

Charles Templeton had once called himself a Christian, but he had become an ardent atheist. Yet, even as an atheist, he admired the life, the words, the integrity, the wisdom and the love of Jesus. In the end, it seemed that the greatest loss of his life was the loss of Jesus: "I . . . miss . . . him!" Five years after his interview with Lee Strobel, on June 7, 2001, Charles Bradley Templeton died of complications related to Alzheimer's disease. Before he died, one of the last people to visit him was his old friend, Billy Graham.

I want you to know from the outset that Jesus is the most important thing in my life. He is the source of everything I know that is good, decent and pure. The ultimate goal of my life is to be like Jesus. Like Charles Templeton, I admire Jesus. Unlike Charles Templeton, I also believe in him.

I didn't write this book to persuade you to be a Christian, but at the same time, I don't want you to reach the end of your life and say with sadness and regret, "I . . . miss . . . him!" So I will simply tell you the story of Jesus, the story of a man whom even one of the world's most devoted atheists couldn't help but admire.

No one can be like Jesus. Yet we can *all* be like Jesus. The world would be profoundly richer, more loving and more full of justice and happiness if everyone in the world would be like Jesus.

So put on your sandals and come with me as we walk alongside the greatest human being who has ever lived. Let's discover together this unique man, Jesus of Nazareth.

CHAPTER TWO

HOW TO HAVE INTEGRITY LIKE JESUS

Jesus was about thirty years old when he left his home in Nazareth. From this point forward, none of the four Gospels mentions Joseph, his adoptive father, so it is likely that Joseph was dead by this time. However, his mother, Mary, appears at several significant points in the story of Jesus.

From Nazareth, Jesus went to the place beside the Jordan River where a man, John the Baptist, was preaching (this was not the same John as the disciple who wrote the Gospel of John). Finding John the Baptist preaching and baptizing people, Jesus called to him and said, "I want you to baptize me."

"Baptize *you!*" John said. "It is *you* who should baptize *me!*"

"Do as I ask," Jesus said. "It is good for us to do this in order for all righteousness to be fulfilled."

John agreed. Together, they stepped into the water of the Jordan, and John plunged Jesus in so that the waters covered him. As Jesus came up out of the water with a prayer on his lips, the sky opened and John saw the Spirit of God, which had the appearance of a white dove, descending upon Jesus. Then, John heard a voice. "This is my dearly loved Son. I am very pleased with him."

John was a second cousin of Jesus. His mother, Elizabeth, and Jesus' mother were first cousins. John was six months older than Jesus. Some time after baptizing Jesus, John told a crowd of people, "I have seen the Spirit come down and rest upon him. I tell you publicly, he is God's son."

Immediately after Jesus was baptized by John, God's Spirit led Jesus out into a desert region, probably the wilderness of Judea, west of the Dead Sea. If you visit that wilderness today, you find a desert that is parched, forbidding and littered with rounded stones that resemble loaves of bread. It was there, in that wilderness, that the integrity of Jesus was first tested.

The word *integrity* comes from the Latin *integer,* meaning wholeness or completeness. Integrity is the quality of having the reality of one's life match the claims of one's words. In contemporary terms, it means walking the talk even when we are hurting and needy, even when we are under pressure and even when no one else is looking.

> *I believe Jesus had to go into the wilderness to find out who he was—that a wilderness experience was as much a part of his shaping and destiny as it is of yours and mine.*
> Laurie Beth Jones
> AUTHOR AND SPEAKER

At the very beginning of his ministry, Jesus went into the wilderness, into the most extreme situation imaginable. There he spent forty lonely days with no food to eat and no company except the wild animals.

The Gospel accounts tell us that at the end of that forty-day period, when he was hungry and weak, the devil came to test Jesus.

The First Test of Integrity: The Temptation of the Easy Path

Many people today do not believe in a real, personal devil, just as many do not believe in a real, personal God. Perhaps this is because some people picture unbelievable caricatures and stereotypes when they hear the words "God" and "devil." To some, the word "God" suggests an old man with a white beard sitting on a throne among the clouds, and the word "devil" or "Satan" conjures up the image of a man wearing red tights with horns on his head and brandishing a pitchfork. Neither of these images is found in the Bible, of course, but they are common stereotypes in our culture.

The Bible presents Satan as an intelligent but malignant spirit who orchestrates evil events and evil systems behind the scenes of the world. Psychiatrist M. Scott Peck, the author of such books as *The Road Less Traveled* and *People of the Lie,* came to the conclusion that the devil is a real, living entity after he met that entity face-to-face:

> Having come over the years to a belief in the reality of benign Spirit, or God, and a belief in the reality of human

evil, I was left facing an obvious intellectual question: Is there such a thing as evil spirit? Namely, the devil? I thought not. . . . I did not think the devil existed. Still, priding myself on being an open-minded scientist, I felt I had to examine the evidence.[1]

So Peck began to seek out evidence for the existence of the devil. He contacted other psychiatrists and sought referrals of cases that appeared to involve the presence of devils or demons. In *People of the Lie,* he said that the first two cases that were referred to him clearly involved "standard psychiatric disorders," not demons. But he became convinced that the third case he encountered involved "genuine possession" by a malignant spirit. He concluded, "I now know Satan is real. I have met it."

It was this kind of spirit, the devil, who came to Jesus in the desert, according to the Gospel accounts. Jesus was famished after forty days of fasting. He was weak. He was lonely. He was probably emotionally drained. He had reached the lowest point in his thirty years of life on Earth, and it was at that moment that the devil came to test him. In this encounter, we witness Jesus as he faced the first great test of his integrity.

"If you are the Son of God," the devil said, "tell these stones to become loaves of bread."

"I will not," Jesus answered. "It is written in the Scriptures: 'Human beings cannot live by bread alone, but must live by every word that comes from God's own mouth.'"

---

[1] M. Scott Peck, *People of the Lie* (New York: Simon & Schuster, 1983), 182.

How did Satan test Jesus? By tempting him to doubt what God himself had said of him.

Remember that at the baptism of Jesus, the voice of God had said, "This is my dearly loved Son. I am very pleased with him." But then, Jesus went out into the desert to be tested, and in the first test, the voice of Satan subtly questioned the identity of Jesus. "*If* you are the Son of God . . ." The devil's attack was sly and indirect and struck Jesus at a point when he felt weak, hungry and totally alone. It was an attempt to goad Jesus into performing a miraculous work of not only alleviating his hunger but also proving himself to the devil.

Jesus replied that it wasn't *physical* food he most needed at that moment. What he needed was *spiritual* sustenance, the kind of "food" that only comes from God's own mouth, the very words of God himself. Jesus was saying, in effect, "I don't rely on short-lived things like food to sustain my life. I rely on God himself. I don't have to turn stones into bread. My bread is the love of God, and God's own affirmation of my identity in him. You tried to plant doubt in my mind about who I am in God's sight, but I refuse to doubt what God has said about me. I am his beloved Son, and I don't have to prove anything to you."

Temptation comes to us in many forms. Obviously, you and I will never be tempted to turn stones into bread. But we are often tempted to doubt our own identity as people made in God's image, as people who live according to the moral and ethical framework God has given us with his words. We are tempted to take the easy path of self-gratification instead of the rugged road of growing the soul.

We may be tempted to gain some short-term advantage by cheating or lying in our business dealings, by cutting ethical corners in order to turn stones into bread that we haven't earned. We may be tempted to cheat on our taxes and lie to the government. We may be tempted to cheat on relationships and lie to our families.

There are many ways we are tempted, and those temptations often come to us, as they did to Jesus, when we are at our weakest point, when we are needy and hurting and hungry for something. Temptation attacks us at our vulnerable points, and we think, *It would be so easy to just take this thing, or tell this lie, and I would gain the advantage I need—and no one would ever know.*

When we yield to temptation, however, we ignore what God has said about us and we reject our identity as his creations, his children. When we are tempted, we need to reach for *spiritual* sustenance instead of *physical* sustenance. To be like Jesus, we must choose the rugged road of faith in God over the easy path of self-gratification. We need to remember that Jesus faced temptation, he conquered it and he fed

> *God is better served in resisting a temptation to evil than in many formal prayers.*
>
> William Penn
> FOUNDER OF THE
> PENNSYLVANIA COLONY

himself on the words of God, not on short-lived bread made out of stone.

The Second Test of Integrity: The Temptation to Recklessness

For the second test of Jesus, the devil took him out of the desert and up to the city of Jerusalem. There, the devil set Jesus on the highest ledge of the Temple —the towering House of God built by King Herod the Great—where Jesus had once questioned the religious scholars when he was twelve years old and where he would later write with his finger in the dust and spare an adulterous woman from a death sentence. Some scholars believe that the place where Jesus stood was at the top of Herod's royal portico on the southeast corner of the Temple. It not only towered over the city walls, but rose 450 feet above the floor of the Kidron Valley, offering a breathtaking view all the way to the horizon.

As Jesus stood on this high place atop the Temple Mount, the devil said to him, "If you are the Son of God, jump— throw yourself down. It is written in the Scriptures: 'God will command his angels to protect you, and they will support you on their hands, so that you won't even strike your foot against a stone.'" The devil was quoting from the Psalms; he knew the Bible well.

Jesus, however, knew better than to be taken in by a fast-talking, Bible-quoting fraud. Jesus answered the devil's Scripture with Scripture of his own: "It is also written: 'Do not put the Lord your God to the test.'" In other words, don't conduct reckless experiments with God. Don't act foolishly and carelessly and expect God to get you out of a jam.

Actions have consequences. If you break God's laws, then you'd better be prepared to pay the fine. This doesn't mean that God wants to hurt you or get even with you for breaking his laws. It means that God has created an orderly universe that operates on certain principles, and he has told us how to live orderly and productive lives based on those principles. If we choose to overstep God's boundaries, then there are natural consequences that follow.

This is certainly true of God's physical laws. If we defy the law of gravity by leaping off a tall building, there will be certain natural consequences, and we all accept this.

The same holds true for God's moral laws. If we break God's moral laws by, say, lying or stealing or expressing our sexuality in inappropriate ways, then we create pain, disorder and damaged relationships. God's moral laws are just as natural as God's physical laws, and they operate in the same cause-and-effect way. Behaving recklessly by defying God's moral laws is the moral equivalent of defying the law of gravity. When you crash and hit bottom—either morally or physically—it is not because God wanted to hurt you. It is simply the way the universe works.

So Jesus rejected the temptation to act recklessly, and once more he resisted the devilishly subtle challenge to his credentials: "*If*

> *When we are troubled with temptation and evil thoughts, then we see clearly the great need we have of God, since without him we can do nothing good. No one is so good that he is immune to temptation; we will never in this life be entirely free of it.*
>
> Thomas à Kempis
> GERMAN MONK

you are the Son of God . . ." Jesus saw through Satan's twisted use of Scripture and responded with Scripture of his own, placing the whole moral contest between the devil and himself into a proper perspective. "Yes," Jesus said, in effect, "God does offer us protection, but he will not protect us from foolish, reckless self-endangerment. Your suggestion that I take a flying leap from the top of the Temple was a nice try, but I'm not buying it."

If we want to be like Jesus, we need to live prudently by exercising sound judgment and rejecting recklessness. We need to respect the physical laws of the universe and the moral laws of God.

The Third Test of Integrity: The Temptation of Power

Next, the Gospels tell us that Satan took Jesus to a mountain peak—though how the devil accomplished this we are not told. From that high place, he showed Jesus all the kingdoms of the world in their power and splendor. This time, the devil didn't bother challenging the identity and credentials of Jesus. He didn't try to decoy and goad Jesus with that same sly line, "*If* you are the Son of God . . ." This time, the devil threw aside all subtlety. Showing Jesus the worldly power that he controlled as the invisible prince of evil, Satan said, "I will give all of these kingdoms to you—if you will bow down and worship me."

Here, Satan tipped his hand. He is the malignant spirit that works behind the scenes and events of this world. He is the invisible, diseased will behind racism, hate, intolerance, slavery, genocide, oppression, war, and terror. He rules the kingdoms of greed and power, the kingdoms of splendid palaces and mighty armies, and the kingdoms that enslave minds, souls and bodies around the world. His claim to this kingdom was not refuted by Jesus.

Satan offered Jesus an easy road to become the ruler over all the splendid and powerful kingdoms of the world. Of course, there were strings attached. All Jesus had to do was bow down and worship the prince of evil. Jesus could have had a kingdom without having to go to the cross. He could have had power over millions by simply bowing down and acknowledging the power of the prince of evil.

Instead, Jesus answered, "Get away from me, Satan! Leave me alone! For it is written in the Scriptures: 'Worship the Lord your God, and serve him only.'" At that moment, the devil left Jesus, and angels came and saw to his physical and spiritual needs.

Jesus rejected the temptation that was put to him. He refused the power that was offered him. He chose instead to persevere in his mission. Three years later, just hours before the Crucifixion, Jesus stood before a Roman governor named Pilate, and he said to Pilate, "My kingdom is not of this world."

That, in essence, is also what Jesus told a spirit ruler named Satan. "You can keep your kingdoms and all their splendor. You can keep your worldly power. My kingdom is not of this world. Go away! I will serve God only."

If we want to be like Jesus, we need to reject the easy path to power. We must resist the temptation to sell out to "the dark side" in order to gain power, status, advantage or control over others. Yes, it is right and good to be people of influence, people who lead, but we should exercise leadership in the right way, for the right reasons, in humility and never for the sake of power, status or ego.

Satan offers power and pride, but, as we will see in chapter 13, Jesus demonstrates a radically *new* form of leadership that is about humility, not pride; about service to God, people and society, not power. If we want to be like Jesus, we will reject the devil's bargain and follow the example Jesus gave us.

The conclusion of this account gives us an insight into just how intense and exhausting the temptation of Jesus was. After the devil left him, angels came and ministered to him. The only other time the Gospels tell us that angels came and ministered to the spiritual and physical needs of Jesus was when he was praying in the Garden of Gethsemane just before he was arrested and taken to be crucified. On that occasion, his agony was so great that he "sweated great drops of blood."

After forty days of fasting, forty days of isolation and loneliness, Jesus went through a time of testing and temptation that is beyond our ability to comprehend. Jesus passed the test, and he did so in large part by knowing and repeating the Scriptures. He had prepared his mind and his soul by steeping himself for years in the words that

> *As Jesus armed himself with "the sword of the Spirit, which is the word of God," so must we. Armed with the puny sword of reason, we stand impotent before an archfiend who has studied us thoroughly and is intimately acquainted with all of our vulnerabilities. Armed with the sword of the Spirit, however, we are a terror to Satan and can stand strong in the face of his fiercest temptations.*
>
> Hank Hanegraaff
> AUTHOR AND RADIO HOST

God himself had spoken. And when he was tested and tempted, Jesus maintained his integrity.

You and I face the same adversaries Jesus faced, and sometimes we find ourselves in wilderness experiences like his. We become weak, hungry, exhausted and vulnerable to attack and temptation. But we want to be like Jesus. So when tests and temptation come, we must look to his example, and we, too, must maintain our integrity.

How to Maintain Your Integrity

This incident from the life of Jesus contains a wealth of insight we can apply to our own struggles with temptation, so that we can maintain our integrity like Jesus. Some of those insights are:

1. *Keep your guard up at all times.* Remember that temptation rarely comes to us as an obvious assault, but usually as a sly subterfuge, a deceptive ploy. Instead of saying, "Do something evil," temptation says, "It

wouldn't be so wrong, would it?" Temptation makes things that are wrong look attractive; it makes destructive behavior seem acceptable, even noble. Temptation has won at the moment you start rationalizing, making excuses or relaxing your moral and ethical standards. Be like Jesus—keep your guard up.

2. *Be especially careful about temptation when you are at an emotional or physical low point.* The devil attacked Jesus at exactly such a time in his life. You know that when you are feeling discouraged, needy, lonely, abandoned and dejected, it is easy to reach for something to fill that emptiness or relieve that pain. It is easy to rationalize the irrational and justify the unjustifiable. When you are depleted or exhausted or feeling sorry for yourself, don't yield to temptation. Be like Jesus—stand your ground.

3. *Set clear boundaries and limits for yourself ahead of time.* You cannot make good moral and ethical decisions under the pressure of temptation. You must make a deliberate decision about the way you will live your life *before* temptation comes, and then it will be easier for you to stick to a decision you have already made. We see this principle in the life of Jesus. When temptation came to Jesus, he did not have to sort through a series of morally ambiguous options. He clearly knew who he was and what he believed in, and he had a well-thought-out answer ready for every attack.

4. *Avoid situations where you know you are prone to*

temptation. If a certain place, a certain activity or certain people have often been your downfall in the past, then you must make sure you avoid those situations in the future. Don't flirt with temptation—shun it completely! Turn around and run away from it. Be like Jesus—don't entertain temptation for an instant!

5. *Fill your life with good things and good people so there is less room for temptation.* We are more prone to temptation when we are feeling empty and unfulfilled. So the answer is to fill our lives with good things, meaningful activities and healthy relationships with positive people so that temptation won't be able to gain a toehold in our lives. Saying "yes" to good things helps you say "no" to the bad.

6. *When tempted, pray.* Ask God for help in maintaining your integrity. When you feel you lack the strength within yourself to resist temptation, rely on God's strength. Also, consider asking other trusted friends to pray for you and hold you accountable.

7. *Recite Scripture.* Jesus used Scripture to combat temptation. Three times he was tempted, and three times his response was, "It is written. . . ." If you study and memorize the Scriptures, you will be armed in advance against the enemy of your integrity. So be like Jesus—fight temptation with Scripture.

8. *When you fail, learn and grow from your failure.* Jesus, of course, didn't fail when he was tempted in

the wilderness, but in the life of Jesus, we see him dealing again and again with people who did fail— with Peter and the other disciples, with the woman caught in adultery in chapter 1, with a Samaritan woman in chapter 5, and with many others. In each instance, his message was the same: Learn from your moral failure, stop sinning and straying, put your failures behind you, and walk in a new direction.

This same principle is true for your life and mine. So make a commitment to build safeguards into your life that will protect your integrity. If you make a genuine commitment based on a serious desire to change, then that commitment is called *repentance.* When you repent, confess your moral failure to God and ask for his forgiveness. If your area of temptation involves serious issues, such as substance abuse or sexual addiction, consider joining a support group where other people who struggle with the same issues will understand and hold you accountable in a firm but compassionate way.

There is great power in a lifestyle of integrity. When people live out what they say they believe, the world is changed for the better. If we want to be like Jesus, we must be people of integrity. We must learn how to maintain our integrity and resist temptation in even the most extreme situations.

The future is always uncertain, but there is one thing we can be sure of: We *will* go through times of testing and temptation, just as Jesus did. We *will* be tempted to take the easy path to possessions or self-gratification or power. We *will* be tempted to recklessly defy God's laws, which exist to protect us, not to hurt us.

No matter what temptations we face, we know that Jesus has endured his own time of wilderness testing. In his testing and temptation, he is able to identify with us, and we are able to identify with him. We can be like Jesus if we keep our integrity as he kept his.

CHAPTER THREE

HOW TO OBEY LIKE JESUS

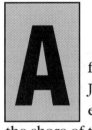**A**fter facing his temptation in the wilderness, Jesus returned to the Galilee region in northern Israel. Walking along the Jordan River and the shore of the Lake of Galilee, he called his first few disciples—a core group that would eventually become the Twelve. Those first disciples were Andrew and his brother Simon Peter, James and his brother John, plus Philip and Nathanael. Accompanied by these men, Jesus left the shores of the Lake of Galilee and walked west to the village of Cana, which was about eight miles north of his hometown, Nazareth.

There was a wedding celebration in Cana, and Jesus was invited. His mother was also at the wedding. We don't know who was getting married, but we do know that it was a huge party that drew people from all around the region of Galilee. In that culture, a wedding celebration was a huge feast, with lavish food and drink, laughter and dancing, joy and jubilation. The host of the wedding party was the bridegroom. If anything went wrong at a wedding celebration, the bridegroom would be disgraced.

As we join the celebration in Cana, we see that something

has gone terribly wrong. The wine has run out! How could this have happened?

It may have happened because Jesus was at the wedding.

When John the Baptist baptized Jesus, he introduced him to all the people as the Son of God, the Messiah who had been promised in the ancient Jewish Scriptures. Even though Jesus had not yet performed a miracle, the people all around the region of Galilee were buzzing with gossip and excitement about the man from Nazareth: Was he truly the Messiah, as John the Baptist claimed? Would he announce his messianic kingdom and the end of Roman oppression? Would he perform a miracle to establish his credentials?

> *Jesus takes water—an inorganic, non-living, commonplace substance—and without a word, without a gesture, without any laying on of hands, in utter simplicity, he causes the water to become wine, an organic liquid, a product of fermentation, belonging to the realm of life. Thus he demonstrated his marvelous ability to master the processes of nature.*
>
> Ray C. Stedman
> PASTOR AND AUTHOR

Rampant curiosity about Jesus may have swelled the guest list by two or three times the planned number. The bridegroom *thought* he had provided enough food and wine to feed all his guests, with plenty left over. Instead, the wine ran out.

Water of Renewal, Wine of Life

When Mary, the mother of Jesus, heard of the shortage of wine, she was concerned that the bridegroom would be disgraced. So Mary went to Jesus, took him aside and said, "Son, they have no more wine."

"Dear woman," Jesus said, "why are you telling me about this problem? My time has not yet come."

Take note of his last statement. Throughout the story of Jesus, he says again and again, "My time has not yet come." His time for what? In a later chapter, we will discover exactly what he meant, and why this is such a significant statement.

In a gentle way and with respectful words, Jesus tried to avoid getting involved in the matter of the wine shortage. Notice how he addressed Mary: "Dear woman." This is a term of affection. Jesus politely and lovingly tried to deflect his mother's request.

But Mary would not be deflected.

What did she think Jesus could do about the wine shortage? Did she expect him to perform a miracle? The Gospel account does not tell us, but clearly she expected her son to solve the problem. She turned to the servants of the bridegroom and pointed to her son. "Do whatever he tells you," she said.

The servants looked to Jesus and awaited his command.

Not far away were six stone water jars. These jars were to be used for the ceremonial washing of hands before and after the meal. They were huge jars, each holding twenty to thirty gallons. Jesus acknowledged the stone jars and said to the servants, "Fill the jars with water."

The servants did as Jesus directed, filling the jars brimfull with clear water.

Next, Jesus said to the servants, "Put in your cups and draw from the jars, and take it to the master of the banquet." The master of the banquet was not unlike the best man at a wedding today. It was his job to make the toasts to the bride and groom and to make sure everyone was enjoying themselves at the party.

The servants took the water to the master of the banquet, and he tasted it—but it was no longer water. It was *wine*.

The master of the banquet had no idea where the wine came from. Only the servants knew. So the master of the banquet took the bridegroom aside, held up the cup of sparkling wine and said, "Everyone else brings out the strong, choice wine first, then hands out the weak, inferior wine when the guests are full and not as discerning in their taste, so they won't know the difference. But you, my friend, you have saved the best wine until now!"

This was the first miracle Jesus ever performed, and he performed it quietly, reluctantly, almost shyly. Jesus was content to let the bridegroom get all the credit for supplying a magnificent vintage to his guests. No one knew what Jesus had done except the servants, the disciples, Mary and Jesus himself. The disciples were so profoundly struck by what they saw Jesus do that they became completely convinced that they were following the promised

Messiah. Any lingering doubts they might have had disappeared in that instant.

There may be significant symbolism in the jars of water. Those jars were special containers consecrated for a specific purpose—ceremonial cleansing. Jesus, of course, had only recently been baptized, and baptism is symbolic of cleansing, renewal and new life. Among Christians, wine is also a significant symbol. In the Sacrament, wine symbolizes the Blood of Christ that flowed down the cross so that we might find forgiveness and live forever. Jesus took the cleansing waters of renewal and transformed them into wine, the symbolic lifeblood of eternal life.

> *Through the obedience of the one [Jesus], the many will be made righteous.*
> Romans 5:19

The Meaning of Obedience

This story brims with powerful truths that are applicable to our lives.

First, we gain some insight into the character of Jesus. He loved celebrations. He enjoyed parties. Jesus was enjoying himself at the wedding in Cana, where his mother Mary imposed on him. There are additional incidences in the story of Jesus that show his light, joyful and exuberant side.

Second, we see that Jesus was obedient and respectful to his mother. Obviously, Jesus, as a thirty-year-old man, was not obligated to obey his mother. Jesus, though, was steeped in the Jewish Scriptures and traditions, including the Ten Commandments. Jesus was obedient first and foremost to the law of God, and he knew that the fifth commandment is:"Honor your father and your mother."

Mary had created a situation that restricted Jesus' options. She told Jesus, "Son, they have no more wine." When Jesus gently tried to remove himself from the situation, Mary turned to the servants and told them,"Do whatever he tells you." At that point, Jesus was stuck. His own mother had boxed him in. He was faced with a dilemma: He could either refuse his mother and embarrass her in front of the servants, the disciples and any others who were watching—or he could obey the fifth commandment and find a way to honor his mother. He chose the path of honoring his mother and obeying the Scriptures.

What was Mary's motive in forcing this situation on her son? She probably hoped that Jesus would perform a spectacular, show-stopping miracle. Perhaps she thought that since there was a huge crowd gathered at this wedding, this would be the perfect time and place for her son to publicly reveal himself as the promised Messiah. After all, she had been convinced of his identity ever since his miraculous birth.

Jesus, however, knew his time had not yet come, so he found a way to solve the wine shortage without creating a spectacle or disgracing his mother. He performed a quiet little miracle with very few witnesses, and he allowed the bridegroom to receive the credit for the wine.

In short, Jesus was obedient. He was obedient to God the

Father, to the Scriptures and even to his mother. Mary's motives may have been good, but her timing was off. Even so, Jesus treated her graciously and respectfully and avoided causing her embarrassment.

Notice that there is another aspect of obedience in this story: the obedience of the servants. Jesus didn't create wine out of nothing. He created wine out of water. He needed the water in order to produce the wine. Jesus told the servants to fetch some water, and they obeyed.

It's important that we see ourselves in this story. We should identify not only with the obedience of Jesus, but with the obedience of the servants. What Jesus said to them, he also says to us in a very real way. "Fill the jars with water."

All around us are empty jars, empty lives and, in fact, a whole world of emptiness. As mere human beings, we can't produce the wine of everlasting life, but we can reach out to people with love, compassion, forgiveness and understanding, and we can begin to fill their lives with water. Jesus will then come along after us and turn that water into wine—into lifeblood and everlasting life. This parched and empty world is longing for a taste of new wine, and we can be a part of the process of touching that need. We can bring the water.

Notice, too, that when the master of the banquet tasted the wine, he commented on its quality, telling

> *Obedience to God's will is the secret of spiritual knowledge and insight. It is not willingness to know, but willingness to do God's will that brings certainty.*
> Eric Liddell
> OLYMPIC CHAMPION
> AND MISSIONARY

the bridegroom (who was undoubtedly the most baffled person in the room), "This wine is wonderful! You have saved the best wine until now!"

Of course, this is just like Jesus. It is what he invariably does. He always gives the *best.* As people who want to be like Jesus, so should we.

A Lifetime of Obedience

The life of Jesus was characterized by obedience. In chapter 1, we saw an incident when Jesus was twelve years old. Mary and Joseph searched all over Jerusalem for the missing boy, and finally found him at the Temple, where he was discussing the Scriptures with the Temple scribes. When Mary rebuked him for making them worry, the boy Jesus respectfully explained that he was where he ought to be—in his Father's house, the Temple. Then, the Gospel account tells us, Jesus *obediently* returned home to Nazareth with Mary and Joseph.

In chapter 17, near the end of the story of Jesus, is an example of obedience to the utmost. There, Jesus was in the Garden of Gethsemane. His soul was filled with horror, knowing he was about to be crucified. He prayed, "Father, if there is any way possible, please let this cup," that is, the horrible experience of the cross, "be taken from me."

Yet he obediently ended his prayer with these words: "Yet, let it not be as I will, but as you will." Jesus desperately wanted to escape the horror of the cross. Who wouldn't? The Gospel accounts tell us that the terrors he faced were so monstrous that an angel came and strengthened him. The agony of his spirit was so great that the sweat ran down his face like blood.

Jesus often told his disciples that his mission on Earth led through the cross—there was no other way. So Jesus obediently carried out the will of his Father. It was not his own will, but he made God's will *his own* through an act of sheer obedience. In the process, Jesus chose obedience, even to the point of death by torture.

The entire life of Jesus, from boyhood through manhood to the very moment of his death, was characterized by obedience. So, if we want to

> *He humbled himself and became obedient to death— even death on a cross.*
> Philippians 2:8

be like Jesus, then we have to obey like Jesus.

Obedience and Love

Obedience is a word we rarely hear anymore. The concept of obedience is not popular in our culture. Instead, rebellion, defiance of authority and lawlessness are glamorized as "cool."

Over the years, many people with revolutionary agendas have tried to paint Jesus as a rebel or a revolutionary. Those people have not only missed the point of his life and his message, but they have stood his message on its head.

Did Jesus oppose the authorities of his day? Of course he did, as we will see in later chapters. Did he do so as a rebel or a revolutionary? Absolutely not. Jesus came as a king, not a rebel. He didn't rebel against the authorities of his day. He was the authority. He pronounced judgment on the scribes and religious rulers as though they were criminals and dissidents against the true and rightful authority. Whose authority? God's—and his own.

Jesus came preaching about a kingdom. Who was the king of that kingdom? He was. When he was born, wise men from the East came seeking him, asking, "Where is he that is born King of the Jews?" In his preaching, Jesus repeatedly explained what his kingdom was like. In his parables—the stories he told to explain his preaching—he often told about kings and kingdoms, and the king in the story was usually Jesus himself. "My kingdom," he told the Roman governor Pontius Pilate, "is not of this world."

So those people who want to picture Jesus as a revolutionary are mistaken. Wishing to enlist Jesus in their cause, they reinvent Jesus in their own image. Jesus, though, will not be forced into anyone else's mold. He has already defined himself. Our job is not to conform Jesus to our image, but to conform ourselves to his. Jesus told us what he is like. He is not a rebel, but a king who has adopted the role of an obedient servant.

> *Obey God in the thing he is at present showing you, and instantly the next thing is opened up. . . . The tiniest fragment of obedience, and heaven opens up and the profoundest truths of God are yours straightaway.*
>
> Oswald Chambers
> MINISTER AND AUTHOR

As a king, Jesus issued commands and demanded obedience. He once told his disciples, "If you obey my commands, you will remain in my love, just as I have obeyed the commands of God, my father, and remain in his love."

Obedience and love are intertwined. The ultimate motivation for obedience is not fear but love. Jesus leads the way to God by setting an example of loving obedience. Our job is to respond to his example by lovingly obeying him. Only by walking in obedience, just as he walked, can we be like him and demonstrate our love for him.

Obedience Is Its Own Reward

There are many arenas in life where obedience is indispensable. Children must learn obedience. A child who disobeys the command, "Don't play in the street," risks tragedy.

Employees must learn obedience. Workers must obey managers, managers must obey executives, executives must obey the board of directors and the board of directors must obey the wishes of the stockholders and the laws and regulations of the government. When members of an organization cannot or will not obey, the results can be disastrous.

Warriors must learn obedience. The ability to obey is as important in a military general as in a lowly private. As Benjamin Franklin observed, "He that cannot obey cannot command." Disobedience may be the result of simple negligence or outright mutiny. Either way, disobedience can bring down a military campaign or even a nation.

What does obedience consist of? Here are the components of authentic obedience, as we observe them in the life of Jesus:

1. *Prayer.* Through prayer, Jesus maintained continuous contact with God. Through this connection with God, Jesus was able to discern God's will for his life. Once he had a clear and firm picture of God's will, he was able to obey God with unswerving devotion. If Jesus needed so much prayer in his life, do we need any less?

2. *Reliance upon God's strength.* When the horrors of the cross overwhelmed him, Jesus had to be sustained and strengthened by angels as he prayed. The same principle applies to us. We are easily overwhelmed by the tasks God gives us. In our human frailty, we often lack the strength to obey. But even if you do not have the strength to obey God, you can rely on him through prayer, and he will supply his own strength to sustain you.

3. *Total surrender.* Jesus held nothing back from God the Father. When God demanded that he submit to the cross, Jesus surrendered completely: "Not my will, but yours." That must be our answer, too. We cannot truly obey God until we have totally and unconditionally surrendered to him.

4. *Continual surrender.* Obedience was more than a

momentary choice for Jesus. It was his lifestyle. On a daily, habitual basis, he surrendered his thoughts, words and actions to God the Father. Like Jesus, we must surrender our lives to God on a daily, even hourly, basis.

5. *Hope of a future blessing.* God always rewards those who obey. Jesus knew that, and he looked beyond the cross to the reward and the blessing that would follow. For us, too, obedience will not always be pleasant. Sometimes, it will be painful and costly, but the lesson of the life of Jesus is that God always rewards obedience with blessing.

Ultimately, obedience is its own reward. The life of obedience is a life of blessing. It is a blessing merely to follow where Jesus has led, to place our feet in his footsteps. It is a blessing merely to be like Jesus in some small way. It is a blessing merely to know that we are living the life God designed us to live. When we live in obedience to God, we not only bring blessing into our own lives, but we spread blessing to those around us—family, friends, coworkers, neighbors and others.

Jesus walked a narrow road, a difficult road. He walked the road of obedience. You and I must choose between many roads. There are difficult roads of obedience, and there are easy roads of rebellion and self-will. Jesus set the pattern for your life and mine when he said to God the Father, "Not my will but yours." He took the rugged road to the cross. Which road will you choose?

An anonymous philosopher once observed that the

world is a better place because of the obedience of a few. The world is a better place because Michelangelo didn't say, "I don't do ceilings." The world is a better place because Noah didn't say, "I don't do boats." The world is a better place because Jesus didn't say, "I don't do crosses."

If we want to be like Jesus, then let's obey like Jesus.

CHAPTER FOUR

HOW TO BE ANGRY LIKE JESUS

fter the wedding in Cana, Jesus and his disciples stayed for a while in Capernaum, a town on the northern shore of the Lake of Galilee. When it was nearly time for the annual Passover festival, Jesus and his disciples went to Jerusalem, about eighty miles to the south and a four- or five-day walk. The journey to Jerusalem for the Passover celebration had been an annual ritual for Jesus ever since he was a boy. Passover had a special and recurring significance in the life of Jesus—and in his death.

Passover is the great Jewish celebration commemorating the deliverance of the people of Israel from slavery in Egypt. During the Passover season, the Jewish people recite the Haggadah, the narrative of the Exodus from Egypt. In Jesus' time, on Passover Eve, a special Passover lamb—a male lamb without a blemish—was sacrificed. The lamb was roasted and eaten with unleavened bread.

The Gospel accounts tell us that after Jesus was baptized, John the Baptist told two different groups of people that Jesus was "the lamb of God, who takes away the sin of the world." In other words, John saw Jesus as God's

Passover sacrifice. Historians also tell us that the shepherds in the fields near Bethlehem—the ones who visited the newborn Baby Jesus—would have been *priestly* shepherds. They were in charge of tending the flocks of sacrificial lambs that were ceremonially slaughtered at the Temple in Jerusalem. The symbolism of the sacrificial lambs reminded people that innocent blood had to be shed to atone for the sins of the people.

All of this, perhaps, weighed on the mind of Jesus as he passed through the gates of Jerusalem. Accompanied by his disciples, he walked the winding streets that led up to the Temple Mount. The city was crowded, filled with religious pilgrims who had come from all around Israel for the Passover season. Jostled by the crowds as he walked, Jesus kept his eyes pointed east, toward the towering columns of the Temple.

> *It is the creative anger of Jesus again and again that turns hearts and minds.*
>
> *While he will not return evil for evil he will draw a boundary, as when he turns the tables over at the Temple....*
>
> *He will go the way of the cross, the way of love, rather than destroy and be destroyed by anger. And that is an art.*
>
> Stephanie J. Nagley
> THEOLOGIAN

As he continued, accompanied by his disciples, Jesus may have pondered all of the sacrifices that were made every day upon the altars of the Temple. Perhaps he thought about the warm lifeblood of countless innocent animals, blood that spilled down the altars and filled the ceremonial bowls. So much blood.

Reaching the foot of the

steps that ascended the Temple Mount, Jesus and his disciples heard strange sounds, irreverent sounds—shouts,
arguments and coarse laughter. They were sounds that
should be found in a marketplace, not in the House of
God. Jesus and his disciples climbed the marble steps.
Reaching the Temple courtyard, Jesus stopped and stared
in shock.

A Right to Be Angry

The courtyard was lined with booths and tables as well
as cages and pens. Everywhere Jesus looked, he saw
greedy men hawking sacrificial sheep, cattle and doves.
The air was fouled by the stink of animal waste. It was
noisy with the sound of bleating and cooing and the
harsh clink of metal coins. Money changers bickered over
exchange rates and reaped obscene profits by exchang-
ing profane Roman coins (stamped with the blasphemous
image of Caesar) for Temple coins, which was the only
coinage acceptable for paying the Temple tax. Price-
gouging was a pervasive practice, since the merchants
and money changers had a monopoly on all trade in the
Temple courtyard. Caiaphas, the corrupt high priest of
the Temple, encouraged this flea-market atmosphere by
allowing merchants and money changers to operate on
the Temple grounds in return for a percentage of the
profits.

The disciples looked at Jesus and saw his eyes

smoldering. The Master was angry. They had never seen him like this before.

Jesus found some rush plants that had grown between the cracks of the Temple stones. The plants had long, tough reeds, and Jesus braided them into a scourge, or whip. Then he stormed through the Temple courtyard, driving the animals out and overturning the tables and benches of the merchants and money changers. Coins and people scattered. "Get these animals out of here!" he told the men who had caged doves for sale. "How dare you turn my Father's house into a marketplace!"

The money-grubbers didn't have to be told twice. They scooped up their money and wares, and they fled.

Jesus was angry. He was not cruel, not vengeful, not out of control. He was angry. Many people have misunderstood this scene by thinking that Jesus flogged people with a whip made of leather cords. But the whip he made was braided from weeds, and he used it not to inflict pain on men or beasts, but merely to herd the animals out of God's house.

Watching this, the disciples of Jesus were dismayed and embarrassed. After the miracle at Cana, they became convinced that they were following the promised Messiah, the one who would lead Israel to victory over the Roman occupation forces. Suddenly, Jesus was attacking the Jewish religious establishment and challenging the power of the priests and scribes right on the Temple grounds! That wasn't the behavior the disciples expected of their Messiah.

Then, a realization flashed through the minds of the disciples. They suddenly recalled a passage from Psalm 69, which predicted the sufferings of the promised Messiah: "Zeal for God's house has seized me and consumed me, driving me to action! And the outrages and indignities of those who insult God have fallen upon me." When the words of that Scripture passage came to their minds, the disciples began to realize more clearly what Jesus was all about: He would make no compromise with evil.

As Jesus cleared the Temple, he didn't fly into a wild rage. He demonstrated a righteous indignation toward evil and injustice. His response was measured and controlled. Jesus was angry, and he had every right to be.

But Jesus wasn't the only one who was angry. The religious men who ran the Temple for their own profit were furious with this upstart Galilean. How dare he come into the Temple and shut down their religious racket! They had a good thing going! They were raking in huge profits by fleecing the faithful.

After the animals and merchants stampeded away and the dust began to clear, the religious leaders marched up to Jesus and confronted him. "If you have the authority to do all this, then prove it! Show us a miraculous sign!"

"You want a miracle, do you?" Jesus said. "Very well. Destroy this Temple, and I will raise it up again in three days."

The religious leaders were stunned. The man from Nazareth was talking nonsense! They looked around them at the towering Temple structure, with its massive

Corinthian pillars carved out of single pieces of stone. "It has taken forty-six years to build the Temple!" they said. "And you say you will raise it in three days? Are you mad?"

But the "Temple" Jesus spoke about was not a building made of stone. He was talking about his own body.

> *Nothing provoked the holy anger of Jesus Christ more than empty religion.*
> David Wilkerson
> PASTOR AND AUTHOR

The disciples who stood beside Jesus were just as astonished as the religious leaders. They didn't know what to make of their Master's strange words. Nevertheless, those words stuck in their minds, and the meaning of these words would later become powerfully clear.

The Pharisees Set a Trap

Some months after the clearing of the Temple, there was another incident in which Jesus became visibly angry. He was attending a Sabbath worship service in a synagogue, and there was a man in the congregation with a crippled, deformed hand. There were also a number of Pharisees present, and they were watching every move Jesus made.

By this point in his ministry, Jesus had made some powerful enemies among the religious rulers, especially the Pharisees. The ultra-strict Pharisees were experts in the Law of Moses, and they were also the dominant political force in Israel. They followed Jesus around in his travels and often argued with him and opposed him. They continually tried to catch him breaking one of their rules and traditions so that they could discredit him. Some of the most important rules had to do with the Sabbath.

The Sabbath, of course, was the day of rest that God had set aside for humanity. The fourth commandment that God gave Moses was, "Remember the Sabbath day, to keep it holy." God had given humanity one simple law regarding the Sabbath in order to ensure that people would have a healthful amount of rest and spiritual reflection each week.

By the time of Jesus, however, the Pharisees had created thousands of rules, regulations and restrictions that controlled people's lives. It wasn't enough that God said to keep the Sabbath holy. The Pharisees believed that people needed a complex network of laws to govern *how* they would keep the Sabbath holy in every conceivable situation.

For example, the Pharisees had a rule that it was all right to spit on a rock on the Sabbath, but it was a violation to spit in the dirt. Why? Because spitting on dirt produces mud, and mud was used as mortar for bricklaying. Making mortar is work. A man caught spitting in the dirt on the Sabbath was considered as guilty as if he were building a house on the Sabbath! It's clear that the rules of the Pharisees were absurd, and they violated God's original intention of enabling people to rest from their labors one day of the week. The Pharisees had turned a day of joy and spiritual refreshment into a burden.

On this particular day, Jesus had come to the synagogue

to worship, and he saw a man in need, the man with a crippled hand. The Pharisees watched Jesus intently, hoping to catch him violating one of their rigid Sabbath rules. Jesus knew this, and he decided to flush them out into the open and expose the hatred in their hearts.

He walked to the front of the synagogue and stood before the entire congregation. Turning to the man with the crippled hand, Jesus said, "Stand here in front, so everyone can see you." The man came up to the front of the synagogue.

Jesus turned and looked directly at the group of Pharisees. "Which is the right and lawful thing a person should do on the Sabbath?" he asked. "Would it be better to do good on the Sabbath or evil? Would it be better to save a life or to kill someone?"

The Pharisees glared at him, but said nothing.

At this point in the story, the Gospel accounts make a remarkable observation. They record that Jesus looked at the Pharisees in *anger*—and that he was deeply *grieved* by the stubbornness of their hearts. The injustice of these religious men stirred his righteous indignation, yet their callousness broke his heart. He was deeply hurt by the fact that these men had put up an impenetrable wall inside themselves to keep out the love of God.

This image evokes a strange image in our minds, an image of the face of Jesus, his eyes burning with indignation yet also brimming with tears of grief. With this strange swirl of emotions churning within him, Jesus turned to the crippled man.

"Put your hand out," Jesus said.

The man stretched out his hand.

The people in the synagogue gasped.

They could all see that the once-crippled hand was now whole and restored.

If you had been in that synagogue, how would you have reacted? Would you have been amazed? Filled with excitement? Filled with awe? Totally convinced of the claims and credentials of Jesus?

That wasn't how the Pharisees responded. They saw Jesus as a threat. He threatened their power over the people. He threatened their pride and self-righteous egos. He exposed the evil and hateful motives that lurked inside them. They couldn't stand to have Jesus walking around on the same planet with them. It didn't matter to them that Jesus had done a good thing on the Sabbath. It didn't matter to them that a man had been healed or that the power of God had been displayed.

No, only one thing mattered to the Pharisees: *Jesus threatened their power.* When he healed, he rose in popularity with the people. And his popularity eclipsed their own.

The Pharisees left the synagogue in a murderous rage. They went out to find the members of a political sect called the Herodians, who were followers of King Herod Antipas.

This was a supremely ironic moment, because the Pharisees and the Herodians hated each other with a vengeance. The Pharisees were strict, observant, religious

men who despised Roman rule. The Herodians were sec-
ularists who favored accommodation with the Romans.
But the Pharisees wanted Jesus dead, and they knew they
could not have Jesus executed without the secular power
of King Herod and the Herodians.

It is instructive to contrast the anger of Jesus with the
anger of the Pharisees. When
Jesus looked upon the
Pharisees, his righteous
anger was mingled with
grief and sorrow. Jesus actually felt *compassion* for his
enemies, even while he was angry with their attitudes and
actions. Yet, when the Pharisees looked at Jesus, all they
felt was a murderous, red rage.

> *Only Christ can free us
> from the prison of legalism,
> and then only if we are
> willing to be freed.*
> Madeleine L'Engle
> NOVELIST

Why Was Jesus Angry?

There is a clear parallel between these two stories from
the life of Jesus. In both stories—the cleansing of the
Temple and the healing of the man with the crippled
hand—Jesus became angry and he confronted religious
corruption.

In the cleansing of the Temple, Jesus was angry because
the Temple, which he called "my Father's house," had been
defiled and turned into a marketplace that was filled with
the stink of animals and the ugly clamor of human greed.
The worship of God had been turned into a commercial

enterprise. Evil men were taking advantage of the poor. The Temple of God was turned into a carnival of evils: blasphemy, sacrilege, extortion, racketeering and corruption.

Later, in the synagogue, Jesus was again confronted by religious corruption and opposed by men who wanted to turn God's gift of the Sabbath into a spider web of rigid, pointless rules. The Pharisees thought that doing good on the Sabbath was a sin, yet they rationalized their hatred and blood lust on the Sabbath. Again, Jesus saw oppression and exploitation disguised as religion, and he was sickened, disgusted and angered.

Clearly, the anger of Jesus is a righteous, holy anger. Many people see the phrase "righteous anger" as a contradiction in terms. Isn't anger a sin? Not always. In fact, there are times when it would be wrong *not* to get angry!

Whenever there is injustice and evil going on around us, we *should* be angry. When people are oppressed, mistreated and exploited, or when the name of God is dishonored, it should make our blood boil. There's something wrong with us if we can witness evil and injustice without feeling indignant.

Jesus demonstrated for us what righteous anger looks like. It is controlled. It is focused. It is channeled into healing and helping, not destroying others. The purpose of righteous anger is to defend those who are defenseless. It is protective of others, not defensive of oneself or one's own ego.

As we continue on through the story of Jesus, we will see him attacked, accused, abused and defamed. We will even see him beaten, tortured and put to death. If you look closely at his story, you will never once see him become angry on his own behalf. Jesus only becomes angry in the defense of others and in the service of God. His anger was a righteous, holy and selfless anger. He never lost control, and he never lashed out to hurt anyone.

The anger of Jesus was so unlike the anger that you and I wrestle with so often. We get angry when we feel offended on our own behalf, frustrated in our own plans, deprived of our own rights and entitlements. Our anger is usually selfish and it easily overwhelms us. All too often, we do not control our anger; our anger controls us. Human rage is fueled by self-centered resentment, and resentment easily spills over into bitterness and hate.

> *When you are angry, do not sin. Don't let the sun go down while you are still angry.*
> Ephesians 4:26

Jesus taught us, by word and example, that this is not how his followers should respond. If we want to be like Jesus, we need to understand how Jesus wants us to behave in times of anger and conflict.

How Should We Handle Anger?

In his most famous speech, the Sermon on the Mount (which we will explore in chapter 6), Jesus talked about anger and hate. He explained how his followers—all who sincerely want to be like Jesus—should respond to difficult and offensive people.

In the Sermon on the Mount, Jesus said, "You've heard that the people were commanded long ago, 'Do not murder.' But I'm telling you that anyone who is even angry with a brother or sister [that is, any other person in the human family] is guilty of murder. If you thoughtlessly slander your brother as an 'idiot' [or some similar insulting name], you may find yourself having to answer to a court of law. But I'm telling you that if you use destructive name-calling in your dealings with other people, you are really in danger of God's judgment."

Jesus made it clear that our love of God is inseparable from the way we treat other people. He put it this way. "If you are in a house of worship and you are giving praise and offerings to God, stop and think about how you have treated other people during the week. If you remember someone you have offended, then stop what you're doing, leave the house of worship, go apologize and be reconciled to your brother—and *then* come back and give your praise and offering to God."

What about disputes? Jesus said, "Settle your disputes quickly, and make peace with your adversaries, even the ones who are taking you to court. Find ways to make peace with people before you reach the courtroom, or the judge just may put you in jail. If it comes to that, believe me, you won't get out until you have paid the last penny you owe."

What about unreasonable people, nasty people, obnoxious people, people who are just plain *mean?* "You've heard that the people were commanded, 'An eye for an eye, and a tooth for a tooth.' But I'm telling you that you should not resist an evil person. If someone hits you on the right cheek, turn the left cheek to him as well. If someone sues you in order to take the shirt off your back, give him your overcoat as well. If someone forces you to walk one mile, be willing to go an extra mile with him. Give to the person who asks you to give. Don't turn your back on people who want to borrow from you."

That may sound like Jesus wants us all to be doormats and let people walk all over us and wipe their feet on us, but I don't think that's what he meant. For example, let's say you are a mother of two kids who lives with an abusive husband. Jesus is not telling you, "If your husband blackens your right eye, give him a shot at your left eye, as well." Jesus would never tell you to put yourself or your children at physical risk. We have to use good judgment. We have to protect ourselves and our children from danger. If you are in a relationship with a person who is dangerous, you need to get out of that relationship. You shouldn't hate or seek revenge, but you do need to make a safe home for yourself and your children.

Jesus is saying, in effect, "When people do things to make you angry, I want you to learn a new way to respond. Instead of thinking of ways to get even, seek ways to change the dynamics of the relationship." Suppose someone struck you, and instead of hitting back, you turned the other cheek. How would that person respond? Well, he might hit you again, but on the other hand, he might be completely dumbfounded by your unexpected act of grace and nonviolence. He might be stricken in his conscience. He might feel like a complete fool. In the end, you might influence that person to change. You might win that person over, so that he, too, would want to be like Jesus. At the very least, you will be subtracting some of the rage and conflict from the world and adding a bit of love, tolerance, kindness and peace.

Jesus went on to say, "You've heard the old saying, 'Love your neighbor and hate your enemy.' But I say to you: love your enemies and ask God to bless those who persecute you. If you do this, then you will truly be children of your Father in heaven." In other words, when we are confronted with angry people and angry situations, we should not respond with hatred. Instead, we should respond with kindness, forgiveness and a prayer of blessing. That is how to be like Jesus.

> *Did you know the Bible describes more than twenty different emotions that Jesus felt? And they weren't all happy feelings either! Among others, Jesus felt affection, anguish, anger, compassion, distress, grief, gladness, indignation, joy, love, peace, sadness, sympathy, troubled and weary....*
>
> *Christ is our model of perfect spiritual and emotional maturity.*
>
> Bruce Narramore
> PSYCHOLOGIST AND
> UNIVERSITY PROFESSOR

Two thousand years ago, Jesus showed us a completely new way of dealing with feelings of anger. The world didn't know what to make of it then. Today, the world still doesn't know what to make of it.

A Grieving and Sorrowful Anger

It is important that we grasp the full range of the personality of Jesus, including the broad range of his emotions. Jesus was an intensely human man, and the better we understand how Jesus expressed his own emotions— including the emotion of *anger*—the better we can understand our own emotions so that we can express them in a way that is healthy and holy. Bible teacher G. Walter Hansen made this insightful observation about the emotional life of Jesus:

> The gospel writers paint their portraits of Jesus using a kaleidoscope of brilliant "emotional" colors. Jesus felt compassion; he was angry, indignant, and consumed with zeal; he was troubled, greatly distressed, very sorrowful, depressed, deeply moved, and grieved; he sighed; he wept and sobbed; he groaned; he was in agony; he was surprised and amazed; he rejoiced very greatly and was full of joy; he greatly desired, and he loved.
>
> In our quest to be like Jesus we often overlook his emotions. Jesus reveals what it means to be fully human and made in the image of God. His emotions reflect the image of God without any deficiency or distortion. When we compare our own emotional lives to his, we become aware of our need for a transformation of our emotions so that we can be fully human, as he is.[1]

The way Jesus expressed his emotions is the way we should express emotion. His was a righteous anger

[1] G. Walter Hansen, "The Emotions of Jesus," *Christianity Today,* 3 Feb. 1997. Electronically retrieved at *www.christianitytoday.com/ct/7t2/7t2042.html.*

directed at evil and injustice. Jesus demonstrated a way to be angry that heals and restores.

If you have ever read John Steinbeck's *The Grapes of Wrath*, you know that it is an angry novel about the Great Depression. Steinbeck first came face-to-face with the plight of California's migrant farmworkers while writing a series of newspaper articles in the 1930s. As a reporter, he visited the squalid migrant labor camps. He watched the workers in the fields and listened to their stories of mistreatment and injustice. He climbed inside their skin and felt their misery and pain.

John Steinbeck became angry.

He began writing *The Grapes of Wrath* in June 1938, and he kept a journal as he wrote. In that journal, he kept a log of his progress on the book and of his emotional ups and downs, including his anger. He was determined to write the book quickly so that the entire world would soon hear of the evils he had seen in those camps and fields.

Whenever Steinbeck's energies lagged, he remembered the misery in the workers' faces and the horror stories they had told him. Instantly, his anger would surge and revitalize him. By October 1938—just five months after he had begun—Steinbeck's book was finished. The work had been fueled and driven by Steinbeck's righteous anger against injustice.

The Grapes of Wrath was Steinbeck's masterpiece, winning him the Pulitzer Prize in 1940. It was also the catalyst that brought social change and justice into the lives of many migrant laborers and their families.

That is what the anger of Jesus is like, and it is what our anger should be like. In our anger, let us not sin. Instead, if we must be angry, let it be a grieving and sorrowful anger, a brokenhearted anger, an anger that loves even unjust people while hating their injustice. Let's make a daily choice to transform every experience of conflict and anger into another opportunity to become more like Jesus.

CHAPTER FIVE

HOW TO TALK LIKE JESUS

esus did not have a home of his own, so he stayed with friends wherever he went. On one particular night, not long after the Passover, Jesus was staying with friends in Jerusalem when a visitor came to see him. Jesus stepped out of the house and greeted the stranger under the star-strewn canopy of night. The stranger checked over his shoulder and along the darkened street, making sure no one was watching. Then he introduced himself.

"My name," he said, "is Nicodemus."

Nicodemus! Jesus knew that name. Nicodemus was a powerful man, a Pharisee and a member of the supreme ruling council, the Sanhedrin. From the earliest days of his ministry, Jesus had been opposed by these strict religionists, the Pharisees. Now, late at night, one of the leaders of the Pharisees had paid Jesus a visit. Why? What did he want?

For a few moments, these two men appraised each other. There was no sound but the night song of the crickets. Even though the face of Nicodemus was shrouded in shadows, Jesus had no trouble reading the man's edgy emotional state.

It was obvious that Nicodemus had come late at night, under the cover of darkness, because he did not want to be seen talking to the preacher from Nazareth. Nicodemus was taking a huge risk in coming to Jesus. The Pharisees had decreed that anyone who followed Jesus would be banished from the Temple. If Nicodemus had been seen, he would not only have lost his high office as a leader of the people, he would have been banished from Jewish society.

> *Jesus' good news, then, was that the Kingdom of God had come, and that he, Jesus, was its herald and expounder to men. More than that, in some special and mysterious ways, he was the kingdom.*
>
> Malcolm Muggeridge
> AUTHOR AND JOURNALIST

No wonder the man kept checking over his shoulder.

Born from Above

"Rabbi—honorable sir," Nicodemus said, addressing Jesus with a term of deep respect reserved for great Jewish teachers. "Some of us in the Pharisee sect know that you are a teacher who has come from God. No one could produce the miraculous proofs that you have done unless God was truly with him."

The "miraculous proofs" Nicodemus talked about were miracles that Jesus performed while he was in Jerusalem during the Passover festival. After cleansing the Temple, he had stayed in the city, teaching and healing. Those healings were the miraculous proofs Nicodemus referred to.

Was Nicodemus sincere in saying he believed Jesus was a teacher sent from God, or was he merely trying to flatter Jesus? It's impossible to know for sure, but one thing is clear: Nicodemus was deeply troubled. There was an unspoken question on his mind. When Jesus replied to Nicodemus, he went unerringly to the heart of that unspoken question, which was, *How can I enter the kingdom of God?*

"I tell you the absolute truth," Jesus said. "No one can see the kingdom of God unless he is born again from above."

Nicodemus was shaken. It was as if Jesus had read his mind! But what did Jesus mean? "What you're saying makes no sense to me," Nicodemus said. "How can someone be born who is already growing old? How can a man return to his mother's womb and be born a second time?"

"Again, I tell you the absolute truth," Jesus said. "Unless a man is born of both water and the Spirit, he cannot enter the kingdom of God. A flesh-and-blood mother gives birth to a flesh-and-blood baby. But only the Spirit gives birth to spirit. So you shouldn't be surprised when I say to you that you must be born again from above! I'm talking about a spiritual birth, not a flesh-and-blood birth."

When Nicodemus still looked baffled, Jesus tried another way of explaining it. "Think about the wind," he said. "Where does it blow? Anywhere it pleases! You can hear the wind, you can feel the wind, but you can't see it, you can't tell where it comes from or where it's going. That's the way it is with every person who is born from above, who is born of the Spirit. The spiritual birth is as invisible as the wind, but it's just as real."

"But how can this be?" Nicodemus said. "I still don't understand how a person becomes 'born from above.'"

Jesus challenged Nicodemus with a blunt question. "Here you are, a well-educated religious teacher of Israel, yet you still don't understand what I'm talking about? After all, we are discussing commonplace things that we have both seen or experienced. I have explained it to you in terms you should be able to understand, comparing spiritual birth to childbirth, comparing the life of the Spirit to the motion of the wind, but you still don't grasp what I'm telling you. If I explain it to you in earthly terms and you don't believe, how will you believe if I explain it in heavenly terms?"

Jesus continued explaining to Nicodemus what he meant about being "born again from above." In the course of that explanation, Jesus made a statement that has resonated down through the centuries and all around the world. "God loved the world so much," Jesus said, "that he gave his one and only Son, so that everyone who believes in him shall not perish but have everlasting life."

That statement—John 3:16—is probably the best-known, best-loved verse in the entire Bible. Nicodemus was the first human being to hear the words that have changed the course of millions of lives. And imagine this: Nicodemus didn't hear those words from Billy Graham or some other evangelist. He heard them from the lips of Jesus himself!

Jesus went on to say, "God's reason for sending his Son into the world was not to condemn the people of the world, but so that they might be saved through him. Any person who believes and trusts in the Son is not condemned, but whoever will not believe stands condemned already, because he will not believe in the name of God's one and only Son."

Tradition tells us that Nicodemus was a wealthy man. The Scriptures tell us he was a powerful man. Yet, as we read between the lines, we can see that he was also an empty and unfulfilled man. He had everything a person could want in life, except peace, meaning and satisfaction. Nicodemus, the proud and powerful Pharisee, had come to Jesus privately, under the cover of darkness, asking for the secret to eternal life. And Jesus, the preacher from Nazareth, told him the secret: You must be born again, born from above—and you do that by believing and trusting in the Son of God.

All of this was strange and new to Nicodemus. What Jesus told him was nothing at all like the religion of rules and regulations that the Pharisees lived by. Rules are external. What Jesus talked about was an internal, invisible transformation. How did Nicodemus receive this message? How did he respond?

At first glance, it appears that their conversation ended inconclusively. However, this is not the last we will hear from this Pharisee named Nicodemus. He makes two more appearances in the story of Jesus. Those two appearances show that Nicodemus was profoundly affected by

> *There is almost no "letter" in the words of Jesus.*
>
> *Taken by a literalist, he will always prove the most elusive of teachers.*
>
> *Systems cannot keep up with that darting illumination. No net less wide than a man's whole heart, nor less fine a mesh than love, will hold the sacred fish.*
>
> C. S. Lewis
> NOVELIST AND ESSAYIST

his late-night conversation with Jesus. The change in Nicodemus didn't happen overnight, but the words of Jesus clearly stuck in his mind and produced a gradual but profound transformation in his life.

Could one conversation change the course of your entire life? Yes—if the person you are talking with is Jesus of Nazareth. He touched and changed hundreds and hundreds of lives—and he did it by talking. If we want to influence lives the way Jesus did, then we must learn to talk the way Jesus talked.

Living Water

A few days after the late-night encounter with Nicodemus, Jesus and his disciples left Jerusalem and went out into the countryside of Judea, the region around Jerusalem. This place was not far from where John the Baptist was preaching and baptizing. Some of John's followers came to him, upset that many of the people who had once come to hear John were now following Jesus instead.

Far from being upset about losing followers to Jesus, John was actually *pleased*. "I've told you all along," he said, "that I'm not the Messiah. I was only sent to *announce* the Messiah. If all the people follow him instead of me, then my joy is full. His reputation must grow; mine must diminish."

John the Baptist was true to his word. Though he didn't disappear entirely from the story of Jesus at this point, he did begin fading from view. The next time we see John will be at his tragic and premature death, not many months before the Crucifixion of Jesus.

At the same time, the Pharisees in Jerusalem were becoming increasingly disturbed over reports that growing numbers of people were following this upstart preacher, Jesus of Nazareth. Jesus knew that the religious leaders wanted him dead, so he led his followers out of Judea in southern Israel and north to Galilee. In order to reach Galilee, he had to pass through Samaria, in central Israel.

Jesus and his disciples walked to a Samaritan town called Sychar. It was near Jacob's Well, a plot of ground with a sacred history to both the Jewish and Samaritan people. According to tradition, Jacob, the father of the Jewish people, had given that plot of ground to his son Joseph. It was noon when Jesus sat down beside the well. He was hot, thirsty and road-weary. His disciples

> *I know now that there is one God.*
>
> *When I was younger, I tried to please my father by not believing.*
>
> *I tried to become a Buddhist, but I wasn't one by nature. . . .*
>
> *Then, one night, I experienced Jesus; after that, I converted, and now I just love Jesus and see him in me and around me.*
>
> Anne Lamott
> AUTHOR

left him and went into Sychar to buy food.

Jacob's Well was deep and lined with chunks of limestone. Those who drew water from the well had to bring a clay pot, which was let down into the well on a rope. The well was fed by a spring—or what the people of that time called "living water," as opposed to still water that sat in a cistern. As Jesus sat beside that spring-fed well, he was about to have a conversation about water—and he was about to give that phrase "living water" a profound and surprising new meaning.

Never Thirsty Again

Before long, a woman came to the well to draw some water. She was a Samaritan woman—a woman whose race was looked down upon by most Jewish people of the time.

The Jews viewed the Samaritans as pagans from Babylon who some seven centuries earlier had been settled in Israel by the conquering Assyrians. The Samaritans had adopted many Jewish customs and beliefs, but they refused to accept Jerusalem as a holy site. Instead, they worshiped at Mount Gerazim, north of Jerusalem. They believed that the original Books of Moses had been corrupted by later Jewish scribes. As a result of their ancestry and beliefs, Jews viewed Samaritans as Gentile cultists who practiced a false religion.

Because of the deep cultural and religious division between Jews and Samaritans—not to mention the cultural taboos that divided men from women—it was completely unthinkable that a Jewish man would speak to a Samaritan woman. So Jesus did the unthinkable.

"Please," he said to her, "give me a drink of water."

The woman was startled. "How can you ask me that?" the woman said. "How can you—a Jewish man!—ask for a drink from me, a woman of Samaria?"

"If you only understood the loving generosity of God," Jesus said, "and who I really am, *you* would ask *me* for a drink—and I would give you *living* water."

The Samaritan woman eyed Jesus with suspicion. This Jewish stranger *seemed* harmless enough, but she didn't trust him. In fact, she suspected he was making fun of her with his talk of "living water."

"Sir," she replied sarcastically, "you have nothing to draw water with, and the well is very deep. Tell me: Where would you get this living water? You seem to think you are greater than Jacob, the father of the Samaritan people. After all, this well was his, and he drank from it, along with his sons and his cattle, and he left it to us, his descendants."

With those words, she flung her Samaritan culture and religion in Jesus' face.

One reason the Jews hated the Samaritans was the way the Samaritans claimed to be true Israelites, true children of "Father Jacob." The Samaritans claimed to be descendants of Jacob through his grandsons, Manasseh and Ephraim, the sons of Joseph. This Samaritan claim set Jewish teeth on edge. In effect, the Samaritan woman was sneering at Jesus and showing her contempt for him. She had no more use for the Jews than the Jews had for Samaritans.

But Jesus smiled as if he hadn't even noticed her insulting tone and contemptuous words. He nodded toward Jacob's Well. "You know," he said, "everyone who drinks of the water in that well will eventually become thirsty again. But whoever drinks of the water I give will never be thirsty again. The water I give is like a well inside one's soul, cool and refreshing, bubbling up and producing eternal life."

Now the woman *knew* that this Jewish stranger was making fun of her! Two could play at that game! "Sir," she said, "why don't you just give me some of this 'living water' of yours? Then I won't ever have to be thirsty again! I won't even have to walk all the way out to this well to get water!"

A New Kind of Religion?

Jesus had been smiling up to now, but suddenly his face became serious. "I want you to do something," he said. "I want you to go back to town and tell your husband to come here."

My, the woman thought, *but this Jewish stranger is full of surprises!* She decided to see where this verbal sparring match was leading. "I don't have a husband," she said.

"That's right," Jesus said. "You phrased it accurately when you said, 'I don't have a husband,' because the truth is that you have had five husbands in the past."

The woman gasped and her eyes widened.

"And," Jesus continued, "even now you are having an affair with a man who is not legally your husband. So everything you have said is *technically* true."

Suddenly, all the sarcasm and mocking went out of the woman's voice, and the sneer left her face. She was shaking. This man had just revealed the deepest, darkest secret of her life—something *no one* could have known!

"Sir," she said in a frightened voice, "I can tell that you must be a prophet—a true prophet of God!" Even as she said this, a frightening possibility opened before her: If this *Jewish* man was a true prophet, then her entire belief system, including her religious beliefs, must be a lie!

"Sir," she said, "I don't know what to believe anymore! For generations, we Samaritans have worshiped on that mountain." She pointed north toward Mount Gerazim. "Yet you people—the Jews—say that Jerusalem is the true place of worship. What should I believe?"

"Woman," Jesus said, "believe *me.* A time will come when people will approach the Father directly to worship him. They won't have to go up onto that mountain nor down to Jerusalem. You have worshiped in ignorance, not realizing that the hope of salvation for the entire human race comes from among the Jews. But a time is coming—in fact, the time is now!—when true worshipers can worship God the Father in spirit and in truth. In fact, the Father is already seeking people who will worship him in truth—not with mere outward rituals, nor in this place or that place. God is *spirit,* and those who worship him must do so honestly, truthfully, in the reality of their own inner being."

The only religion this woman had ever known was a religion of rules, rituals and traditions. What did this stranger mean, declaring some new kind of religion, a religion where it didn't even matter whether you worshiped on a mountain or in a certain city? What kind of religion was this man talking about? The words of this Jewish stranger sounded attractive and inviting, but they violated all she had ever been taught. She couldn't accept such a radical new way of worshiping God, not on the say-so of one Jewish stranger!

"I know that the Messiah is coming someday," she said. "When he comes, he will make everything easy to understand. Until the Messiah comes, I don't know what to believe."

"Messiah *has* come," Jesus said. "I, the very one who speaks to you, am he."

The Samaritan woman was so stunned by those words that she left her water pot at the well and hurried back toward the town. This Jewish stranger had just told her the deepest secrets of her own life. Then he had claimed to be the long-promised Messiah! Could it be true? As she hurried toward the town, she passed the disciples who were returning to the well, having purchased food in Sychar.

Jesus looked at the returning disciples, and he noticed the shocked expressions on their faces. He knew exactly what they were thinking, even though they didn't say a word. *The Master was speaking to a woman—and a Samaritan woman at that!* The disciples approached him and took some bread from their bags. "Master," they said, "here is the bread we bought. You should eat some."

Jesus didn't even look at the bread. He was watching the Samaritan woman as she disappeared down the dusty road toward Sychar. "I have food to eat that you don't know anything about," he said, smiling to himself.

The disciples looked at each other in bewilderment.

"My food," Jesus continued, "is to do the will of him who sent me, and to bring his work to completion."

Soon after, the Samaritan woman returned with a group of people from the town of Sychar. "Come meet the man who knew all my deepest secrets," she told them. The Samaritan townfolk invited Jesus to stay with them in Sychar, and he stayed there two days. The people heard what the Samaritan woman had to say, and they also listened to

> *It is characteristic of the preacher that he simultaneously questions and proclaims.*
>
> *He must ask along with the congregation and form a "Socratic Community," otherwise he could not give any reply. But he can reply and he must, because he knows God's answer is Christ.*
>
> Dietrich Bonhoeffer
> THEOLOGIAN AND AUTHOR

Jesus. As they listened, many became convinced that he truly was who he claimed to be—the Messiah, the Savior of the world.

The Communication Style of Jesus

What was it about the way Jesus talked that made him so convincing and persuasive? What was it about the way he talked that persuaded Nicodemus—a Pharisee, a member of the opposition—to become a follower? What was it about the way he talked that persuaded a Samaritan woman—and most of her town—to believe in him?

As we look closely at the speaking style of Jesus, we can see that there was something about the way Jesus talked that moved hearts and minds. Although there has never been a communicator like Jesus, and never will be again, there are certain things that Jesus did when he spoke that we can all learn from. No one can talk like Jesus, yet we can all talk like Jesus more than we do. As we examine the communication style of Jesus, these principles emerge:

1. *Jesus asked questions.* Throughout his ministry, Jesus asked tough questions as a means of communicating truth. He asked probing questions that forced people to think for themselves. He asked rhetorical questions that made the answers stand out with clarity. He asked confrontational questions that forced people to get off the fence and choose sides.

   In his dialogue with Nicodemus, Jesus sensed that the Pharisee was avoiding crucial truths that were staring him in the face. Nicodemus needed some tough questioning to penetrate his thick armor of denial. So, Jesus hit Nicodemus right between the eyes with a challenging question. Jesus said, in effect, "Think, man, think! You're an educated teacher of Israel! Don't you get what I'm telling you? If I explain it to you in earthly terms, in simple analogies, and you still don't get it, how will you grasp the truth if I explain it to you directly in spiritual terms?"

Jesus used a method of teaching called the Socratic Method after the Athenean philosopher Socrates, who lived four centuries before Jesus. In the Socratic Method, the teacher does not dispense information but instead asks questions that stimulate the student to think and search within to find the truth for himself or herself. The Socratic Method should really be called the Jesus Method, for, though Socrates used that method earlier than Jesus, no one ever used it more effectively than Jesus. Jesus used questions to expose false assumptions, to penetrate denial, to illuminate new ideas and to stimulate thought.

Jesus is renowned, of course, as a preacher and teacher, but he was, above all, a questioner. In the Gospel of John, we find 161 recorded questions of Jesus. In our first encounter of Jesus as a boy, we saw him in the Temple in Jerusalem listening to the scribes and teachers of the Law and asking them many questions. In fact, the scribes and teachers found that his questions reflected a keen under-standing and knowledge of the Scriptures.

In chapter 4, we saw Jesus in a dispute with the Pharisees over whether it was right for Jesus to heal on the Sabbath. In that dramatic confrontation, Jesus asked the Pharisees, "Which is the right and lawful thing a person should do on the Sabbath? Would it be better to do good on the Sabbath or evil? Would it be better to save a life or to kill someone?" Though the Pharisees refused to answer his question, the question answered itself. With those questions, Jesus had rendered the moral issue clear beyond question.

2. *Jesus provoked questions.* He not only asked questions, he inspired and provoked questions from the people around him. What form of speech are people the most receptive to? Lectures? Sermons? Or answers to their own questions? I can tell you that I sit up straight and pay attention when a speaker answers the questions that are on my mind. I'm sure most people respond the same way.

How do we get people to ask us questions? As we look at the example of Jesus, we see that he provoked questions in two ways.

First, Jesus provoked questions through his *actions.* He continually did things that raised the interest and piqued the curiosity of people. One of the things Jesus did was perform miracles—in particular, miracles of healing. When Nicodemus came to Jesus, he began by saying, "No one could produce the miraculous proofs that you have done unless

God was truly with him." The miracles got the attention of Nicodemus and motivated him to approach Jesus by night with his questions.

Now, you and I can't perform miracles, but there are many things we can do to attract attention and provoke questions. Our accomplishments—from running a successful business to running a marathon, from writing a book to righting a social wrong—inspire interest and provoke questions. An animated, energetic speaking style also grabs attention and makes people interested in what we have to say. Using dramatic visual aids also rivets attention and invites questions. So when you speak, think of exciting, dramatic, entertaining things you can do to provoke questions from your listeners.

The second way Jesus provoked questions was with his words. Jesus said things that provoked questions. When he was speaking to Nicodemus, he made a provocative statement. "No one can see the kingdom of God unless he is born again from above." This statement grabbed the attention of Nicodemus and provoked him to ask, "How can someone be born who is already growing old? How can a man return to his mother's womb and be born a second time?" At that point, Jesus had a captive audience and an opening to share his message in a powerful and persuasive manner.

Jesus used a similar approach when he spoke to the

Samaritan woman at the well. When she asked him, "How can you—a Jewish man!—ask for a drink from me, a woman of Samaria?" Jesus sidestepped the question and made a profound, attention-getting statement. "If you only understood the loving generosity of God, and who I really am, *you* would ask *me* for a drink— and I would give you living water." Once Jesus said that, the woman *had* to keep listening!

So when you speak, think about startling, attention-getting words and statements you can use. Frame your words in ways that capture the attention of your audience and provoke your listeners to ask questions.

3. *Jesus used every occasion as an opportunity to communicate his message.* When Jesus sat down at Jacob's Well, he was hot, tired and thirsty. Who would have blamed him for just taking a rest in the shade? He and the woman could have easily ignored each other like strangers on an elevator.

But when Jesus saw the Samaritan woman approaching with her waterpot, his mind and heart were instantly engaged: *Here is a woman who is world-weary and hurting,* he thought. *How can I help her? How can I reach her? What can I say to her that will meet her need?* Jesus did not let an opportunity pass him by, no matter how tired he might have been. He took the time to open a conversation with the woman. He seized the opportunity to make a difference in her life, and the result was that a whole town was changed.

4. *Jesus used anything handy as a tool to communicate his message.* Jesus didn't have a megaphone or a lectern. He didn't have an overhead projector or a PowerPoint presentation system. All he had was his voice and a well with some water at the bottom. And that was enough.

Notice how Jesus used the water to open the conversation: He asked the woman for a drink. He asked for a favor. He placed himself in her debt. This is an excellent way to connect with other people. Something wonderful happens when you say to someone, "Would you please do me a favor?"

When there is an inequality between two people—boss to employee, teacher to pupil, parent to child, speaker to audience—there is a distance that must be bridged. If you want to dialogue with a child, a good way to do that is to get down on your knees so you can talk on the same level. Asking a listener for help is a symbolic way of doing the same thing—descending to another person's level. It's an endearing act, a display of humility. It puts people at ease and makes them more ready to receive what you have to say.

The inequality between Jesus and the woman was a cultural barrier of that era: A Jewish man could have nothing to do with a Samaritan woman. But by asking the woman for water to drink, Jesus revealed that he had no prejudice toward her. He erased that cultural barrier and placed himself on her level. Before the conversation was over, the tables were turned, and the woman was asking Jesus for water! This is a profound example of the genius of Jesus' communication skills.

5. *Jesus listened.* When Jesus talked with both Nicodemus and the woman at the well, he had conversations, not monologues. When people spoke, Jesus listened. That, in turn, guaranteed that when Jesus spoke, people listened. People always listen when they feel listened to; people always try to understand when they feel understood. Jesus was a master at making people feel listened to, understood, affirmed and cared for.

In the story of Jesus and the Samaritan woman, we clearly see that Jesus listened just as intently for what the woman *didn't* say as for what she *did* say. He listened for her unspoken emotions, fears and guilt. He listened to her pauses and hesitations. He listened to her body language, to the world-weariness and quiet desperation that was conveyed in her eyes, her facial expression and the way she carried herself.

Jesus was a great communicator because he was a great listener.

6. *Jesus was never rushed.* Jesus was never in too much of a hurry to talk with people. Nicodemus came to him late at night and might have even interrupted Jesus' sleep. No matter, Jesus made time to talk with him. The Samaritan woman approached

Jesus when he was hot and tired after a long journey, and he probably didn't feel like talking. No matter, Jesus simply turned his exhaustion and thirst into a conversation starter by asking the woman for a drink.

As he talked, Jesus did not rush to score his favorite, prerehearsed debating points. He was patient. He listened. He gently moved the discussion in a direction that would reveal the truths that his listener needed to grasp. If Jesus had started each of those conversations with the statement, "I am the Messiah, take it or leave it," the conversation would have been over in a hurry. Instead, he used questions, intriguing statements and patient listening to build rapport so that genuine communication could take place.

7. *Jesus stayed "on-message."* In these two conversations, the late-night talk with Nicodemus and the noontime talk with the woman at the well, we see that there are numerous points when each conversation could have veered off in some other direction. Nicodemus opened with flattery. "We know that you are a teacher who has come from God. No one could produce the miraculous proofs that you have done unless God was truly with him." The Samaritan woman, too, offered flattery to Jesus. "I can tell that you must be a prophet—a true prophet of God!" Neither time did Jesus respond to words of flattery.

He never said, "Why, thank you! How good of you to notice!" He simply let the flattery roll off of him, and he stayed on-message.

The same is true of controversy. At one point in his conversation with the woman, she became combative and contentious, saying, "You seem to think you are greater than Jacob, the father of the Samaritan people. After all, this well was his, and he drank from it, along with his sons and his cattle, and he left it to us, his descendants." She knew that the Jewish people considered that statement an abominable lie, and she seemed to be going out of her way to offend Jesus.

But he calmly brought the conversation back to his original theme. "You know," he said, "everyone who drinks of the water in that well will eventually become thirsty again. But whoever drinks of the water I have to give will never be thirsty."

In our own communication, we encounter people who try to distract us, change the subject and pull us off our message. At such times, we need to remember the example of Jesus. He never let other people move him away from what he came to say. People could not distract him with flattery nor could they disrupt him with controversy. He had a message for the world, and he didn't let anyone keep him from saying it.

8. *Jesus avoided the "fork."* There is a ploy that the enemies of Jesus tried on him again and again—a ploy

that chess players know as the "fork." In chess, it is sometimes possible to move your knight into position to threaten two of your unwary opponent's pieces at the same time. For example, your knight might threaten both a castle and a bishop of your opponent, so that even if he saves one, he will surely lose the other. When you are caught in a fork, you are faced with two no-win alternatives. That is exactly how the opponents of Jesus continually tried to trap him.

We saw an example of the fork in chapter 1. There, the enemies of Jesus brought to him a woman caught in adultery. They said, "According to the Law, Moses commanded us to stone such women to death. What do *you* say should be done with her?" In effect, they tried to trap Jesus by forcing him to choose between the Law of Moses and the law of Rome.

Jesus eluded the trap and put the onus back on them by saying, "Let the one among you who is without sin throw the first stone at her." With that, his enemies were defeated.

Another example of his brilliant ability to avoid the fork is found in the story of the woman at the well. I don't think the Samaritan woman *intentionally* set out to entrap Jesus with a fork, but there was an unintentional fork in her words. It comes at the place where the woman said to Jesus, "For generations, we Samaritans have worshiped on Mount Gerazim. Yet you people—the Jews—say that

Jerusalem is the true place of worship. What should I believe?" She asked him an either/or question.

Again, Jesus wouldn't give an either/or answer. Instead, he said, "A time will come when people will approach the Father directly to worship him. They won't have to go up that mountain nor down to Jerusalem."

The woman was focused on worshiping in a certain *place.* Jesus opened her eyes to a completely new way of looking at worship: Worship is not some ritual performed in this place or that. Worship is a relationship with God that takes place within the human spirit. By avoiding the either/or fork of her erroneous assumptions, Jesus opened her eyes to a new way of understanding what it means to love God. As a result, her life was changed and her village was transformed.

> *Debate has ensued through the centuries about the best title for Jesus.*
>
> *Should we refer to Him as Lord, or Christ, or Son of Man, or Son of God?*
>
> *Maybe we need to remember Jesus as the Storyteller, one who threw common, real-life stories next to eternal, spiritual truths.*
>
> Brian L. Harbour
> PASTOR AND AUTHOR

Jesus, the Master Storyteller

There is one crucial aspect of the communication style of Jesus that we haven't discussed: Jesus was a master *storyteller.* The stories he told are called *parables,* short stories

that illustrate a moral or spiritual truth. In the two incidences we just examined, the encounters with Nicodemus
and the woman at the well, Jesus does not use any parables.
He typically used parables in settings involving groups of
people, such as when he was teaching his disciples, when
he was preaching to great crowds or sometimes even when
he was contending with his opponents.

No discussion of the speaking and teaching style of
Jesus would be complete without a discussion of his parables. The Gospel of Matthew recorded a series of parables
that Jesus told to a crowd by a lake, and the passage con-
cludes with this statement: "Jesus taught the crowd
entirely in parables. He didn't say anything to the people
without using a parable." Amazing! On that occasion, he
didn't use grand oratory. He didn't lecture. He just told
stories. Everything he wanted to convey to the crowd
beside the lake was conveyed through parables.

The parables of Jesus are simple stories on the surface,
yet they often yield multiple layers of meaning. A story
might proceed along predictable lines, then suddenly veer
off in a surprising direction. These twists and turns often
challenge an audience to reflect on the story, to set aside
preconceived assumptions and to look at reality from a
new perspective.

The parables of Jesus remain powerfully relevant to our
lives today. A good example of the enduring relevance of
his stories is the Parable of the Weeds Among the Wheat:
"The kingdom of heaven," Jesus said, "is like a field that was
planted by a farmer. The farmer planted good seed in the

field. But while he and his workers were asleep that night, his enemy came and planted seeds of a weed in the field, then sneaked away. Later, when the wheat stalks came up out of the ground and began to ripen, the weeds appeared as well. The workers went to the farmer and said, 'Sir, didn't you plant wheat seed in your field? Where did all of these weeds come from?' The farmer replied, 'An enemy has done this to sabotage me.' So the servants said, 'Do you want us to go out and pull up the weeds?'"

Now, this is where the surprise appears. The workers made a suggestion that seems as sensible today as it was then. One of the main focuses of any farming operation is weed control, because weeds are harmful to crops. Jesus, however, said that the farmer's wisdom transcended conventional wisdom.

"'No,' the farmer answered, 'don't pull up the weeds. If you try to remove all the weeds from the field, you'll probably pull up a lot of good wheat along with the bad weeds. Let the wheat and the weeds grow together until harvest time. When that time comes, I will tell the harvesting crew, 'Collect all the weeds first and tie them into bundles to be burned. Then harvest the wheat and store it in my barn.'"

What did Jesus mean by this story?

Well, in a few moments, I'll tell you how Jesus explained it. But first, reread it; think about it; meditate on it. What insights do you find as you imagine yourself in the sandals of that farmer? What does the field represent? What does the wheat represent? What do the weeds represent? Who is the enemy of the farmer? Why do you think it is wiser, in the view of Jesus, to let the weeds grow rather than pull them up? We'll come back to these questions in a moment.

Now, think about your own communication style. How do you usually convey your message to the people around you? How do you talk to the people in your office, your place of worship, your home, or in your club or organization? Do you use stories to inspire, to provoke thought, to explain, to clarify, to create flashes of insight? If you want to talk like Jesus, then you must become a storyteller.

Often, you will find yourself in situations of conflict between two points of view. Stories can be used to clarify the issues and create understanding between these two sides. The stories of Jesus often clarified two sides of an issue by presenting us with characters who represented two points of view—a rich man and a beggar, a master and a servant, a loving father and a wandering son. These stories challenge the listener to understand the viewpoint of the other side.

The stories of Jesus make his lessons and teachings unforgettable. Parables instruct in a way that no other form of instruction can match. Stories stick in the mind. They create memorable images and evoke memorable emotions. "The best way to learn is through stories," says leadership expert Ken Blanchard. "I know that because of the way people respond to my stories in my lectures. Stories permit the audience and readers to identify and get into the characters and learn right along with the characters. It makes learning effortless and enjoyable."

Business writer Tom Peters agrees. "Numbers are

numbing," he says. "Stories are personal, passionate and purposeful."

When I speak before groups, I keep an eye on the audience. If I see people begin to yawn or check their watches, I always use a phrase that is guaranteed to rivet their attention: "Now, let me tell you a story."

At the same time, I think we miss the point of the parables of Jesus if we assume they are just inserted into his preaching to highlight a point or hold his listeners' interest. The parables of Jesus speak for themselves. They are intended to evoke a flash of sudden insight, an experience of "Aha!" within the listener. They are intended to create that wonderful moment of clarity when a deep and mysterious truth suddenly becomes real in our minds.

The parables deal with realities that were commonplace to people in the land of Palestine some two thousand years ago. Yet they still communicate with power and clarity to our computer-age, Internet-speed culture. Why? Because in two thousand years, the nature of God and the deep needs and yearnings of people remain unchanged. God still meets us in the ordinary, commonplace realities of life.

Jesus told many parables. Some he explained, but most he did not. The Parable of the Weeds Among the Wheat is a story he explained very simply and clearly.

After Jesus had left the crowd along the lake shore, his disciples came to him and asked him what the story meant. So Jesus explained it to them. "The one who planted the good wheat seed is the Son of Man," he said. "The wheat field is the world, and the wheat seed represents the children of the kingdom of heaven. The weeds are the children of the Evil One, the devil, and the enemy who plants the weeds is the Evil One himself. The harvest time is the end of human history, and the harvesters are the angels." Notice that, as we saw in chapter 1, Jesus used the term "the Son of Man" to refer to himself.

He continued. "The weeds that are uprooted and burned in the fire represent what will take place at the end of human history. At that time, the Son of Man will send out his angels. The angels will uproot all who cause sin and evil, and will remove them from his kingdom. The angels will throw the evildoers into the fiery furnace, where there will be weeping and unquenchable sorrow and regret. Then the righteous ones will shine like the sun in the kingdom of God, their Father. If you are listening to this story, make sure you truly hear what I'm telling you."

How should we apply this parable of Jesus to our lives today? Well, one layer of meaning that jumps out at me is this: I've heard many people say, "I don't go to church because churches are full of hypocrites. Many churchgoers don't practice what they preach." And that's true! Jesus predicted that the church would be like this. He said that his kingdom is like a field planted with both wheat and weeds, with good believers that he himself has planted and with hypocrites and evildoers who have been planted there by the Evil One.

Is that any reason to avoid becoming involved in the church? Of course not. Fact is, the whole world is planted with wheat and weeds, with both righteous people and hypocrites. You'll find wheat and weeds in the government, in the office where you work, in the neighborhood where you live, in the stores where you shop and in the clubs where you have a membership. Does that mean we should avoid those places?

Jesus is saying that God will not uproot the hypocrites and evildoers until the end of human history. In the meantime, wherever you go, wheat and weeds grow together. That's just the way it is.

This story from nature teaches us that God is patient, but we must make a choice: Wheat or weeds? Which do we choose to be? "If you are listening to this story," Jesus said, "make sure you truly hear what I'm telling you."

This is what parables do: They reveal spiritual issues and force the listener to make a choice and take a stand.

Jesus, the greatest communicator of all time, has left us an instructive example. To talk like Jesus, we must learn to ask questions, provoke questions, take advantage of every opportunity, use anything handy as a communications tool, listen authentically, never be rushed, stay on-message and avoid getting "forked." Above all, if we want to talk like Jesus, we must become storytellers. We must learn to use the power of a story not just to entertain or get attention, but to reveal *truth*.

If we want to *be* like Jesus, we must learn to *talk* like Jesus.

CHAPTER SIX

HOW TO THINK LIKE JESUS

fter his encounter with the woman at the well and his two-day visit in Sychar, Jesus and his disciples left Samaria and continued north into Galilee. When they arrived in Galilee, Jesus found that his reputation had spread far and wide.

Many people from Galilee had been down in Jerusalem for the Passover festival, and they had seen the things Jesus did there. Returning home, those people told their neighbors about the healings he had performed and his cleansing of the Temple.

Jesus stayed for a while in Cana, the town where he had turned water into wine. While he was there, a government official arrived from the neighboring town of Capernaum. The man's son was extremely sick and near the point of death, so his father had come to Cana on foot. It was about one in the afternoon when the man from Capernaum found Jesus and begged him to come heal his son.

"You won't believe," Jesus said, "unless you see me perform some miracle."

"Sir," the official pleaded, "just come before my boy dies—that's all I ask!"

Jesus smiled. "You may go to your son," he said. "He's going to live."

The man believed what Jesus said, thanked him and left. The next day, the official was still on the road to Capernaum when he was met by some of his servants. "Your boy is well!" they told him. "He's going to live!"

"When did he start to get better?" the official asked.

"The fever left him yesterday," they said, "at about one in the afternoon." The man realized it was the same hour that Jesus had said that his son would live. As a result of that healing, the official from Capernaum became a believer, and so did everyone in his household, from his family to his servants.

After that, Capernaum became the "home base" for Jesus—the town where he rested from his travels. Though the Gospel accounts do not tell us why Jesus chose Capernaum, it is likely that the government official, in his gratitude, made his own home available as a place where Jesus could stay whenever he wanted.

> *The apostle Paul tells us today in no uncertain terms that we are to strive to have the same mind in us that was in Christ Jesus.*
>
> *We are to think like Jesus thinks in order to do what Jesus did....*
>
> *Humility and unconditional love are the thoughts of God. Think not of your own interest, but also to the interests of others. Think like Jesus thinks.*
>
> Frank Logue
> PASTOR

The Rejection of Jesus

News travels fast. Word of the healer from Nazareth quickly spread across Galilee, north into the province of Syria, south into Decapolis (the Region of the Ten Greek Towns) and east across the Jordan River. People came from all around and brought their loved ones to Jesus to be healed, from the demon-possessed and insane to the sick, blind, deaf and paralyzed. So, Jesus traveled around Galilee, healing people and teaching in the synagogues.

On one Sabbath, Jesus went to the synagogue in Nazareth, the town where he had grown up (Nazareth was about thirty miles south of Capernaum, about a two-day walk). It was customary to have members of the congregation read from the Scriptures on the Sabbath. Since Jesus had just returned to town, he was given the honor that day. He stood up to read and was handed the scroll of the prophet Isaiah. Jesus opened it and read:

"The Spirit of the Lord is upon me, because he has anointed me to preach the good news to the poor. He has sent me to announce freedom for those who are in chains, the recovery of sight for the blind, and deliverance for those who are oppressed—to announce that this is the year of God's good favor."

Then Jesus closed the scroll, handed it back to the attendant and sat down. Everyone in the synagogue watched him closely, because he had done something highly unusual: *He had stopped reading in mid-sentence.* He had left out part of the passage. This was a famous text from

Isaiah, and many of those in the congregation knew that text by heart. The part Jesus left out was significant. The last phrase should have read, "to announce that this is the year of God's good favor, *and the day of vengeance of our God.*" Everyone wondered why Jesus omitted that last phrase.

Then, with all eyes riveted on him, Jesus did something even more shocking. He said, "Today, this Scripture has been fulfilled, at the very moment you were hearing it read."

In other words, Jesus applied those words to *himself!* He was saying that God's Spirit had anointed *him* to preach the good news to the poor, to set captives free, to heal the blind, to deliver the oppressed and to announce the time of God's blessing to humanity. The people in Nazareth had heard of his preaching throughout Galilee. They knew that he had healed many people in Capernaum and all around the region. And they knew what the word "anointed" meant.

To anoint someone is to bless and commission a person for a holy ministry by means of a ceremony in which oil is applied to the person's head. In Jewish history, olive oil was used to anoint prophets, priests and kings. There was one person, though, who the Scriptures said would one day fulfill all three of these roles at once. In the Hebrew language, this person was called *Mashiach,* meaning, "The Anointed One." The English form of Mashiach is *Messiah;* the Greek form is *Christos,* from which we get our English word *Christ.*

So when Jesus took upon himself the messianic description of an "Anointed One" who would preach, heal and deliver the oppressed, everyone in the synagogue understood exactly what he was claiming to be: the Messiah, the Anointed One of God.

The people of Nazareth were astonished and impressed by his words. Some seemed inclined to believe his claim, since they knew he had, in fact, given sight to the blind and delivered people who were oppressed by demons, just as the prophet Isaiah had written. They turned to each other and said, "Isn't this the son of Joseph the carpenter? When he lived here in Nazareth, we never knew he was capable of such things!"

Jesus heard the approving words that were said about him. He turned to them and said, "You'd probably like me to perform healings here in Nazareth, just like I've been doing in Capernaum." From the looks on their faces, he could see that this was exactly what they wanted. Jesus shook his head. "I tell you the truth," he continued. "A prophet is never welcomed and honored in his own country. At first, people may like to hear him speak, but after they hear what he has to say, they reject him."

The people who had spoken so approvingly of Jesus a moment before now sat in stunned silence. "Look at it this way," Jesus continued. "Back in Elijah's day, when there was a severe drought, and it didn't rain for three and a half years, the whole country went through a horrible famine. Many people died, and there were many needy widows just barely surviving in Israel. Yet God didn't send the prophet Elijah to help any of them. Instead, God sent Elijah to Sarepta, a widow in the Gentile city of Sidon. And there was the time God sent another prophet, Elisha, to heal a man with leprosy—yet the leper he healed was not an Israelite, but a Syrian called Naaman."

Hearing this, the crowd suddenly turned against Jesus. They jumped to their feet, shook their fists and shouted at him. Why? What did Jesus say that made them so angry? Actually, there were two things Jesus said that offended this crowd.

First, you recall that he left out Isaiah's phrase, ". . . and the day of vengeance of our God." Earlier, the people of Nazareth weren't troubled by that. Yes, it was odd that he had stopped reading in mid-sentence, but at first they didn't know what to make of it. Only later, after Jesus reminded them of the stories of the prophets Elijah and Elisha, did they get the point he was making. If Jesus had finished that sentence about God's vengeance, the people in the synagogue would have taken it as an indication that Jesus, in claiming to be the Messiah, was about to lead an insurrection against the Roman government. They would have taken it as a declaration of God's vengeance against the oppression of Rome.

Jesus, however, did not see his purpose that way. He had not come to lead a political and military revolution, so he stopped short of completing that sentence. His role as Messiah, he said, was to proclaim good news, healing, freedom and deliverance. In other words, he had come to bring *spiritual* salvation, not *political* salvation.

When he told the stories of Elijah and Elisha, and how these prophets had reached out to help non-Jewish people from Sidon and Syria, he made it plain that his kingdom was not going to be confined to the people of Israel. No, his kingdom would encompass the whole world, both Jews and Gentiles. It would be a kingdom in which Jewish people and non-Jewish people would live together in freedom and harmony.

That was a radical message, a shocking message. Just as Jesus had predicted, the people were angry when they heard it. A prophet is never welcome in his own country, and at that moment, Jesus was not welcome anymore in Nazareth.

The congregation of worshipers suddenly became a bloodthirsty mob. The people grabbed Jesus and dragged him out of the synagogue. They hustled him through the narrow streets where he had played as a boy. They took him to the steep cliff at the edge of town and were about to throw Jesus into the canyon below.

But Jesus simply shrugged out of their grasp, walked through the middle of the crowd and went on his way. Rejected in his hometown, Jesus left Nazareth and returned to Capernaum.

In the lakeshore town of Capernaum, people responded favorably to his teaching. On one Sabbath, while he was teaching in the synagogue in Capernaum, a man came into the building, shouting, "Hey, Jesus of Nazareth! What do you want with us? Have you come to destroy us? I know who you are! You're the holy one of God!"

"Be silent!" Jesus said sharply. "Come out of him!"

The man fell down violently in front of all the people, then suddenly became still. The man had been possessed by a devil, and the devil had left him at the command of Jesus! The man wasn't even hurt.

All the people who saw it were amazed. "This man speaks to evil spirits with authority," they said, "and the evil spirits obey him!" And the reputation of Jesus continued to spread like wildfire across the country-side.

> *Most of the Beatitudes are single, short sentences.*
> *They are cogently stated—originally in poetry—and could scarcely lose a word without losing the meaning.*
> Roger Shinn
> THEOLOGIAN

Many people brought loved ones to Jesus so that he could command evil spirits out of them. When the evil spirits came out at his command, they shouted, "You are the Son of God!" Jesus always silenced them because they were trying to disrupt his ministry by announcing him before his time had come.

Paradoxical Blessings

The region around the lakeshore village of Capernaum is rolling with hills. One large hill overlooking the Lake of Galilee is known today as the Mount of Beatitudes, which is the place where Jesus is thought to have delivered the Sermon on the Mount. Other traditions suggest that the actual site of the sermon was just south of Karn Hattin, a pair of cone-shaped mountains west of the town of Magdala. If we want to think like Jesus, then the place to begin is the Sermon on the Mount. If we understand the deep meaning of that sermon, then we are well on our way to understanding the mind of Jesus.

Because of his spreading fame, Jesus was followed by crowds wherever he went. One day, he walked up on a mountain with his disciples, and the crowds followed him. Reaching a level place that could accommodate a large crowd, Jesus sat down and began to teach the people.

"Those who are lowly and humble minded are blessed," he began, "for the kingdom of heaven belongs to them. Those who sorrow are blessed, for they will receive an extra measure of comfort and encouragement."

This word "blessed" deserves a second look. In the original language, it does not mean what we usually understand the English word "blessed" to mean—that is, to be richly endowed with material prosperity, good fortune and a sense of well-being. Nor does it exactly mean "happy," as the original Greek word is often translated. No, in the original language, to be "blessed" is to be *spiritually and eternally prosperous.*

"Those who are gentle are blessed," Jesus continued. "They rely on God as their strength and protection, and the whole Earth will belong to them. Those who hunger and thirst for a right relationship with God are blessed, because their hunger and thirst will be satisfied. The merciful are blessed, because they will receive God's mercy. Those who have pure hearts of integrity are blessed, because they will see God. Those who make peace are blessed, because they shall be God's own children. Those who suffer persecution for doing what is right are blessed, because the kingdom of heaven belongs to them. Those who own nothing at all are blessed, because all of God's kingdom shall one day be theirs."

So Jesus began his talk by telling the people how to be truly blessed, how to be spiritually and eternally rich. The spiritual prosperity Jesus talked about has nothing to do with material blessing and financial prosperity. In fact, Jesus was presenting a strange and paradoxical teaching: If you are humble, if you suffer, if you seek to do good, even when treated badly, then you are *blessed!* That teaching goes completely against the grain of human logic.

Common sense tells us that being blessed means being lucky, rich, powerful and connected. This logic says that the most blessed people are either born with a silver spoon in their mouths, or they are born with a gift for making connections and making money. To be blessed, says conventional wisdom, is to be lucky and rich.

In the Sermon on the Mount, however, Jesus turned conventional wisdom upside-down. He said that true blessing is a paradox. Sometimes, what outwardly looks like a curse is blessing, and what outwardly looks like a blessing is a curse.

"But as for you who are rich," Jesus went on to say, "how miserable you will be! For in this life you have already received all the comforts you will ever receive, and no comfort awaits you in the life to come! And you who have full bellies and bulging wallets now—how miserable you will be, for you shall suffer hunger and want! And you who laugh now—how miserable you will be, for you will mourn, weep and wail in torment! When people praise you and flatter you, how miserable you will be one day, for that is how people praised and flattered the evil, lying prophets of old, and they have gone down to their well-deserved fate!"

True blessing is not having a lot of possessions, power or pride. These "blessings" fade and pass away. True blessing is spiritual prosperity that lasts for all eternity. True blessing is something only God can give, and he gives lasting blessings only to the humble, the pure in heart, the needy and the sorrowing.

> *Each of us has a mission in life. . . . We seldom fully realize that we are sent to fulfill God-given tasks. We act as if we were simply dropped down in creation and have to entertain ourselves until we die. But we were sent into the world by God, just as Jesus was.*
> Henri J. M. Nouwen
> AUTHOR AND PRIEST

Salt and Light

"You are the salt of the Earth," Jesus continued. "But what if salt loses its saltiness? Can it be made salty again? No! It is no longer good for anything, except to be thrown out on the ground and walked on."

What did Jesus mean when he said that people who follow him are "the salt of the Earth"? He was speaking to people like you and me, people who want to be like Jesus. Salt is a flavor enhancer, so Jesus is telling us that we must add taste and flavor to everything and everyone we come in contact with.

Jesus may have also meant that salt acts as a preservative. It retards spoilage and corruption. Salt was commonly used in ancient Palestine to preserve dried meat and dried fish. If we are "salty" people, if we are truly like Jesus, then we will act as preservatives in our society, retarding the spoilage and corruption that takes place all around us. We will spread our saltiness around so that other people will want to be like Jesus. The more people in the world who think, talk and act like Jesus, the less corruption and spoilage there will be in our society.

Notice that Jesus also warns us that we must never lose our flavor, our "saltiness." We must be real, genuine salt. If we lose our saltiness, we are no longer worth anything. We might as well be tossed out into the street. So be salty, says Jesus. Be flavorful and act as a preservative, and never lose your distinct and precious saltiness.

"You are the light of the world," Jesus went on to say. "A city that stands on a hill cannot be hidden; it rises high and shines its light far into the night. And people never light an oil lamp, then hide it under a bowl. Instead, they put the lamp on a stand, so that it will shine its light throughout the house for everyone to see. So be like that city on a hill, be like that lamp on a lampstand. Let your light shine so that everyone can see the goodness of your works. When your life is a shining light, people will see how you live and will give praise to God, your Father in heaven."

We live in a dark world. But those who follow Jesus are people of the light. Their light shines most brightly in a dark place. Just as the moon reflects the light of the sun in the night sky, those who are like Jesus reflect the light of God in a dark world. If you and I choose to follow Jesus and be like Jesus, then we reflect the light that he brought into the world.

Jesus warns that it is not enough to merely be a light. The light of our lives must be visible to the world. We must stand tall, like a city on a hill, like a burning lamp on a lampstand, so that we can illuminate our surroundings. Our light must radiate into the dark corners of the world. When our light shines, people see that the source of our light is not ourselves, but God. The result, as Jesus said, is that "people see how you live and they give praise to God, your Father in heaven."

It is important that we do not separate what Jesus said about salt and light from the previous section on the paradoxical blessings. Jesus is telling us that when we undergo trials of sorrow and persecution, then we have an opportunity to be salt and light.

This is what it means to be salty for God and to shine for God. In the difficult and trying circumstances of life, we demonstrate character traits that are like the character of Jesus. Look again at that list of paradoxical blessings *because this is the heart of the entire book.* All the traits that Jesus says are blessings are actually nothing more or less than the character qualities of Jesus himself! Humility, gentleness, mercy, integrity, the endurance of sorrow and persecution for doing what is right—that's the life of Jesus in a nutshell. So if we are like Jesus in all of these traits, we will become salt and light. We will add flavor to the lives of people around us. We will illuminate their lives so that they can see reality more clearly.

In June 1937, a German pastor named Martin Niemöller preached a sermon to his dwindling congregation in Berlin-Dahlem. The title of his sermon was "You Are the Salt of the Earth," and it was based on this section of the Sermon on the Mount. Niemöller was one of the courageous few who dared to speak out against the Nazi regime. More than seventy people from his congregation had already been arrested for opposing the Nazis, and Niemöller himself had been threatened many times. As he preached his sermon, members of Hitler's secret police were sitting in the congregation taking notes.

At one point in the sermon, Niemöller said, "Jesus told us, 'But what if salt loses its saltiness?' It is not for us to worry about how the salt is used. Our job is to see that it doesn't lose its saltiness! Our flavor must remain distinct from the flavor of the world. We must not try to make our salt taste like the world around us. Our salt must remain salty!"

Niemöller also talked about what Jesus meant when he spoke of the light of the world. "We remember those in our congregation who have been arrested," Niemöller said, "and we think, 'Alas, this storm wind that is blowing through our world—will it not blow out the candle of our message? We must take our message in out of the storm and hide it in a safe nook.' But it is only in these days that I have truly understood what Jesus meant when he said, 'Do not cover up the light!' He is telling us, 'I have not lit a candle in Germany for you to hide it under a bowl to protect it from the wind. Away with the bowl! Place the light on a lampstand! Let your light shine before all people!'"

Two weeks after preaching that sermon, Pastor Martin Niemöller was arrested by the Gestapo. This man, who loved his country, who had even commanded a German U-boat during World War I, was sent to a concentration camp. He survived eight years of forced labor and near starvation at the camps in Sachsenhausen and Dachau. When Dachau was liberated in 1945, Niemöller emerged as little more than a walking skeleton. But he had survived, and he went on to a long postwar career as a Christian spokesman, as true salt and light, before his death in 1984 at the age of ninety-two.

If we want to be like Jesus, we must not be afraid to stand out in contrast to the world around us. Make no mistake: It's not safe to be salt and light! In fact, it can be costly and dangerous! But nowhere in the Sermon on the Mount does Jesus tell us that we should seek safety. Instead, he tells us that we are to stand tall, like a city on a hill, like a lamp on a lampstand, and we are to shine.

> *It is not enough to believe in Jesus. We must learn to think like Jesus.*
> *Once we learn to think like Jesus, we'll begin to act like Jesus.*
> Brooks Bryan
> PREACHER

Jesus Attacks Sin

There were many other issues that Jesus talked about in the Sermon on the Mount. He talked about anger and settling disagreements, as we discussed in chapter 4. He taught about issues we will examine soon, including how to pray (see chapter 7) and how to forgive (see chapter 8).

Jesus talked extensively in the Sermon on the Mount about the problem of sin, a word we don't hear very much these days. We live in a postmodern world that doesn't believe in such absolute concepts as right and wrong. Today, morality is widely seen as relative and changeable. Wrong is wrong only if you get caught, and there is no such thing as sin. Jesus, however, talked about sin a lot, and you cannot think like Jesus unless you believe in clear moral standards. You cannot be like Jesus unless you grasp the meaning of *sin*.

The Hebrew Old Testament uses a dozen different words to describe sin. The Greek New Testament uses five. Sin is a deliberate violation (sometimes called a transgression) of one of God's laws. Some sins take place not merely with our actions but in the realm of our thoughts, such as the sin of lust (a sinful sexual desire), the sin of coveting (wanting another person's possessions or spouse) and the sin of unbelief (a deliberate rejection of God's truth, not to be confused with honest doubting or questioning). Some sins involve neglecting to do what we know is right.

Jesus addressed all of these forms of sin in the Sermon

on the Mount. He said, "You have heard the old commandment, 'Do not commit adultery.' You may think you have avoided sinning by not having sexual relations outside of marriage. But I say to you that everyone who looks at someone else with a lustful mind has already committed adultery with that person in his or her heart."

These days, we hear people rationalize sexual sin, saying, "Well, it wasn't really adultery—we only did this kind of behavior or that kind of behavior. We didn't have actual intercourse." Jesus, though, will not let us excuse ourselves with rationalizations and denials. He makes it clear that the sin is not just in the act of adultery. The sin begins when we first dwell on lustful thoughts! Certainly, it is not a sin to be momentarily tempted, but the moment we invite temptation to take up residence in our thoughts, we are committing sin.

"The lamp of the body is the eye," Jesus went on to say. "If your eye is healthy, then your whole body will be filled with light. But if your eye is unhealthy, then your whole body will be filled with darkness. And if you surround yourself with darkness, so that the only 'light' you ever see is darkness, then the darkness that fills you will be dark indeed! So be very careful that the light that fills your being never becomes darkness. Make sure your eye is healthy, and your body is filled with light."

Jesus tells us here that we must be careful about what we focus on. What is the eye? It is a device that receives light from the outside world, focuses it through a lens, and transmits that light into our brains via the retina and optic nerve. The eye is the window of the soul. We receive our information about reality through our senses, especially through the eyes. So we must be careful about what we focus our eyes on and what kind of light we allow to pass through our eyes and into our bodies.

This counsel of Jesus can be applied to our lives in many ways. One of the more obvious applications has to do with what we literally *look at* with our eyes. Do we focus on input that stimulates our lusts? Do we focus on movies, books, magazines and Internet images that cause us to dwell on sinful thoughts? The culture around us tells us that there is no right or wrong, so it becomes easy for us to rationalize and justify our sin. When we rationalize, we are calling darkness "light." Once we start down that road, we lose the ability to distinguish between light and darkness, right and wrong, good and evil.

There is also a less obvious layer of meaning in these words. I believe that Jesus is not only addressing what we literally *look* upon with our eyes, but what we *take into our souls* via the mind's eye—our mental and spiritual focus. Certainly, having a healthy mind's eye includes avoiding sinful, destructive images such as pornography. But it goes much deeper than that. It also means that we should be careful not to adopt the world's values with regard to money, greed and power. It means we should be careful of the philosophies and belief systems that we feed our minds. It means that we should be aware of the deception and false values that pervade the political arena, literature, entertainment and the arts.

In short, we must make sure that our mental focus admits only light, because if we let the world pull the wool over our eyes, our darkness will be dark indeed! We need to see clearly in order to be like Jesus and think like Jesus.

Next, Jesus talked about temptation. The world is full of temptations, and Jesus wanted us to be aware that yielding to temptation can destroy us. This issue is so important that Jesus uses a series of shocking metaphors to make sure we don't miss the point.

"If your right eye tempts you to stumble into sin," Jesus said, "then gouge it out and throw it away! It's better for you to lose an eye than for your whole body to be destroyed in the ash heap of hell. It's better to go one-eyed through life than to have both eyes as you go down to destruction. Yes, and if your right hand tempts you to stumble into sin, then cut it off—amputate it and throw it away! It's better for you to lose an arm than for your whole body to be destroyed in the ash heap of hell. It's better to go maimed through life than to have both hands as you go down to destruction."

These words sound harsh to our postmodern ears, but these are actually words of intense love and compassion.

> *My experience of life is that it's a mixed grill.*
>
> *It's not predictable. It's not pretty. It's messy. You can have very deep faith and still experience deep disappointment and confusion. Jesus doesn't promise to take away the pain, confusion or disappointment. But he'll enter into it with you and keep you company till you cross over to the other side.*
>
> Anne Lamott
> AUTHOR

Today we call this "tough love." Jesus is telling us that our bodies are temporary, but our souls are eternal. He wants us to do whatever it takes to guard our souls, even at the expense of our bodies if need be—that is how important the issue of eternity is. Obviously, Jesus was speaking in metaphors. We do not need to blind or maim ourselves in order to avoid sin. Temptations can be overcome through prayer, meditating in Scripture, asking others to hold us accountable and, as necessary, meeting with groups such as Alcoholics Anonymous or Narcotics Anonymous.

Jesus wants us to get serious with temptation. He doesn't want us to destroy ourselves with sin. He loves us enough to tell us the truth about sin and its destructive effect on our eternal souls.

How to Treat One Another

Next, Jesus tells us how we are to treat each other. "Don't be critical of other people," he said, "if you don't want people to criticize you. Don't condemn other people if you don't want to be condemned. You will be judged by the same standards you use to judge other people. The same measuring stick you use on others will be used to measure the way you live your life. So make allowances for the faults and frailties of others, and people will make allowances for you."

Many people take this to mean that no one has a right to criticize anyone else for a major moral or ethical lapse or for corruption or immorality. However, this is not what Jesus is saying. He is talking about people who are hyper-critical of the faults of others while failing to examine their own faults. He is talking about people who condemn others when they themselves are committing even worse sins. If we think we have the right to judge another person's life, then we had better have our own lives in order, because the same standard we apply to others will surely be applied to us.

People must be held accountable for the sake of a livable community and a just society. Criminals must be caught, tried and punished for their crimes. Unethical business-people must be held accountable for wrongful actions that harm investors, customers and employees. Corrupt politicians must pay a price for their corruption, which hurts us all and destroys good government. Corrupt judges must be removed from the bench. Bad teachers, clergymen, police officers, coaches, executives, doctors and lawyers should be forced to find other employment. If they are *criminally* bad—if, for example, they harm or molest children—then they should pay the heaviest price the law allows.

Jesus is not advocating an amoral, nonjudgmental society. That would be anarchy. He is telling us that we should stop gossiping about other people and criticizing them behind their backs. He is saying that we should stop fault-finding and obsessing over the minor flaws and foibles that are common to us all. Let's just cut each other a little slack! He is saying we should stop mind reading and pretending we know the inner motivations of other people. He is saying that we should honestly search our own lives and root out every trace of hypocrisy and arrogance—the desire to build ourselves up by putting others down.

As he did when he talked about gouging out our eyes and hacking off our arms, Jesus made this point clear with the use of another exaggerated metaphor. "Why," he continued, "do you make such a big deal about a tiny speck of sawdust in your brother's eye, yet you completely fail to notice a huge wooden plank in your own eye? How can you say to your brother, 'Here, let me remove that tiny speck from your eye,' while there is a huge plank in your own eye? You arrogant fraud! First, take the plank out of your own eye, and then you'll be able to see to remove that speck of sawdust from your brother's eye."

The image here is so extreme it's cartoonish. A man with a six-foot-long wooden plank protruding from his eye thinks he can remove an infinitesimal speck of dust from the eye of another person. The people who sat on the mountainside must have laughed out loud at how ridiculous it was, but the point was not lost on them. Jesus was not saying we should never try to help other people see themselves and their faults more clearly. Helping remove sawdust from each other's

> *One of the dangers of having a lot of money is that you may be quite satisfied with the kinds of happiness money can give and so fail to realize your need for God. If everything seems to come simply by signing checks, you may forget that you are at every moment totally dependent on God.*
>
> C. S. Lewis
> NOVELIST AND ESSAYIST

eyes *can* be an act of love. But it is absurd—and grossly hypocritical—to think we can do such delicate work on the eyes of other people when our own vision is blocked by a massive two-by-four of sin!

Next, Jesus made a statement that sums up his teaching on the subject of how we should treat one another. "In every situation," he said, "always do to other people what you would have them do to you, for this is what genuine religion boils down to." That principle is known today as the Golden Rule; if everyone in the world would live by that simple rule, imagine how our world would be transformed!

Money and True Security

The next theme of the Sermon on the Mount has a special meaning for us in the days in which we live. Here, Jesus deals with the true meaning of life, and he contrasts true meaning with what most people *think* life is all about: accumulating as much wealth as you can, or, as a bumper-sticker philosopher once put it, "He who dies with the most toys wins."

"Don't pile up treasures in this world," Jesus said, "where moths and worms can eat them, where rust can corrode them and where thieves can break in and steal them. Instead, keep your treasures in heaven where there are no moths, no worms, no rust and no thieves. Where do you keep your treasure? In some dark hiding place, where you worry and fret over it? Or in heaven, where it is eternally safe? Wherever you store your treasure is where your heart will be, for the thing you treasure is the focus of your life."

At first, these words of Jesus sound radical and shocking. Are we to take a vow of poverty, get rid of our homes, our wardrobes, our cars, our 401(k)s, our stock portfolios? Well, in a word, yes. If all of these things are our treasures, if our hearts are set on possessing all of this stuff, then we are not thinking like Jesus. Our thinking has been captured by this world. Our minds have been enslaved by the almighty dollar.

But is this statement of Jesus truly so radical or shocking? Actually, it's merely a restatement of something we all know deep down inside: You can't take it with you. We came into this world with nothing; we will exit this world the same way. You'll never see a hearse pulling a U-Haul trailer.

So while we are here, during these brief few decades of life that have been given to us, we must learn to loosen our grip on the things of this world. We must set our hearts on storing up eternal treasures in heaven and not on accumulating corruptible treasures here on Earth.

Now, there's nothing wrong with owning a house or a car or having a big investment portfolio. These are an important part of taking care of our families, which is a God-given responsibility. Riches and possessions are not evil, but as the apostle Paul once wrote, the *love* of riches leads to all sorts of evil. And as Jesus says in this sermon, the love of riches ultimately leaves you spiritually bankrupt.

I can tell you in all honesty that I own and enjoy some very nice possessions—a house, a car, a collection of mementos and sports memorabilia and much more. If it all

disappeared in a fire or a Florida sinkhole, I would be saddened and disappointed, but I would be okay. I enjoy those
things, but they are not my treasure, they are not where
my heart is. My treasure is in heaven.

Jesus went on to say, "No one can be loyal to two different masters at the same time. If there are two masters
seeking control of your life, you must choose to serve one
and reject the other. God is a master, and so is money—
and there is no room for two masters in one life. You can't
serve God and money at the same time."

If your treasures are in heaven, then God is your master.
If your treasures are in this world, then money is your master. There is no compromise between the two. You must
choose one or the other.

Ultimately, the only true security we have in life is found
in God, not in money and possessions. This is the point
Jesus made as he continued. "So don't worry about money
and the cost of living. Stop wondering where your next
meal is coming from or if you'll have enough to drink or if
you have something stylish in your closet to wear. The
essence of life is not food or your outward appearance."

As Jesus spoke, a flock of birds soared overhead. "Look
up there!" he said, pointing skyward. "See those birds? Do
they plant seeds in the ground? Do they harvest grain and
store it away in barns? No! Your Father in heaven feeds
them, and they have all they need. Aren't you more
valuable to God than the birds are? So why are you so worried about the necessities of your life? Why are you so
anxious about food and clothing?"

Next, Jesus pointed to the wildflowers that carpeted the mountainside. "And look at all of those wildflowers," he continued. "Do they work at being beautiful? Do they weave clothes for themselves? Of course not! Yet I tell you that even King Solomon never wore a kingly robe that was as glorious as the simple, natural beauty of those wild-flowers! Now, if God clothes the flowers of the field in such beauty—and flowers are here today and a shriveled memory tomorrow—then won't he care for you and clothe you appropriately? Is your faith too small to trust him for even that?"

A short man in the front of the crowd attracted his attention. "You, my friend," Jesus said, pulling the short man to his feet. "Can you make yourself an inch taller by worrying about it?" The man grinned and shook his head, and Jesus clapped him on the shoulder.

"Of course not," Jesus continued, addressing the entire crowd. "Then why do you all spend so much time worrying about what you cannot change? Why do you keep asking yourselves, 'What shall I eat? What shall I drink? What shall I wear?' That is what the unbelievers are always fretting about, because they have no God in whom to place their trust. But you are not

> *"The Jesus of dogma I do not understand,"* a Hindu professor once said to Stanley Jones, *"but the Jesus of the Sermon on the Mount and the cross I love and am drawn to."* Similarly, a Muslim Sufi teacher told him that when he read the Sermon on the Mount he could not keep back his tears.
>
> John Stott
> BIBLE SCHOLAR AND AUTHOR

unbelievers! You know that your heavenly Father loves you and knows your needs. So set your heart on his kingdom and on doing the right things and living the right way. If you do that, then God will give you everything you need in due course."

What, then, is the answer to our worries? Trust, simple trust, in God. "Don't worry about tomorrow," Jesus said. "Instead, focus on what God is doing in your life right now. When tomorrow's troubles arrive, God will give you the grace to deal with them. But until then, deal with today's problems today, and place your trust in God."

How to Think Like Jesus

Do you want to think like Jesus? Then the Sermon on the Mount is the key. If you understand it, then you'll understand how to think like Jesus. If you don't, you won't.

What is the Sermon on the Mount all about? In one sense, it's about a lot of different things: It's about how to be spiritually, eternally, paradoxically blessed. It's about how to be salt in a tasteless world and light in a dark world. It's about how to deal effectively with the problem of temptation and sin. It's about how we are to live together and treat one another. It's about placing our trust in God instead of seeking security in money and possessions.

In another sense, the Sermon on the Mount is really about just one thing: How to be a citizen of the kingdom of heaven. A citizen of heaven is a person who thinks and acts the way Jesus thinks and acts. Every thought and behavior that Jesus tells us we should practice in this Sermon is simply an example of the way Jesus thinks and behaves.

Jesus tells us that he himself is a king, but his kingdom is not of this world. His kingdom is the kingdom of heaven, and it operates by a different set of principles than any kingdom on Earth. But notice something important about the principles of this kingdom: They are not *laws*. They are actually *promises*. In most cases, they are paradoxical promises that make no sense according to worldly thinking.

Again and again, Jesus pits worldly expectations against heavenly principles. The world says it is the powerful, the exalted, the aggressive, the conquerors, the successful who are happy and blessed. But Jesus stands on the mountain and he blesses the lowly, the humble, the sorrowing, the gentle, the righteous, the merciful, the pure, the peacemakers, the persecuted and the powerless. These are the citizens of his kingdom. These are the people he calls "blessed."

The Sermon on the Mount is a study in contrasts. The world is tasteless, but those who think like Jesus are the salt of the Earth. The world is dark, but those who think like Jesus are the light of the world. You've heard it said, "Do not murder," but Jesus says, "Do not even hate!" You've heard it said, "An eye for an eye," but Jesus says, "Bless your enemies. Turn the other cheek." You've heard it said, "Do not commit adultery," but Jesus says, "If you even lust in your heart, you are already guilty." Again and again, throughout the Sermon on the Mount, Jesus challenges our thinking with his thinking. He challenges our viewpoint with paradoxes and contrasts.

If we want to think like Jesus, we have to stop thinking the way the rest of the world thinks. We have to think in new ways, and our lives have to reflect these new ways of thinking. People who think like Jesus go against the flow. Their views and values are at odds with the culture around them. This is the point Jesus made as he brought his wide-ranging sermon to a close.

"You enter my kingdom through the narrow, hidden gate," he said. "Most of the people in this world are taking an easy road through a broad gate that leads only to destruction. But the gate is narrow and the road is difficult that leads to life, and only a few people find it.

"Look out for false teachers and leaders who come to you and outwardly seem as innocent as sheep—but inwardly, they are wolves, waiting for the chance to rip into you and devour you. How do you know the false from the true? Teachers and leaders are like trees in an orchard. A true tree bears good fruit; a bad tree bears bad fruit. A tree that doesn't bear good fruit is fit only to be cut down and used for firewood. You'll know whether your teachers and leaders are good or evil by the fruitfulness of their lives.

"A lot of people will say to me, 'Jesus, my master!'—but talk is cheap. Only those who do the will of my Father in heaven will actually enter the kingdom of heaven. In the final analysis, at the end of human history, many people will say, 'Jesus, my master! Remember all the great things I did in your name? I declared the truth in your name and commanded demons out of people in your name, and I did many other powerful works in your name!' But I will say to them,

'I never knew you. Get out of my sight, you evildoers!'

"If you hear my words and live according to them, you'll be like a wise man who built his house on a solid foundation of stable rock. When the rains came, when the floods rose, when the winds pounded on the walls, the house didn't fall, because it was built on a firm foundation. But those who hear my words, ignore them and go on about their lives will be like a foolish man who built his house upon sand. Rains, floods, winds—these forces will easily destroy a house with an unstable foundation. It will collapse like a house of cards!"

When Jesus had finished speaking these words, the crowd on the mountainside sat in stunned silence. Never had they heard such teaching. Jesus didn't teach like the religious scribes who offered their opinions, which were based on the opinions of other scholars and scribes. Jesus taught them as if he was the final authority on all matters relating to life and faith.

Moreover, he challenged them. He confronted them with a tough choice: Take the narrow road, the hidden gate. Don't just hear the words of the Sermon on the Mount, but do them. Don't build your life on the unstable foundation of this world's values and philosophies, but build your life on the stable foundation of the words of Jesus. In essence, Jesus said, "If you want to enter my kingdom, you have to think like me, live like me and be like me. So what is your decision?"

Two thousand years later, his question to us is still the same.

CHAPTER SEVEN

HOW TO PRAY LIKE JESUS

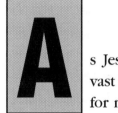s Jesus came down from the mountainside, vast crowds followed him. Some were hungry for more words like those of the Sermon on the Mount. Others hoped to see him perform a miracle. But as Jesus and the crowd walked back from the mountain, they were met along the road by a scene of unspeakable horror and ugliness when a mutilated and disfigured man approached on the road. Jesus saw the man and continued walking toward him, but the crowd stopped and drew back in disgust.

The man looked like a walking corpse. His face was covered with patches of livid discoloration and dark nodules. His nose, lips and ears were swollen and misshapen. Patches of his scalp were hairless, replaced by blackened, sickly flesh. Yellowish eyes stared wildly from a face without eyebrows and eyelashes. His fingers and toes were rotting and lumpish.

The man was a leper, a victim of what we now call Hansen's disease, a bacterial infection that destroys the skin and nervous system. Those infected with the disease were shunned by the rest of society.

As the people around Jesus backed away and hid their

eyes, the leper came up to Jesus and knelt at his feet. "Master!" the deformed man cried out. "If you are willing, you can heal me!"

Jesus looked at the man, and his eyes brimmed with tears of compassion. In a voice choked with emotion, Jesus said, "I am willing." Then he reached out and touched the man, saying, "Be clean!"

Immediately, the leprosy fell away from the man. The discoloration left his face. The dark nodules turned to smooth, healthy skin. His nose, lips and ears returned to their normal shape. The whites of his eyes lost their yellow appearance. His fingers and toes were whole once more. He was clean.

> *The great tragedy of life is not unanswered prayer, but unoffered prayer.*
> F. B. Meyer
> BIBLE SCHOLAR

The Touch of Jesus

This is a profound story with several layers of meaning for our lives. The first thing to notice about this story is that the leper approached Jesus with the words, *"If you are willing,* you can heal me!"

Does that request remind you of another event in the life of Jesus? We talked about it in chapter 3, and we'll explore it in detail in chapter 17. It's an event that takes place shortly before the Crucifixion—the prayer of Jesus in the Garden of Gethsemane. "My Father," Jesus prayed, "if there is any way possible, please let this cup be taken from me." Facing the bitter "cup" of the cross, his soul recoiled in horror. Even so, he ended his prayer with, "Yet, let it not be as I will, but as you will."

"If you are willing . . . ," the leper prayed to Jesus. "Let it not be as I will, but as you will," Jesus prayed to God the Father. Somehow, this leper intuitively understood what it means to pray like Jesus!

This man may have been horrible to look upon, but his spirit and his attitude were beautiful. Think about what these few simple words express: "If you are willing." The leper wasn't saying, "Jesus, if it wouldn't be too much trouble, please heal me." He wasn't saying, "Jesus, if you're in a good mood right now, please heal me." No, this leper sensed that everything Jesus did was part of a greater purpose, a larger plan. So his question was, "If my request is in harmony with your will and your purpose, please heal me."

So the first thing we see in this story is the prayerful attitude of the man with leprosy. He didn't come with any demands. He simply carried a request and a submissive heart. He was ready to accept the will of Jesus, whatever it might be: "If you are willing."

This is the first lesson in what it means to pray like Jesus. Prayer is not about getting God's will to align with ours. Prayer is about getting our will to align with God's. Prayer begins with an attitude of submission to the will of God. If we come to God and we are not willing to humbly align our will with his, then it is not prayer.

The second thing we notice in this story is the *compassion* of Jesus. The Gospel account tells us that

Jesus looked at this man and was "filled with compassion." Jesus saw a tortured human soul trapped within that diseased flesh. The man had once been a mother's beautiful baby. He had grown into a little boy who ran and played with his friends and who had dreams of a future. Perhaps he was married. Perhaps he even had children. He once had so much to live for.

Then an infectious microorganism called *Mycobacterium leprae* had invaded his flesh. It had destroyed his life, his career, his relationships, his dreams of the future. This horrible disease had made him an outcast, repulsive to everyone around him, repulsive even to himself.

Jesus saw all of this in a flash of insight. In that moment, his heart broke for this man. His eyes flooded with tears. Jesus took this man's pain into his own being, and he made it his pain. He had compassion.

The third thing we notice in this story is that Jesus did something that no one else would ever have done: He *touched* a leper. How could Jesus bring himself to touch this man? There are few things more ugly and disgusting than flesh that is diseased with leprosy. We know that this man was not in the early stages of the disease, for the Gospel account tells us that he was "covered with leprosy." His condition was advanced.

There was more than mere revulsion and disgust at stake here. This man was not merely sick. He was *unclean,* according to the Law of Moses. It was a

> *True prayer is asking God what he wants.*
> William Barclay
> BIBLE SCHOLAR

violation of the Law to touch a man with leprosy. But Jesus didn't hesitate to answer the man's prayer and touch his diseased flesh.

And with that touch, the man was healed.

A Failure to Obey

After healing the man, Jesus took him aside and said to him, "I don't want you to spread around what has happened to you. Instead, I want you to go show yourself to the priest and offer the sacrifices to God that Moses commanded. Do this in gratitude for your cleansing and as a testimony to the priests."

Jesus had a clear purpose in mind for this healing. This was the first time a man had been cured of leprosy since the prophet Elisha had cured Naaman, the Syrian army commander, in the Old Testament's Book of Numbers. Jesus wanted to use this healing to demonstrate the power of God to the religious leaders. He planned for this healing to stand as a fulfillment of the prophecy of Isaiah—the same prophecy he had read in the synagogue in Nazareth (see chapter 6). In short, Jesus was offering this healing as a sign that he was who he claimed to be—the promised Messiah.

In those times, leprosy was considered a symbol of sin. The disease symbolized the spiritual deformity that sin produces in human lives. So, when a man came along with the power to cleanse people of leprosy, performing miracles of healing as the prophet Isaiah had predicted, these actions were considered signs of the Messiah. Jesus wanted the religious leaders to see these signs, so he told the healed man to present himself to the priest.

The leper, however, didn't do as Jesus told him. Instead, he went all around, spreading the news of his healing! The news quickly raced through the countryside. From that time on, Jesus was no longer able to enter a town without attracting vast crowds.

It's understandable that this healed leper would have a hard time containing himself and doing exactly what Jesus commanded. The man probably thought he was doing Jesus a favor by praising him to everyone he met. But it wasn't praise that Jesus wanted. After all, when he commanded evil spirits out of people, they also praised him and said, "You are the Son of God!" Jesus silenced them because they were trying to announce him before his time had come. Jesus wanted obedience, not praise.

When the leper came to Jesus for healing, he said, "If you are willing." But in all the excitement after he was healed, the man forgot about obeying the will of Jesus! Here is a lesson for us all: It's not enough to pray, "If you are willing." *After* we pray, we have to *continue* living according to his will. While we pray, we should also obey.

With the best of intentions, the healed man hindered the plan and program of Jesus. His disobedience barred Jesus from

> *What if the main object in God's idea of prayer be the supplying of our great, our endless need—the need of Himself?*
>
> George MacDonald
> PREACHER AND NOVELIST

traveling freely in towns and forced Jesus to spend much of his time out in the wilderness to escape the pressure of the crowds. The story of the healed leper tells us that it is always a mistake to substitute our plans for God's plan.

The Prayer of a Roman Centurion

After healing the leper, Jesus made his way back to Capernaum in hopes of resting from the stresses and pressures of the recent days. The crowds not only followed him to Capernaum, but there were crowds waiting for him when he arrived. He had no sooner entered the town, accompanied by his disciples, when he was met by a Roman centurion—the commander of a division of about one hundred men (roughly the equivalent of an Army captain today).

"Master," the Roman officer said, "I have a servant in my home who is paralyzed and suffering terribly."

"Then I will go to your home and heal him," Jesus replied.

"Master," the Roman said, "I'm not important enough for you to even set foot under my roof. But if you'll just say the word, I know my servant will be healed. For I myself am a man who is under the authority of others, even as I am in authority over soldiers. I can say to one man, 'Go!' and he goes, and to another man, 'Come!' and he comes. I say to my servant, 'Do this,' and he does it. So I know that if you give the word, whatever you say will be done."

Jesus gazed in astonishment at this Roman officer, who represented the hated Roman occupation forces. Then he turned to the crowd and said, "I tell you the truth, I have not found anyone with such great faith in all of Israel!"

Then he said to the centurion, "Go on your way. Everything will happen just as you have believed it would."

The centurion's servant was healed at that very moment.

Here again, we see a man who seemed to intuitively understand what it means to pray like Jesus. The centurion was a man who understood the issue of authority—and submission to authority. The attitude of this Roman soldier was almost identical to the attitude expressed by the leper's words, "If you are willing."

This Roman placed no demands on Jesus but simply stated his request and left the results to Jesus. When Jesus offered to go to his home and heal the servant, the centurion said, in effect, "That won't be necessary. I know the authority you have over diseases, and I know that you don't even need to be physically present for this authority to be exercised. I am familiar with authority and submission, because I am both a soldier and a commander of soldiers. I obey authority and I exercise authority—and I willingly submit to your authority. Do as you will, and I will accept it."

> *The essence of request, as distinct from compulsion, is that it may or may not be granted. And if an infinitely wise Being listens to the requests of finite and foolish creatures, of course he will sometimes grant and sometimes refuse them.*
>
> C. S. Lewis
> NOVELIST AND ESSAYIST

"Such great faith" indeed!

The Prayers of Jesus

Whenever Jesus faced a major problem or decision, he would spend an entire night in prayer. One night, not long after the Sermon on the Mount, he faced such a decision: Who would he choose as his inner circle of disciples?

He had scores and scores of disciples following him, but Jesus knew he needed a core group of ultra-disciples called *apostles,* which means "people sent out with authority to perform a mission." His plan was to mentor them and pour his life into them so they could carry on his work after he was taken out of the world.

So Jesus slipped away from Capernaum and walked up a mountainside under the moon and stars. In the stillness of the night, away from the pressure of the crowds, Jesus went to his knees and prayed. Hour after hour, all through the night, he talked to God and listened to what God was saying within his inner being. When the sun arose the next morning, Jesus got up, descended the mountain and returned to Capernaum with his mind made up.

He chose twelve men to be his apostles. Some of the Twelve Apostles became his closest friends and leaders of the group—men like Simon Peter and the two sons of Zebedee, James and John. But one of the Twelve was a man named Judas Iscariot—the traitor who later betrayed Jesus. It might seem, at first, that Jesus made a terrible mistake in choosing Judas. After spending an entire night in prayer over a crucial decision, he chose a traitor! What a terrible miscalculation on the part of Jesus!

Or was it?

By the end of the story, it is clear that Jesus was walking a road that was carefully mapped out for him. He was following the will and the plan of the Father, and everything that happened—including the treachery and disloyalty of Judas—was used by God to further that plan. There was no mistake, no miscalculation. Jesus spent the night in prayer, and the result was that he chose twelve men. Each of those men had a role in advancing God's plan. Eleven played their parts as obedient apostles and representatives of Jesus. One played his part as a traitor. Taken together, the Twelve were an answer to Jesus' prayer that night.

Another lesson about prayer in the life of Jesus is that he continually prayed for others. Two key examples occur shortly before his death. In the first example, Jesus meets with his disciples in an upper room. Knowing in advance that all of the disciples will abandon him at his arrest and that Simon Peter will deny even knowing him, Jesus takes Peter aside and tells him, "Simon, Simon, Satan has demanded permission that all twelve of you be given over to him so that he might sift all of you like so much grain. But I have prayed especially for you, Peter, that your own faith may not fail during this time of testing. You will disown me, Peter, but when you have returned and regained your faith, I want you to strengthen and establish your brothers."

Here we see Jesus praying for the men in his inner circle, and in particular for Simon Peter, whom he has designated to lead them in his absence.

The second example occurs later that same night. Hours before going to the cross, Jesus prays again for his close friends and followers, but not only for them. In his prayer, he adds, "I am not praying for these followers only, but for all who will one day come to trust in me as a result of their message."

In other words, Jesus looked ahead, over the centuries, to all the future followers who would hear the message of Simon Peter and the other apostles. He even looked two thousand years into his future, to people such as you and me. Jesus prayed for us, that we would truly be like Jesus— and God the Father is answering that prayer in your life and mine right now.

These events in the life of Jesus illustrate what it means to pray like Jesus. He prayed daily. He prayed early. Faced with problems and tough decisions, he prayed through the night. He prayed for himself. He prayed for others. Jesus was, above all, a man of prayer.

The question that confronts you and me is this: If Jesus needed such an intense and daily reliance on prayer, how much *more* do you and I need to pray? If we want to pray like Jesus, we need to watch the way he prayed, and we need to listen to everything he said

> *There are many people who speak to God in prayer, but hardly ever listen to him, or else listen to him only vaguely.*
> Paul Tournier
> PSYCHIATRIST, LAY THEOLOGIAN
> AND AUTHOR

about prayer. Let's return, then, to the Sermon on the Mount and hear what Jesus taught about prayer.

The Pattern for Prayer

In the Sermon on the Mount, Jesus taught extensively about prayer. "When you pray," he said, "don't be like those religious phonies—the ones who love to stand up and make a big show of praying in the synagogues and on the street corners, so that other people will see them and notice how 'religious' they are. I tell you the truth, when they get noticed by the crowds, they get all the reward they're ever going to get—and they'll receive no reward from God!

"But when you pray, go into your own room, shut the door, and pray to God the Father in privacy. He sees all things, including your private devotion, and he will give you an eternal reward for praying in truth and sincerity.

"And when you pray, don't make a long, babbling speech of it, like the pagans do. They think their prayers will be heard because of their wordiness. Don't be like them. After all, God, who is truly a loving Father to you, knows everything you need even before you ask him—but ask him anyway. He is your Father, you are his child, and he enjoys fellowship with you."

The disciples had seen Jesus pray on many occasions. They had seen his commitment and consistency in prayer, as he regularly rose early to pray in a solitary place. They had witnessed the intimate relationship Jesus had with his father in prayer. They had seen the power he had in prayer—power to heal, power to command evil spirits, power to persevere under intense opposition. They had seen the peace he had in prayer, even amid the pressures and stresses of his ministry with the crowds. The disciples wanted to pray like Jesus, so they said to him, "Master, teach us to pray."

Jesus taught them a pattern for prayer that is widely known today as the Lord's Prayer. "When you pray," he said, "let this be the basic pattern you follow: Our Father in heaven, may your name be honored. May your kingdom come. May your will be done on Earth, just as it is in heaven. Give us this day the bread we need to sustain us. Forgive us for the wrongs we have done, according to the way we forgive those who have wronged us. Lead us away from the path of temptation, and save us from evil."

There are five elements to this prayer:

1. *Praise.* Jesus tells us that we should begin by recognizing God as our Father and giving honor to his name. We give praise to God not because he wants to be flattered, but because we need to grasp the awesomeness of our Father-Creator. So we offer words of praise, respect and reverence, such as, "Our Father in heaven, may your name be honored."

2. *Surrender and submission.* The leper understood this principle; so did the Roman centurion. We do not come demanding that God bend his will to ours. We come humbly, with yielded spirits, seeking to align our hearts with his. We come asking him to rule over our lives. So we offer words of surrender and submission, such as, "May your kingdom come. May your will be done on Earth, just as it is in heaven."

3. *Requests and needs.* God is a loving Father, and he wants to give us good gifts. Though there is much more to prayer than, "God, give me this; God, I need that," we should approach him gladly and gratefully, knowing that he cares about our needs. So we offer to him our requests, such as, "Give us this day the bread we need to sustain us."

4. *Forgiveness.* To be like Jesus and pray like Jesus, we need to have the forgiveness of Jesus flowing through us like the air we breathe. We take forgiveness in from God, and we give forgiveness out to others. So we pray, "Forgive us for the wrongs we have done, according to the way we forgive those who have wronged us."

5. *Protection from evil.* Temptation is the risk that is inside us all—the risk of our lusts, our selfishness, our tendency to go our own way and wander from God. Evil is the peril that is all around us—the risk of illness, accident, crime, natural disaster, war, terrorism and so forth. We must rely on God's power to protect us from temptation, and we must trust his love and power to either guard us from harm and trouble or to enable us to endure it. So we pray, "Lead us away from the path of temptation, and save us from evil."

That is the pattern of prayer Jesus gave to his disciples—and to us. He didn't say that we should necessarily pray this prayer word for word, although many people find it helpful to do so. This prayer that we call the

Lord's Prayer is ultimately a pattern or outline to enable us to focus our prayers in a meaningful and effective way.

In the Sermon on the Mount, he also told us the attitude we should have as we pray. "Ask," he said, "and it will be given to you. Seek and you will find. Knock and the door will be opened for you. The one who asks will always receive; the one who seeks will always find; the door will always open to the one who knocks."

Do you believe in the power of prayer? Do you believe that God truly does answer prayer as Jesus said? Herb Miller, in his book *Connecting with God,* tells about one church that wasn't sure what it believed about prayer.

A nightclub opened in a small town, Miller said, and the goings-on in that nightclub were immoral and offensive to the people of the town's largest church. So the church held an all-night prayer vigil. Hour after hour, from sundown on into the night, the people in the church prayed for God to burn down the nightclub. Finally, sometime after midnight, a thunderstorm rolled over the little town. Lightning struck the nightclub after closing time, and within minutes, the place had burned to the ground.

When the nightclub owner heard that the church had prayed for his business to be destroyed, he filed suit against the church. The church claimed it wasn't responsible for his loss. The judge, after hearing both sides of the case, scratched his head and said, "Let me see if I've got this straight. It sounds to me as if the nightclub owner believes in prayer, but the church doesn't!"

Now, I don't agree that prayer should be used to call

down lightning on those we disagree with, but the judge has a point: If we want to be like Jesus and pray like Jesus, then we need to believe that prayer works. When we pray, we need to put our faith and trust squarely behind God, who has promised to answer our prayers.

Which brings us back to the promise of Jesus that if we ask, seek and knock, we shall receive. What is he telling us about prayer? Does he mean that we have a blank check from God, and all we have to do is fill in the amount? Does he mean that if we ask, seek and knock in prayer, God will give us whatever we ask?

> *God loves to hear the sound of your voice.*
> Steve Brown
> AUTHOR AND SPEAKER

For the answer to these questions, listen to what Jesus goes on to say about prayer in the Sermon on the Mount. "If one of your children came to you and asked for bread," Jesus continued, "would you give your child a stone instead? If he asked for a fish, would you give him a snake? If you, as a sin-prone human being, know how to give good gifts to your children, isn't it far more likely that God, your perfect heavenly Father, will give good gifts to those who ask him in prayer?"

Here, Jesus tells us we should approach God in a trusting way, as a child approaches a loving parent. We should ask, seek and knock in prayer, then see how God chooses to answer our prayer. I believe Jesus is telling us that God will sometimes say "Yes" to our prayers and give us what we ask for. I think it also means that God will sometimes say, "Wait, and I will give you something even better."

As a father, I have heard many requests from my kids. Some of those requests were very reasonable, while others were completely ridiculous. Kids want what they want when they want it—that's only natural. They will ask you for ice cream for breakfast. They will ask if they can stay out all night. They will ask for a brand-new Corvette for their sixteenth birthday. They will ask you for the moon and look at you cross-eyed if you don't immediately hand it over.

God, our heavenly Father, has heard a lot of similar prayers. Some of our prayers are sensible and reasonable, while others are completely off the scale—the equivalent of asking for that Corvette at age sixteen. As Jesus said, God loves us and wants to give us good gifts. He wants us to have the bread we need, not a stone. But what if we come to him in prayer and ask for a stone? Should he give it to us, just because that's what we asked for? A loving parent wouldn't do that. A loving parent would answer, "Wait, and I will give you something even better. I'll give you real bread, not just a stone."

I'm glad that God doesn't give us a blank check when we pray. Many times, I've asked God for something that I thought was good, something I thought was the equivalent of "bread." Looking back, I realize that I was actually asking for a stone. I'm glad that God always gave me what was best for me, and that he didn't always give me what I asked for!

Remember the attitude of the leper: "If you are willing." Remember the attitude of the centurion: "If you give the word, whatever you say will be done." Remember the prayer Jesus taught us: "May your will be done." Remember the prayer Jesus himself prayed before he went to the cross: "Not as I will, but as you will."

Finally, remember the first lesson of prayer: Prayer is not about getting God's will to align with ours. Prayer is about getting our will to align with God's. Prayer begins with submission to the will of God.

No human being has ever prayed with more intensity than Jesus prayed the night before the Crucifixion. "Let this cup be taken from me." When God answered that prayer, the answer was, "No." Though it was Jesus' will that he escape the horrors of the cross, God's will was that he endure the cross and die. In the course of that terrible night of prayer, the will of Jesus came into alignment with the will of the Father.

That is what your prayers and mine must be like if we are to pray like Jesus. As we align ourselves with God's will in prayer, we can ask, seek and knock, knowing we will receive God's best for our lives. It may not be what we expected. It may not be what we asked for. But it will be a good gift, the best gift we could possibly receive.

CHAPTER EIGHT

HOW TO FORGIVE LIKE JESUS

Not long after Jesus called the Twelve Apostles as his inner circle, he was in Capernaum, his adopted hometown by the Lake of Galilee. He was speaking to a crowd in a large house—possibly the home of the government official we met in chapter 6. The crowd overflowed through the doorway and onto the street. People huddled around the windows. Inside and outside the house, they strained to hear every word Jesus spoke.

Not far away, four men made their way through the streets of Capernaum, and they carried a burden among them. Each man held one corner of a thick mat. Lying in the middle of the mat was a man who was paralyzed from the neck down. The four men carried their friend to the edge of the crowd and tried to push through, but the crowd wouldn't let them pass.

Finally, one of the men had an idea. He pointed to the roof of the house. The other three nodded, and they went to work on their plan.

Inside the house, Jesus was speaking when suddenly— *thunk-thunk-thunk!*—he was interrupted by the sound of heavy footsteps on the roof. Jesus looked up. So did the crowd. Then, another sound—*scraaaaape!*—the sound of clay tiles being pulled aside. The shadowy interior of the house was split by vertical shafts of sunlight. Jesus peered up at the hole in the roof. The faces of four men gazed down at him—then the four men continued ripping up tiles and enlarging the hole.

A murmur rippled through the crowd. "Who do those men think they are?" some said. "How dare they rip up a man's house?" But the four men on the roof didn't care what anyone said. They would do anything to bring their friend to Jesus.

Within moments, the mat was lowered through the roof and placed at the feet of Jesus. The paralyzed man looked up from his mat with hope in his eyes. Jesus looked up at the four men who crowded around the hole overhead. Their eyes, too, were full of hope and expectation. These five men had complete confidence that God was about to act.

> *Failures for the believer are always temporary.*
>
> *God loves you and me so much that he will allow almost any failure if the end result is that we become more like Jesus.*
>
> George Verwer
> MISSIONARY AND AUTHOR

Jesus bent down to the paralyzed man and said something strange and completely unexpected. "My son, your sins are forgiven."

The Miracle of Forgiveness

Some of the people sitting in that house were leaders of the religious community. As soon as they heard Jesus tell the paralyzed man, "Your sins are forgiven," they went into shock! They turned to each other and grumbled, "Who does he think he is, saying he can forgive sins? That's blasphemy! No one but God can forgive sins!"

Though Jesus couldn't hear what these men whispered to each other, he could read their thoughts in the expressions on their faces. "You teachers of the Law!" Jesus said. "Why are you debating among yourselves this way? Which would be easier to say to this paralyzed man? 'Your sins are forgiven,' or 'Rise up, pick up your mat and walk'?"

Jesus looked from face to face in that room, searching the eyes of those who had accused him of blasphemy. "But," he continued, "just so you'll know that the Son of Man has authority on Earth to forgive sins—watch!" Then he turned to the paralyzed man at his feet, and his voice changed. "Hear me!" Jesus said. "Get up! Pick up your mat and be on your way!"

In an instant, a look of astonishment appeared on the man's face. Arms and legs that had been limp and paralyzed began to move. The man raised himself from his mat and stood in full view of all the people.

For several seconds, there was total silence. The crowd was stunned. Then, a few voices began praising God. Others said, "We've never seen anything like this before!" A cheer went up around the entire house.

The man bent down, picked up his mat and walked out through the crowd of cheering people.

> *He who has not forgiven an enemy has never tasted one of the most sublime enjoyments of life.*
> Johann Kaspar Lavater
> CLERGYMAN AND POET

At first glance, this looks like a story about God's power to heal a broken human body. But if we look closer, we can see an even deeper meaning to this story: It is about God's power to heal the *soul*. This healing of the soul took place through the miracle of *forgiveness*.

The Meaning of Forgiveness

What an amazing thing for Jesus to say! "Your sins are forgiven." What did Jesus mean by those words?

To put this issue into perspective, consider this question: What if I came to you and said, "Your sins are forgiven"? What would that mean to you? Probably nothing at all. Talk is cheap.

I can say to you, "Your sins are forgiven," or, "Abracadabra! You are now a billionaire!" or "Shazaam! You are now ten feet tall!" But would those words mean anything coming from me? Of course not. I don't have any authority or power to say such things and make them come true. So how could Jesus say such a thing to the paralyzed man?

It is important to understand that when Jesus said, "Your sins are forgiven," the words he used had a specific and profound meaning. He was telling the paralyzed man, "The penalty for every sin you've ever committed is hereby removed. You are no longer guilty of any wrong in God's sight. You are now in right standing with God."

What if I said those words to you? You would think I was arrogant to the point of blasphemy! You would think I was playing God. And that's exactly what the religious leaders accused Jesus of doing: playing God.

Jesus had put the question to them, saying in effect, "Which is easier to do, forgive sins or heal a physical illness? You've questioned my authority to declare a man's sins forgiven before God. Fine. If I'm not who I claim to be, then you're right: I'm arrogant and blasphemous. But what if I am who I claim to be? And how would I prove my claim? I tell you what. I'll demonstrate to you that I not only have the authority to forgive sins, but the authority to heal as well. If I have the power to make this man walk, then you'll have to agree that I have the authority to forgive his sins."

Then Jesus healed the paralyzed man right before their eyes. The man got up, walked out of the house on his own two feet and all the people cheered and rejoiced—all, of course, except those religious teachers!

During his three-year ministry on Earth, most of the opposition Jesus faced came from religious people. He could command demons with a word. He got along well with sinners, Samaritans and even a Roman centurion. But the religious teachers and leaders he encountered could be obstinate, bigoted, close-minded and intolerant beyond belief.

This is not to say that religion is a bad thing. Honest, authentic religion that is rooted in a genuine relationship with God is a wonderful thing, and it produces the most loving, openhearted, reasonable people in the world. But counterfeit religion, rooted in self-righteous pride and a desire to see oneself as better than others, was a powerful force in the world of Jesus' day. Counterfeit religion fought Jesus at every turn. It plotted his death and ultimately crucified him.

What's more, counterfeit religion is still in full force today, and some of it parades under the banner of "Christianity." The kind of counterfeit religion I'm talking about is not a particular religious movement, organization or denomination. It is an arrogant spirit. It is a sanctimonious attitude. If we are honest with ourselves, we have to admit that there is probably a bit of counterfeit religion lurking within each of us.

Our goal in wanting to be like Jesus is to root out that counterfeit religion—that prideful, egotistical, self-righteous religion of our own making—and replace it with a real, openhearted, open-minded relationship with God himself. So how do we do that? How do we replace counterfeit religion with a genuine relationship with God?

It all begins with forgiveness.

The reason we tend to be self-righteous is that we know, deep down, that we are *not* righteous! We feel guilt and shame over things we've done. We remember the times we have hurt other people or committed moral failures. We know that we are living with broken relationships in our lives. We know that our character is not what it should be. So we try to cover our guilt and shame with a hopelessly inadequate fig leaf of self-righteous religion.

But a fig leaf of religion can't help us. What we need is a message from God, the same message Jesus gave the paralyzed man: "Your sins are forgiven. The penalty for every sin you've ever committed is removed. You are no longer guilty of any wrongs. You are now in right standing with God."

All healing begins with those words, "Your sins are forgiven." All guilt and shame ends with those words, "Your sins are forgiven." Real life, the abundant life, doesn't truly begin until you hear those words. Only then does the paralysis of guilt lose its grip on your life.

When did the paralyzed man hear those wonderful, liberating, life-changing words from the lips of Jesus? When he and his friends looked at Jesus with eyes of hope and trust. In short, when Jesus saw their faith.

In this story, we see that he deliberately presented himself as God's expression of forgiveness to human beings. Maybe you believe that claim, maybe you don't.

> *True forgiveness never brings up the subject again. Biblical forgiveness treats the offender as if the offense had never happened. The basis for God's forgiveness is the cross of Jesus Christ. The cross enables God to forgive us because it maintains His justice. But the basis upon which we are called to forgive is different: Our basis for forgiving others is the fact that we ourselves have already been forgiven.*
>
> Ray C. Stedman
> PASTOR AND AUTHOR

There were some in that house who believed his claim. One of them got up and walked. The rest cheered and rejoiced.

There were also some who didn't believe his claim. They looked at Jesus and saw an arrogant blasphemer.

By now, you can see that this event in the life of Jesus is not as simple as it might seem on the surface. This event demands of us that we choose sides. It forces us to select between one of two options. Either Jesus is who he claimed to be—the personification of God's forgiveness—or he was an arrogant blasphemer who took it upon himself to play God.

I won't tell you which option you *should* choose. I can only tell you that you *must* choose.

Canceling the Debt

The theme of this chapter is how to forgive like Jesus. From what we've seen so far, however, it appears that we have painted ourselves into a corner. We have just made a convincing case that we *can't* forgive like Jesus! Obviously, you and I can't go around to strangers on the street and say, "Your sins are forgiven." We don't have the authority that Jesus claimed for himself—the authority to declare God's pardon for sin and guilt.

Once again, we find a paradox in the life of Jesus. We see another way in which we *can't* be like Jesus. Yet we must be like Jesus! What's the answer to this riddle? How *do* we forgive like Jesus when we can't forgive like Jesus?

Actually, this riddle has a very simple solution. We simply forgive as Jesus taught us to forgive. Jesus taught extensively on the subject of forgiveness. Let's look at some of those teachings.

First, we got a hint of Jesus' teaching on forgiveness in chapter 7 when we examined the prayer he taught his disciples. In that prayer, the Lord's Prayer, Jesus said we should pray, "Forgive us for the wrongs we have done, according to the way we forgive those who have wronged us." In other words, we need to experience God's forgiveness flowing through us. His forgiveness is to be like the air we breathe. First, we inhale God's forgiveness, drawing it into the center of our being. Then, we exhale forgiveness, breathing out a gracious, forgiving spirit upon everyone around us. We receive forgiveness and we give forgiveness.

Jesus once illustrated this truth with a story. He was alone with the Twelve when Peter (the unofficial leader of the Twelve) asked a question. "Master," said Peter, "how many times should I forgive my brother when he sins against me? Should I forgive him as many as seven times?"

Do you detect a note of spiritual pride in that question? It sounds as if Peter thought he was being oh-so-spiritual in offering to forgive an offending brother as many as seven whole times!

If Peter was demonstrating an inflated spiritual pride, then Jesus wasted no time in deflating it. "I tell you," Jesus said, "you must forgive your brother not merely seven times, but seventy times seven times!"

If you remember your fourth-grade arithmetic, then you can easily calculate the meaning of Jesus' answer to Peter. Seventy times seven equals 490 occurrences of forgiveness! Now, if you think you *don't* have to forgive your brother the 491st time he sins against you, then you've missed the point. Jesus is not raising our forgiveness quota from 7 to 490. He's raising it to *infinity!* He's saying, "Don't even keep track, don't even keep score. Peter, you think you are being generous by offering to forgive your brother seven times. I tell you that you are to keep forgiving and forgiving and forgiving until you completely lose count of how many times you have forgiven!"

Jesus then told Peter and the others a story to illustrate his meaning. "Look at it this way," he said. "The kingdom of heaven can be compared to a king who wanted to settle accounts with his servants. As the king began settling each account in turn, a servant was brought before him who owed him ten thousand silver talents."

When Jesus said this, a collective gasp must have gone up from the twelve disciples. Jesus was describing a shockingly huge debt. A "talent" was a unit of monetary exchange throughout ancient Rome, Greece and the Middle East. In today's terms, one silver talent was worth fifteen hundred to two thousand dollars. So how much did the servant owe the king in this story? Ten thousand silver talents equaled *fifteen to twenty million dollars!*

Jesus continued. "Since the servant was unable to pay back the debt, the king ordered that the servant, his wife, his children and all his possessions be put on the auction block and sold—even though the money from the sale wouldn't begin to cover the debt. The servant collapsed to his knees before the king and begged, 'Please be patient with me and I promise to pay back everything I owe you!' The king took pity on the servant. 'I have reconsidered,' the king said. 'I have decided to cancel the debt and release you. Go in peace.'"

Unfortunately, the story does not end there.

"The forgiven servant went out," Jesus continued, "and he found one of his fellow servants—a man who owed him a paltry hundred denari." This was a sum equal to about twenty dollars. "The servant who had been forgiven by the king grabbed the other servant by the throat and began to choke him! 'Pay me what you owe me—right now!' he demanded. The other servant collapsed to his knees and begged, 'Please be patient with me and I promise to pay back everything I owe you!' But the forgiven servant refused to forgive his brother. Instead, he called for the authorities to haul the poor man away and throw him into prison until he could pay the debt.

"When the other servants of the king saw that their brother was thrown in prison for a debt of a mere hundred denari, they became upset. They went to the king and told him what had happened. So the king called in the servant he had forgiven. 'You wicked, contemptible, ungrateful servant!' the king said. 'I forgave your great debt because you begged me to. Why, then, didn't you show mercy to your fellow servant, as I showed mercy to you?' Then the king handed the servant over to the jailers to be tortured until he had paid back everything he owed. And that is how my heavenly Father will deal with every one of you unless you freely, sincerely forgive your brother when he sins against you."

So the forgiveness of God, Jesus says, is intimately linked to our own willingness to forgive those who offend us. If we truly want to be like Jesus, there is no room in our lives for holding grudges, for criticizing and gossiping about others, or for holding onto unforgiving attitudes of spite, bitterness, resentment, hatred and revenge. When we hold a grudge, we are being like that ungrateful, unmerciful servant. We must forgive—and never even mention the sin again.

I know that God has forgiven me for so many sins, so many debts. How, then, can I hold a grudge against a brother or sister in the human family who has committed some paltry little offense against me? If we have been for-given by God, then we know that he has canceled a debt that we owed him—a debt that is infinitely beyond our ability to pay. If God has so freely forgiven us, then we should freely forgive one another by cancelling the debt that they owe us.

This doesn't mean, however, that we don't hold other people accountable for their sinful actions. Jesus said that when people commit a serious or harmful offense against us, we should speak up! "If your brother sins," he said, "sin-cerely tell him so. Rebuke him gently and humbly. If he repents and is sorry for his offense, forgive him. Even if he sins against you seven times in a day, and comes to you seven times to say, 'I'm sorry,' forgive him, let go of your resentment, and consider his debt against you to be canceled."

What if we don't *feel* like forgiving someone? That's okay. In fact, when someone offends us, it's a sure bet that we won't feel like forgiving—but we have to forgive anyway. How do we forgive when we feel like hating? We do it by making a *decision* to forgive—and then sticking to that decision.

Helen Gahagan Douglas was an actress turned congresswoman who was also a good friend of First Lady Eleanor Roosevelt. She once observed that the former first lady "got even with her enemies in a way that was almost cruel. She *forgave* them."

In his book *Answers to Satisfy the Soul,* my friend and writing partner, Jim Denney, defines forgiveness as "a choice to renounce anger or resentment against an offender." He says that forgiveness is a decision we make, not an emotion we feel. Feelings such as anger and resentment will come and go. "But," he says, "if we make a *decision,* we can *will* ourselves to abide by that decision, despite our wavering feelings."

You've heard the cliché, "Forgive and forget." I'm sure you also know that, when someone has really hurt you, it is almost *impossible* to forget it! "We can't simply press a 'delete' button on our memories," Jim Denney says. "In fact, our brains are constructed in such a way that the most painful memories tend to be the ones that are the most permanently imprinted. So forgetting is *not* a component of forgiving. Fact is, we must forgive precisely because it is *impossible* to forget. The memory of the hurt will come back to us again and again, so we must make a deliberate choice to renounce anger and resentment."[1]

Later in this book, we will look at the Crucifixion of Jesus. We will see him hanging from a wooden cross, the bloody instrument of Roman torture and execution. We will hear him speak these astounding words in his death agony: "Father, forgive them. They don't know what they are doing."

As Jesus spoke those words, he certainly could not have had warm, fuzzy feelings for the religious leaders who had lied about him at his trial, or for the Roman soldiers who had pounded iron spikes through his flesh and bones, or for the crowd that surrounded him, mocking and jeering him as his lifeblood drained onto the ground.

> *"Father, forgive them."* *This may be the most perfect statement spoken at the most perfect time since God gave the gift of language. As unimaginable as his request was, it was so fitting! If the cross is about anything at all, it is about forgiveness. Forgiveness of the most incorrigible and least deserving.*
>
> Beth Moore
> AUTHOR AND SPEAKER

But in that dark and cruel hour, he made a tough decision. He *chose* forgiveness over bitterness and hate. If we want to be like Jesus, we have to make that same tough choice.

---

[1] Jim Denney, *Answers to Satisfy the Soul* (Sanger, Calif.: Quill Driver Books, 2001), 101–2.

What Is God's Forgiveness Like?

People sensed the forgiveness of God in Jesus. When they were in his presence, the love of God radiated from him. People with dark and shameful secrets gravitated to him, because he talked about a God who was ready to cleanse their lives and wash away the stench and stain of their sins. People who were outcasts and hated by society—the tax collectors, drunkards, prostitutes, street people and lowlifes—all crowded around him, because he accepted them and treated them as equals.

When the religious leaders and Pharisees saw how much those sinners loved Jesus and how freely he accepted them, they grumbled and complained about him. "This man from Nazareth actually welcomes these sinners! He receives them as friends and even eats with them!"

When Jesus saw how resentful the religious leaders were, he told them a number of parables to make a point about God's forgiveness. "A shepherd had a hundred sheep," Jesus said, "and he lost one of them. So he left the ninety-nine out in the wilderness and he went searching until he found the one lost sheep. When he found that sheep, he placed it across his shoulders, then returned home happy. Arriving home, he called all of his friends and neighbors together and said, 'Be happy with me, because I have found the one sheep that was lost.' And so I tell you, there will be more rejoicing in heaven over one wicked sinner who repents and is forgiven than over ninety-nine righteous people who do not need to be forgiven.

"And there was a woman who had ten silver coins, each coin worth a full day's wages. One day, she noticed that one of the coins was missing. So she lit a lamp and swept out her house, looking under every stick of furniture until she found the lost coin. Then she called all of her friends and neighbors together and said, 'Be happy with me, because I have found the silver coin that was lost.' And so I tell you, there is rejoicing among the angels of God over one wicked sinner who repents and is forgiven.

"And there was a man who had two sons. The younger son came to his father and said, 'Dad, I want you to give me my share of the property that would come to me as my inheritance.' His father agreed, and divided his entire estate between his two sons. A few days later, the younger son took everything he had and went to a distant country. There, he squandered his fortune on wild and reckless living.

"After he had spent everything he had, a famine fell upon that country, and the young man was needy and hungry. A pig farmer in that country hired him to slop hogs—a miserable and degrading job. As the young man fed carob pods to the hogs, he held back some of the pods for himself, but they didn't satisfy his hunger, and no one gave him anything better to eat.

"Finally, the thought came to him: *My father's hired servants are eating well, and here I am, dying of hunger! I'll get up, go to my father, and say, 'Dad, I have sinned against heaven and against you. I'm not even worthy to be called your son anymore. But I would be grateful if you would just take me back as a hired servant.'*

"So the young man got up and headed home. While he was still a long way off, his father saw him and was overcome with compassion. He ran to the boy and hugged him and kissed him. The son began the little speech he had rehearsed. 'Dad, I have sinned against heaven and against you. I'm not even worthy to be called your son. . . .'

"But the father interrupted and called to his servants. 'Hurry! Bring the finest robe of honor and put it on my son! Place a ring on his hand and sandals on his feet! Kill the fattened calf and let's feast and celebrate! Share my happiness, because my son was dead and is alive again; he was lost and is found!' And the people of the household began to celebrate.

"But the older son was in the field as all this was taking place. He returned to the house and heard the sound of music and people dancing. So he asked one of the servant boys, 'What's all this celebrating about?' The servant boy replied, 'Your brother has returned, and your father has killed the fattened calf because he has received his son safe and sound.'

"The older brother was enraged and would not go near the celebration. So the father came out and pleaded with him to join them. But the older brother angrily replied, 'Look! I've been working hard for you all these years, obeying every order you gave me. You never even let me barbecue a young goat to celebrate with my friends—yet here you are, slaughtering our best calf to throw a party for a disobedient, ungrateful son who spent your estate on prostitutes!'

"'Son, son!' the father said. 'You are always here with me! Everything I have is yours. But it is only right to celebrate and be happy, because your brother was dead and is alive again! He was lost and now he is found!'"

Jesus told three stories about three things that were lost and then found: a sheep, a coin and a wayward son. The third story is the most detailed and dramatic. A son goes to his father and demands his inheritance. Jesus does not spell it out, but everyone who heard him knew what this boy was actually saying to his father. "Dad, I wish you were dead. I'm tired of waiting for you to die, so I can get what's coming to me. I want my inheritance now!" The disrespect and ingratitude of this young man was shocking.

The father was undoubtedly wounded by the callous behavior of his son, yet he agreed to the boy's thoughtless demand. The boy went out to a distant country, where he lived in sin and received the consequences of his rebellious lifestyle. He ended up being, in effect, a servant to a bunch of hogs. The pigs ate better than he did! Finally, humiliated and ashamed, he returned to his father's home.

What was the father's reaction? Jesus said that the father observed the returning boy "while he was still a long way off." I think Jesus wanted us to know that this father didn't just happen to glance up and notice his son. This loving father had a daily habit of going up on a hill, looking down the road, hoping against hope to see his returning son. One day, his lonely vigil was rewarded!

The son was welcomed home, the fattened calf was barbecued, and the people of the household threw a big party. The obedient son, however, refused to celebrate. He was understandably angry, as he felt his loyalty and obedience had been taken for granted. Meanwhile, his brother's waywardness was *rewarded!* It wasn't fair! If anything, the older brother felt he should get the party and his wayward little brother should be *punished!*

The older son certainly had a point, but he failed to grasp the meaning of forgiveness. The forgiveness of God transcends the logic and justice of human beings. Forgiveness isn't fair. Forgiveness isn't even logical. That's precisely the point.

Forgiveness is an act of grace. What is grace? It is a gift or a benefit that is completely undeserved. That is what this father did for the younger son. He gave the boy a completely undeserved gift of grace and forgiveness. That is exactly what Jesus says God the Father offers all of us, including you and me: the completely undeserved gift of his grace and forgiveness.

Though we deserve punishment, penalty and judgment, Jesus says that God offers forgiveness and love, instead. That is what the forgiveness of God is like, and that is what our forgiveness should be like. Instead of demanding justice and fairness when we are wronged, as the elder son did, we must practice grace and forgiveness. It's not fair. It's not logical. But that's what forgiveness is all about.

> *It doesn't matter whether someone deserves to be forgiven. You deserve to be free.*
>
> Diane Hales
> AUTHOR AND JOURNALIST

The Bombardier Who Forgave

On April 18, 1942, Army Corporal Jacob DeShazer left the deck of the aircraft carrier *Hornet* aboard a B-25 bomber. DeShazer was a bombardier, one of the "Doolittle Raiders"—seventy-nine men in sixteen airplanes under the command of Lt. Col. Jimmy Doolittle. These men were on a mission to bomb Tokyo during World War II. It was a one-way mission, since there was not enough fuel for a round-trip. Their orders were to drop their bombs, proceed to China and bail out.

As DeShazer's plane came in low over Japan's capital, he checked his bomb sights and released his ordnance. Below him, factories exploded in billowing flames. Anti-aircraft fire perforated the skin of the airplane, but the plane made its escape toward China. Hours later, as their plane was flying on fumes, DeShazer and his fellow airmen parachuted into the night over Japanese-held territory. DeShazer landed in a Chinese cemetery, breaking several of his ribs in the process.

He was soon captured and taken to a Japanese prison camp for interrogation. There, a military tribunal sentenced him to death by decapitation. The sentence, he was told, would be carried out at sunrise. The next morning, he was taken from his cell, but instead of being executed, he was put onto a plane with some other prisoners from America. They were flown to Tokyo, where they were interrogated and tortured.

Later, DeShazer and his companions were returned to China. He spent the next two years in a tiny cell that was an oven in the summer and a deep-freeze in the winter. He suffered from many illnesses, including dysentery, as well as the brutality of the guards.

Finally, after two years in prison, DeShazer and the other Americans were allowed to have a Bible to read. Each prisoner took a three-week turn, then the Bible was passed on to the next man in line. Reading by the faint gray light from a tiny vent near the top of his cell, DeShazer began in Genesis and read straight through to Revelation. In particular, he pored over the life of Jesus, memorizing as many of the words of Jesus as he could.

One day, just to be cruel, a guard slammed the cell door on DeShazer's foot. As the American prisoner clutched his foot and groaned, he felt nothing but hatred for the sadistic guard. Then, he remembered the words Jesus spoke in the Sermon on the Mount: "Love your enemies and ask God to bless those who persecute you."

The next day, when the guard opened the cell door, DeShazer smiled, greeted the man with a Japanese word of blessing and asked him about his family. The guard seemed startled, shaken and suspicious. Day by day, DeShazer continued to show kindness to the guard. Soon, the guard responded by bringing DeShazer extra food, even candy.

In June 1945, DeShazer and the other Americans were moved to a prison where conditions were even worse. Though Jacob DeShazer became ill and nearly starved to death, his faith in God grew stronger. In August of that year, the war ended, and Jacob DeShazer was a free man.

It is one of the great paradoxes of God that, over the course of his imprisonment, Jacob DeShazer developed a deep compassion and a love for his captors. After the war, he returned to Japan with his wife, Florence, where they served together as missionaries. DeShazer simply wanted to be like Jesus and live among the Japanese people, helping to meet the physical and spiritual needs of the people of postwar Japan.

Ironically, one of those whose life Jacob DeShazer touched was a man named Mitsuo Fuchida, the flight commander who had led the Japanese attack on Pearl Harbor. After hearing DeShazer's story and getting to know him personally, Fuchida decided that he, too, wanted to be like Jesus. Fuchida became an evangelist, traveling the world as the "Japanese Billy Graham."

The story of Jacob DeShazer convinces me that one of the most powerful, visible and life-changing ways we can be like Jesus is to learn how to forgive like Jesus. Forgiveness replaces human hate with godly compassion. Forgiveness transforms lives and relationships.

Forgiveness is not fair, nor is it logical. But forgiveness is powerful beyond measure. If you want to be like Jesus, then let these be the first words from your mouth whenever you are mocked, slandered, beaten or crucified: "Father, forgive them. They don't know what they are doing."

CHAPTER NINE

HOW TO BE HUMBLE LIKE JESUS

In northern Israel, you can visit the towns around the Lake of Galilee where Jesus walked and taught, including the lakeshore towns of Capernaum and Tabgha. Capernaum, the adopted hometown of Jesus, was the site of many of his miracles, such as the healing of the paralyzed man. Tabgha was the fishing town where, according to tradition, Jesus called his first disciples, Simon Peter, Andrew, James and John.

Midway between Capernaum and Tabgha is a small cove, which today is called the Cove of the Sower (after one of the parables Jesus probably told there). The hills rise in an arc around that cove to create a natural theater. Jesus probably did much of his teaching there, either from the shore of the cove or from a boat pushed out a short distance from the shore.

The acoustical properties of the Cove of the Sower are astounding. If you visit that region, go to the cove with a friend and try an experiment on a calm day, a day when no cars are passing on the nearby road. Have your friend stand on the shore while you go far up the hillside. Then have your friend speak to you. He should speak in a strong voice, but there's no need to shout. Though it seems impossible, the person high up on the hill will hear every word spoken from the shore.

The Cove of the Sower is probably where Jesus taught the people after he healed the paralyzed man in Capernaum. Multitudes crowded the hills that rose in a bowl-shaped semicircle from the shore of the cove. Day by day, with the sparkling blue water of the Lake of Galilee as his backdrop, Jesus taught the people about the kingdom of heaven.

One day, as Jesus walked down the road that led south from Capernaum to the Cove of the Sower, he passed a tax collector's booth, which had been set up just outside the city gate. The man in the booth was Matthew Levi, the son of Alphaeus. Jesus walked up to the booth, looked Matthew square in the eye and said, "Follow me." Matthew immediately left his booth and followed Jesus.

> *Throughout the Bible, God shows a marked preference for "real" people over "good" people.*
> Philip Yancey
> AUTHOR AND JOURNALIST

What kind of man was Matthew? To understand him, we need to understand his profession—the profession of a tax collector.

The Lowest of the Low

What was the job of a tax collector like? How were tax collectors viewed by Jewish society?

The Roman government collected three kinds of taxes—property taxes, a per capita (per person) tax and a customs tax on goods transported from city to city. Since Matthew's tax booth was located on the roadside at the city gate, he was probably a collector of customs taxes. When fishermen transported their salted, dried fish out of Capernaum or when farmers shipped their wheat, figs and olive oil through Capernaum, they had to stop at Matthew's booth and pay the tax.

Matthew made a good living, primarily by extorting money from his Jewish brothers on behalf of Rome. Tax collectors were among the most hated people in Israel, because they collaborated with the Roman oppressors. They were notorious for overtaxing the people and keeping as much money for themselves as they could. They were hated not only as traitors to their own people, but as robbers and extortionists, as well.

Now we begin to see what kind of man Matthew was. He was rich but despised, powerful but hated. He was probably crooked. He had friends, but his friends were not respectable people. The only people who would have a man like Matthew as a friend were people who were just as shunned and vilified as Matthew himself: pagans, drunkards, prostitutes, people who had been excommunicated by the synagogue, and other tax collectors.

This is the kind of man Matthew was. So it is nothing less than amazing that Jesus would approach him with the words, "Follow me." Matthew accepted his invitation, left his booth and became a disciple of Jesus of Nazareth. At first we might wonder why Jesus would choose such a hated and disreputable man to be his follower. But on closer examination, we realize that this was his pattern: Most of the people whose lives Jesus touched were outcasts of one kind or another.

> *Humility is not a quiet, reserved super-sanctimonious posture in life. The truly humble person can be appropriately bold and can enjoy life to the fullest— laughing and crying with great expression. Humility is the driving desire to give God the glory in all things and to obey him regardless.*
> Joseph Stowell
> EDUCATOR AND AUTHOR

In chapter 7, we saw Jesus reach out to touch a leper, the most shunned of all social outcasts. We also saw him heal the servant of a Roman centurion, one of the hated oppressors. In chapter 1, he spared the woman caught in adultery as she was about to be stoned. Now, Jesus spoke to a tax collector, a traitor and a thief. Again and again, he reached out to the lowest of the low— outcasts, enemies, sinners, traitors and crooks.

What does it take to reach out to such people, to love them and eat with them, to talk to them and treat them as equals? It takes a special quality called *humility.*

A Friend of Sinners

As a new follower of Jesus, the first thing Matthew did was throw a huge banquet for Jesus. Matthew invited all of his friends. Of course, his friends were the very dregs of society, but that didn't stop Jesus from attending. So what if there were pagans, drunkards, prostitutes and tax collectors on the guest list? These were the very people Jesus wanted to reach! So, Jesus and his disciples dined and drank at Matthew's house with the lowest of the low.

As we have seen in previous chapters, the disciples were not the only ones who followed Jesus. His enemies, too, followed him around and watched his every move. The Pharisees kept Jesus under surveillance, alert for some word or action they could use to discredit him. When they saw him eating and drinking with sinners and tax collectors, they thought they had him.

There were so many people at the banquet that some sat outside the house talking, laughing, eating and drinking. Some of Jesus' disciples were among those outside. The Pharisees angrily accosted those disciples and said, "What is your Master doing in there with those people? Why is he eating and drinking with tax collectors and sinners?"

Inside the house, Jesus was at a table with Matthew when he heard the commotion outside. He got up from the table, walked to the doorway of the house and found the Pharisees arguing with his disciples.

"This man you call 'Master,'" the religious leaders sneered, "this so-called 'teacher' and 'healer' from Nazareth! Look at him! He's a glutton! A drunkard! A friend of tax collectors and sinners!"

Jesus stepped out of the shadows of the house. "Yes," he said. "You speak truly. I am a friend of tax collectors and sinners."

The Pharisees turned, startled by the voice of Jesus. A hush fell on the scene. Both the eyes of his followers and the eyes of his foes were turned on Jesus.

"It is not the healthy who need a doctor," Jesus continued, "but the sick. You should go back to your books and learn what the prophet Hosea was trying to tell you. He said that God desires a heart full of mercy, not sacrifices burned on an altar. He desires compassion, not meaningless rituals and empty religion."

One of the Pharisees stepped forward and jabbed his finger at Jesus. "You have no sense of decency! Look around you! This is a nest of sinners—a bunch of thieves and lowlifes! These are the people God hates!"

Jesus reached out and put his arms around two of those "lowlifes" and looked the Pharisee in the eye. "You have no understanding of God's purpose in the world," Jesus answered. "These people you despise are the ones God sent me to. For I have not come to call the so-called 'righteous' to repentance. I have come to call 'sinners' and 'lowlifes' to turn from their sin, and receive God's mercy."

> *By meditating upon the humility of Jesus, we find how very far we are from being humble.*
> Teresa of Avila
> AUTHOR AND MYSTIC

Before the proud Pharisees could respond, Jesus turned and led his friends back into the house of the tax collector. More enraged than ever, the enemies of Jesus turned and stamped down the street, grumbling among themselves.

If Jesus Walked Through Our World

Imagine yourself in that scene. Imagine that you are one of the disciples of Jesus. You have been invited to a lavish banquet at the house of a wealthy man—but he's not a bank president or a corporate CEO or a respected politician. No, he's gotten his wealth from dealing drugs or from political corruption. Who's on the guest list at his party? Well, you're rubbing shoulders with prostitutes, drunks, drug addicts, illegal aliens, ex-cons—the lowest of the low. There's not a respectable citizen, not a Rotarian, not a minister, not a community leader in the bunch.

How would you feel if the word got out to your friends that you had attended this party? It would be a scandal! You'd be disgraced and humiliated. You'd never be able to show your face in polite society again!

That's the situation Jesus put himself and his disciples in. Yet Jesus was perfectly comfortable there. He welcomed the company of "lowlifes" and they welcomed him. Jesus ate Matthew's food, drank Matthew's wine and thoroughly enjoyed himself. He shook hands that had committed crimes. He put his arm around shoulders that were stooped in shame. He embraced people who have never felt the touch of mercy and compassion before.

He also taught his disciples, and you and me, an important lesson in acceptance and humility. Some of the disciples who were there that day probably felt out of place and uncomfortable. The fishermen who followed

Jesus, men like Simon Peter, Andrew, James and John, may have resented being in the home of Matthew the tax collector. This man had probably cheated them many times over the years, collecting taxes and graft on the dried fish they exported. Like the rest of their society, these fisherman would have looked down on a tax collector as the lowest of the low, a traitor to the nation of Israel.

But Jesus set an example for his followers, showing compassion and acceptance toward the lowest of the low. His message was that everyone is the same. No one is greater, no one is lesser. God loves everyone alike. We must stop giving undue deference to the high and mighty. We must stop treating the low and lowly with contempt. We must begin to see all people as God sees them.

The religious leaders thought that God would be satisfied with the slaughter of animals on stone altars. But Jesus reminded them of what their own Scriptures told them: God is pleased by hearts full of compassion and mercy, not by a lot of dead sacrifices. God is pleased when people live humbly and treat each other as equals. He is not pleased by arrogant, empty religion.

Why do we lavish our attention on the rich and powerful while ignoring the needy and powerless? The answer is obvious: The rich and powerful can do things for us. We lavish attention on them in hopes of getting something in return. What can the needy and powerless do for us? Absolutely nothing.

Yet, the needy and powerless are the ones Jesus gave his time and attention to. Why? Because they were the ones who needed it most! Jesus spent most of his time helping the helpless, and he asked nothing in return. Someone once observed that the best way to size up a person's character is by watching how he treats people who can't do him any good. By that measure, Jesus had more character than anyone else in history.

Truly humble people have open hearts that accept all people. There is no room for bigotry, intolerance or hatred in a humble heart. Humble people are approachable and easy to talk to. Humble people are gracious and understanding. They are good listeners. Humble people are great human beings precisely because they never think of their own importance.

If Jesus were walking through our society today, where would he go? To a power lunch with corporate CEOs and prominent politicians? Would he hobnob with entertainers, rock stars and authors? Would he appear at a state dinner at the White House? Or, would you likely find him at the soup kitchen of the Salvation Army, reaching out to inmates in the jails and prisons, and embracing dying patients in an AIDS ward?

If you and I truly want to be like Jesus, where should we be?

The Demands of Jesus

After the banquet at Matthew's house, the people continued to come to Jesus to hear his words and receive his healing touch. Some were under the influence of demons, and Jesus delivered them from the power of evil spirits. Others were sick, and Jesus healed them. Finally, the pressure of the crowds became so great that Jesus had to withdraw for a while. He had some of his disciples bring a boat to the shore, so that they could cross to the far side of the Lake of Galilee. It was a fishing boat with a single, large sail and was probably twenty-five feet from bow to stern.

The boat was beached, and Jesus and his disciples went aboard. Before Jesus could settle into the boat, however, two men ran up to him. One was a religious leader, a teacher of the Law of Moses. Unlike many of the religious leaders who opposed Jesus, this one had become convinced of Jesus' claims. "Teacher!" the man said. "Let me follow you! I will go wherever you go!"

Jesus turned to the man and said, "Are you sure you know what you are asking? Where do you think I'm going? What kind of life will you have if you follow me? Where will you call home? Even the foxes of the field have holes to live in. Even the birds of the air have nests to call home. But the Son of Man doesn't even have a place to lay his head at night."

The second man stepped forward. "Master," he said. "I want to follow you, too! Only . . ." The man hesitated.

"Only what?" Jesus said.

"It's just that my father has died," the man said. "Let me go and bury my father—and then I will follow you anywhere."

"Follow me now," Jesus said, "and let the dead bury their own dead."

How harsh! How unfeeling! These two men came to him wanting to join the band of disciples. Why, then, did he speak so sharply to them?

Because they needed to know the truth!

To the first man, he said, in effect, "I know you are sincere, but make sure you know what you are getting into. As a religious leader, you are zealous and earnest about following me now, but things are going to get rough. Life will be uncomfortable and dangerous. I have no home, no shelter, and the storms of opposition are coming. If you want to follow me, fine—but you should know that following me will cost you everything, including your home, your comfort and your security."

To the second man, he said, in effect, "I know you are grieving, but your father is already dead, and you can't do any more for him now. Understand, the life of a disciple is a demanding one. If you would call me 'Master,' then you must set aside your agenda and follow mine. If you want to follow me, nothing must hold you back."

Jesus placed tough, uncompromising demands on those who followed him. What he told these two men was only what he had told his disciples all along. "If any person wants to follow me, he must disown himself, carry his cross on his own back and walk every day in my footsteps. Anyone who cares more about his own life than about following me will lose his life. But whoever loses his own life for my sake will save it for eternity. For what good does it do you to gain the world, then lose your own soul? If you do not sacrifice everything for me, you cannot be my disciple."

It takes genuine humility to accept those words. Jesus doesn't ask for our spare change or a moment of our time. He demands everything—total submission, total surrender, total humility.

> *God is attracted to weakness. He can't resist those who humbly and honestly admit how desperately they need him.*
>
> Jim Cymbala
> PASTOR AND AUTHOR

We don't know how these two men responded to the challenge of Jesus. The Gospel accounts don't tell us whether they went with Jesus or turned back in discouragement. We only know that after this encounter, Jesus and his disciples pushed their boat out into the water and set off across the Lake of Galilee.

The Least and the Greatest

Jesus began his life with a humble birth in the village of Bethlehem. He was raised in a humble little town called Nazareth. He lived a humble life—he owned no home, acquired no possessions and had no place of his own to rest his head at night.

There are many words that characterize the life of Jesus—love, courage, obedience, prayer, forgiveness, leadership—but high on that list is the word *humility*. In fact, that is how Jesus defined his own character: "Take my yoke upon you and learn from my example, for I am gentle and humble in heart, and you will find rest and refreshment for your souls."

Notice that phrase, "take my yoke upon you." A yoke is a bar with two collars used to harness two draft animals together, such as a pair of oxen. In the ancient world, oxen were always sold as a pair, as a "yoke of oxen." Jesus tells us that we are to yoke ourselves side-by-side with him. He will share our burden as we share his burden. As we yoke ourselves to him and learn from his gentle, humble example, we will find rest for our souls.

On one occasion, Jesus and the disciples were walking on the road to Capernaum. As they walked, some of the disciples hung back and argued with each other in whispers. What was the subject of their debate? They were arguing about who would be the greatest in the kingdom!

Even though Jesus repeatedly told them what his kingdom was about, the disciples persisted in picturing it as a *political* kingdom. They saw Jesus as a political messiah— a revolutionary who would defeat the armies of Rome and reestablish Israel as an independent kingdom. They saw the miracles he performed as evidence that God would enable him to accomplish military and political miracles, as well. They believed that when Jesus was crowned king, they would all become viceroys, chancellors and prime ministers in his new kingdom.

Peter, the most outspoken of the Twelve, may have started the argument by staking a claim to the position of vice-regent, the second-in-command to Jesus. And then there were James and John, whom Jesus had nicknamed the "Sons of Thunder," perhaps for their zealous and militant personalities. They probably argued over who would be minister of war. Judas Iscariot, who kept the money purse for the disciples, probably expected to be Chancellor of the Exchequer in the coming kingdom—a role that Matthew, the former tax collector, may have coveted for himself.

These twelve men were strong-willed, competitive individuals who would have fit right into our aggressive, dog-eat-dog American business culture. They wanted to get ahead in the world, they wanted to be winners, they wanted to call the shots.

The Twelve kept their voices low as they quarreled, and they thought that their argument went unheard by Jesus. Arriving in Capernaum, they went to the house where Jesus was staying. Once inside, Jesus turned to his disciples and asked, "What were you arguing about on the road?"

The disciples exchanged guilty glances. None dared say a word. But Jesus didn't need to be told what they had squabbled about. He *knew.*

The people who owned the house where Jesus stayed had children, so Jesus called one of those children to himself. "Listen," he said, seating himself before the shame-faced disciples. "If one of you wants to be first in the kingdom, he must be the very last, and the servant of all the rest. And whoever elevates himself in pride shall be humiliated. But he who humbles himself shall be honored. For the one who willingly becomes the

> *People with humility don't think less of themselves. They just think about themselves less.*
>
> Norman Vincent Peale
> SPEAKER AND AUTHOR

least among you is truly the greatest of all."

Then Jesus hugged the child in his arms and added, "I tell you the truth, unless you change your attitude and become like this little child, you will never enter the kingdom of heaven. Does this child compete for power and position? No! And neither should you. So whoever chooses to humble himself like this child shall be the greatest in the kingdom of heaven."

Humility in Giving, Praying and Worshiping

Jesus spoke often about the importance of a humble spirit. On one occasion, as Jesus was teaching the disciples at the Temple in Jerusalem, he pointed to the teachers of the Law who paraded through the Temple courts. "Don't be like the teachers and scribes," he said. "They like to walk around in fine clothes, to be greeted with respect, to sit in the front row at the synagogue or at the head banquet table. They love to be thought of as righteous and religious, so they make long-winded prayers to cover up their crimes of cheating widows out of their homes. They will receive a heavy sentence of eternal condemnation."

After saying this, Jesus led his disciples to a courtyard lined with stone columns, where the Temple treasury was located. Against one wall of the courtyard was a row of thirteen collection boxes with trumpet-shaped receptacles on top. If you dropped large coins into the collection box, they would rattle and clatter loudly down the throat of the trumpet and attract a lot of attention.

There were thirteen collection boxes, because offerings were collected for thirteen distinct purposes: for the purchase of turtledoves or pigeons for sin offerings; for the purchase of wood, incense and golden vessels for the Temple; for offerings by cleansed lepers; and so forth. The very last collection box in line, the thirteenth, was for voluntary offerings.

As Jesus sat across the courtyard, he watched the people file past and drop money into the various receptacles. The rich filed past in their finery, making a show of dropping golden coins into the receptacles. They would drop a few coins at a time to create a long, drawn-out production of their donations. Their heavy coins landed in the chests with a sound like a Las Vegas slot machine. They wanted everyone to see how generous they were.

As Jesus and the disciples watched, a humble widow came through the line. She paused at the thirteenth collection box and took two copper mites from her purse. A mite was the smallest and least valuable coin of all. Together, those two coins were worth about half a cent. She dropped them into the horn of the collection box. The *clink, clink* they made was almost inaudible.

Then she melted anonymously into the crowd and was gone.

Jesus turned to his disciples. "I tell you the truth," Jesus said, "that widow, as poor as she is, has given more to God's treasury than all of the others. The rich contributed what they could easily afford. But that woman, out of her poverty, put in everything she had to live on."

The widow and her two copper mites provided a visual lesson in humility—a lesson that Jesus taught the people in his Sermon on the Mount. On that occasion, he said, "Beware of doing your so-called 'good deeds' so that people will notice and admire you. If self-important pride is your motive, you will receive no reward from your Father in heaven. Instead, when you give to the needy, don't make a big display of it, announcing your 'good deed' with a trumpet fanfare! That's what the hypocrites do in the synagogues and the streets. They just want to be honored and praised. I tell you the truth, the empty praise they receive is all the reward they will ever get!

"But you, when you give to God or to charity, don't even let your left hand know what your right hand is doing. Don't congratulate yourself! Do your good deeds, then forget them! That way, your giving will be secret, even from yourself. Your Father is watching, and he knows all secrets, including the secrets of the truly humble heart. He will reward you openly for giving secretly out of pure and sincere motives.

"The same goes for your worship and religious devotion. Those religious hypocrites who make such a show of their giving also make a show of their religious piety and fasting. They deliberately make themselves look miserable so that everyone will see that they are fasting and being so 'religious.' I tell you the truth, the empty praise

> *Talent is God-given; be thankful. Praise is man-given; be humble. Conceit is self-given; be careful.*
> Tony Dungy
> NFL COACH

they receive is all the reward they will ever get.

"But you, when you devote yourself to prayer and fasting, do so in all humility. When you fast, make sure your hair is combed and your face is washed, so that no one knows you are fasting. Keep it a secret, just between you and God. And your Father in heaven, who knows all secrets, will be watching. He will reward you openly for praying and fasting secretly with a pure and sincere heart."

Humility must be at the heart of everything we do, especially when we are giving, praying or worshiping God. If our motives are tainted, then our religious acts are worse than useless. They are hypocritical and hateful to God.

The Greatest Are the Most Humble

Dr. Billy Graham recalls a time early in his career as an evangelist when he learned the meaning of humility. He had come to a small town to preach the gospel at a local Baptist church. He needed to mail a letter, but he didn't know where the post office was. So he stopped a young boy and asked for directions. The boy told him how to get to the post office.

Billy Graham thanked the lad and said, "If you'll come to the Baptist church tonight, you can hear me tell everyone how to get to heaven."

The boy shook his head. "No, thanks, mister," he said. "How can you tell people the way to heaven when you don't even know the way to the post office?"

Now, that's a lesson in humility!

I once had a conversation with Rick Marshall, a crusade

planner for twenty-three years with the Billy Graham Evangelistic Association. I asked Rick if he could capture the character of Billy Graham in a word. He didn't even have to think about it. "The word for Billy Graham," Rick said, "is *humility*. That's why God has been able to use Billy in such a powerful way for so many years. I think God looked down at Billy and said, 'I can give him success, fame and prestige because I know I can trust him to remain humble. At the end of the day, I know that Billy Graham will never take credit for the accomplishments that only I can do.'"

The greatest leaders are always the most humble leaders. Humility is the great dividing line that distinguishes a boss from a leader. Bosses are proud, vain and intimidating. They demand that people serve them. Leaders are humble, unassuming and encouraging. They see themselves as servants, not bosses.

Dr. Charles Swindoll is a best-selling author and chancellor of Dallas Theological Seminary. When he was a first-year seminarian at Dallas in 1959, Dr. Swindoll studied Greek under Dr. Bert Siegle, a soft-spoken and humble professor. "I didn't know what it was that made such an impact on us as we sat in Dr. Siegle's classroom," Dr. Swindoll recalled, "but at times it was as though we had been lifted into the heavenlies."

Dr. Siegle died in 1963, and Dr. Swindoll attended the funeral. As he sat and listened to various people talk about Dr. Siegle's impact on their lives, Dr. Swindoll was astonished to learn the depths of humility—and the heights of greatness—of his old seminary professor. He learned that

Dr. Siegle began teaching at Dallas during the Great Depression. Many times, the seminary was unable to meet payroll. If Dr. Siegle and other professors had not sacrificed, the school might not have made it through those tough times. In addition to his teaching duties, Dr. Siegle served on the maintenance crew, where he hauled trash, emptied wastebaskets, laid bathroom tile and scrubbed toilets.

"When I heard that," Dr. Swindoll concluded, "I knew what it was about the man that so endeared him to us: His heart of humility had won our respect."

Dr. Bert Siegle knew how to be humble like Jesus. His life is a challenge to your life and mine. If we truly want to be like Jesus, then let's pattern our lives after the one who said, "Take my yoke upon you and learn from my example, for I am gentle and humble in heart."

CHAPTER TEN

HOW TO LOVE LIKE JESUS

Jesus climbed into a boat with his disciples. They pushed off from the shore and set out across the lake. They sailed east, toward the district called Decapolis (the Region of the Ten Greek Towns). Exhausted from dealing with the needs of the crowds, Jesus settled in the back of the boat and quickly fell asleep.

As they cruised across the lake, the disciples saw the gray skirts of an impending storm. Within minutes, they found themselves plunging into a threatening squall. Gusts of spray-laden wind stung their faces. The men wondered if they should turn back, away from the storm. The sail billowed and flapped in the rising wind. The boat rocked sickeningly. The men looked to the back of the boat, wondering what Jesus would have them do. Amazingly, Jesus didn't awaken. He didn't even stir.

The little boat rode into the furious storm. Waves broke over the bow, swamping the boat. Finally, the disciples shook Jesus and woke him. "Master, Master!" they shouted. "We're going to drown!"

Jesus looked up at their worried faces. "Is your faith so small?" he replied. "What are you afraid of?" Sighing, he got up and went to the side of the boat. Leaning on the rail, he shouted at the winds. The original wording of the Gospel accounts tells us that he told the winds, in effect, "Knock it off!" He didn't just *command* the winds. He *scolded* the winds for disturbing his rest!

The winds calmed in an instant.

The disciples were stunned and shaken. They hadn't expected him to do *this!* The men turned to each other and whispered in fear, "What kind of man is this? Even the winds and the waters obey him!"

Jesus and the disciples completed their journey and

> *Jesus says, "I love you just the way you are. And I love you too much to let you stay the way you are."*
> Chris Lyons
> PASTOR

landed on the far shore of the Lake of Galilee. There were just a few fishermen mending nets on the shoreline when they beached the boat. A short distance away, on a bluff overlooking the lake, a number of herdsmen watched over a large herd of pigs.

As Jesus and the disciples stepped ashore, they were startled by screams and shrieks that sounded neither human nor animal-like. They sounded—*unearthly.*

My Name Is Legion

Jesus looked up the shoreline and saw a vaguely human form shambling toward them, naked, bleeding and covered with filth. Its eyes shone with both hatred and terror. The disciples huddled behind Jesus as the drooling, shrieking man-thing ran straight toward Jesus, as if to pounce on him. Jesus didn't flinch.

Instead of pouncing, the creature collapsed in a writhing, stinking mass at the feet of Jesus. "What do you want with me?" the creature shrieked. "I know who you are! You are Jesus, the Son of the Most High God! What do you want with me? I beg you, don't torture me!"

From up the beach, one of the local fishermen approached warily. "Stay away from him!" he warned. "Don't let him near you! He's possessed by an evil spirit!"

Jesus ignored the warning. He bent closer to the wretched man and looked at the open wounds that criss-crossed his naked flesh; wounds that were caked with filth, oozing with blood and swarmed by flies.

"You don't understand!" the fisherman warned again. "He lives outside the town, among the tombs. The evil spirit makes him do things too horrible to mention. He screams through the night and cuts himself with sharp stones. We've tried to chain him up, but he breaks the chains, and the demon drives him into the wastelands."

Jesus waved the fisherman back. Then he turned to the demon-possessed man at his feet. "What is your name?" he asked.

The man's head slowly rose until his hateful stare met the compassionate gaze of Jesus. "Legion," the man-thing replied. His voice was like many voices speaking in unison. "My name is Legion, because we are many."

The disciples shuddered at the sound of that voice.

The face of Jesus turned hard with anger. "Come out of this man, foul spirits!"

"Please!" the demon-voices begged. "Don't send us into the abyss!"

"Come out of him!"

The man went into a seizure. His eyes rolled back and his mouth foamed. He thrashed on the ground. Then his eyes seemed to focus on something far up the shore: The bluff where several herdsmen tended their pigs. "There!" said the demon voice. "Send us there! Let us possess those pigs!"

Jesus looked where the man-thing pointed. From the beach, it was impossible to tell how many pigs were on that hillside, but it was a large herd. The non-Jewish farmers of the Decapolis region raised pigs for their own consumption and for sale to the Roman military garrisons nearby.

"Very well," Jesus said. "Possess the pigs, if you want. But come out of the man now!"

And the man let out a wailing howl. Those who stood nearby sensed a rushing, evil presence that vomited from the man's body and hurried up the beach and toward the herd of pigs. In the next moment, the entire herd flew into a frenzy and moved with a single will toward the edge of the bluff. They bolted down the face of the bluff and tumbled into the lake, squealing and shrieking.

Several stunned pig herders gathered at the edge of the bluff and stared in shock and dismay at the lapping water, where hundreds of drowned hog carcasses floated. Then,

READER/CUSTOMER CARE SURVEY

We care about your opinions! Please take a moment to fill out our online Reader Survey at **http://survey.hcibooks.com**. As a **"THANK YOU"** you will receive a **VALUABLE INSTANT COUPON** towards future book purchases as well as a **SPECIAL GIFT** available only online! Or, you may mail this card back to us and we will send you a copy of our exciting catalog with your valuable coupon inside.

(PLEASE PRINT IN ALL CAPS)

First Name _____ MI. _____ Last Name _____

Address _____ Email _____ City _____

State _____ Zip _____

1. Gender
☐ Female   ☐ Male

2. Age
☐ 8 or younger
☐ 9-12   ☐ 13-16
☐ 17-20   ☐ 21-30
☐ 31+

3. Did you receive this book as a gift?
☐ Yes   ☐ No

4. Annual Household Income
☐ under $25,000
☐ $25,000 - $34,999
☐ $35,000 - $49,999
☐ $50,000 - $74,999
☐ over $75,000

5. What are the ages of the children living in your house?
☐ 0 - 14   ☐ 15+

6. Marital Status
☐ Single
☐ Married
☐ Divorced
☐ Widowed

7. How did you find out about the book?
(please choose one)
☐ Recommendation
☐ Store Display
☐ Online
☐ Catalog/Mailing
☐ Interview/Review

8. Where do you usually buy books?
(please choose one)
☐ Bookstore
☐ Online
☐ Book Club/Mail Order
☐ Price Club (Sam's Club, Costco's, etc.)
☐ Retail Store (Target, Wal-Mart, etc.)

9. What subject do you enjoy reading about the most?
(please choose one)
☐ Parenting/Family
☐ Relationships
☐ Recovery/Addictions
☐ Health/Nutrition

☐ Christianity
☐ Spirituality/Inspiration
☐ Business Self-help
☐ Women's Issues
☐ Sports

10. What attracts you most to a book?
(please choose one)
☐ Title
☐ Cover Design
☐ Author
☐ Content

TAPE IN MIDDLE; DO NOT STAPLE

BUSINESS REPLY MAIL
FIRST-CLASS MAIL PERMIT NO 45 DEERFIELD BEACH, FL

POSTAGE WILL BE PAID BY ADDRESSEE

Faith Communications, Inc.
3201 SW 15th Street
Deerfield Beach FL 33442-9875

FOLD HERE

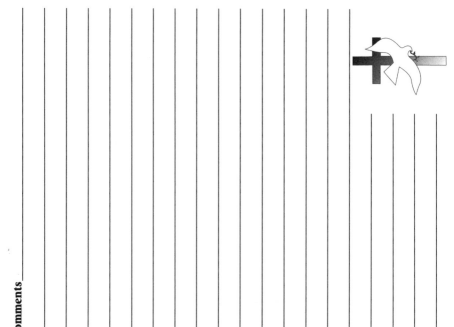

Comments

the terrified pig herders dashed away toward the town.

Minutes later, a crowd poured out of the nearby village and gathered on the beach. They found Jesus, his disciples and a man they didn't initially recognize. When the man looked around at the crowd, the people gasped in recognition. It was the demon-possessed man who haunted the tombs!

But he was no longer possessed. He sat calmly at the feet of Jesus, fully clothed and in his right mind.

The people from the town should have been relieved to see this man suddenly sane and clean, but they weren't. They were *afraid.*

"Leave us!" the townspeople said. "Get into your boat and go back where you came from!"

"Very well," Jesus said. "We'll go." And he and his disciples climbed back into the boat.

"Wait!" called the man who had been delivered from the demons. He ran to the side of the boat and clutched at Jesus. "Please, let me go with you!"

"No," Jesus said, clasping the man's arm. "Stay here. Go back to your home and tell everyone you meet what God has done for you."

The man nodded reluctantly. "All right," he said. "I'll do as you say. I'll tell everyone—everyone in all of Decapolis!"

As he watched Jesus and

> *The love of Christ both wounds and heals, it fascinates and frightens, it kills and makes alive, it draws and repulses. There can be nothing more terrible or wonderful than to be stricken with love for Christ.*
> A. W. Tozer
> PASTOR AND AUTHOR

the disciples sail away from the shore, he rubbed the spot on his arm where Jesus had touched him. It had been a long time since anyone had given him a clasp of friendship like that. It had been a long time since anyone had looked at him with eyes of love and compassion, as Jesus had.

The memory of that touch and those loving eyes would remain with this man for the rest of his life.

Love for the Unlovely, the Unlovable and the Unloving

Jesus loved people no one else would love. He looked past the filth and blood that encrusted the flesh of the demon-possessed man. He looked past the hatred in the man's wild eyes, the curses on his stinking breath, the ugliness of his scarred, naked body, and he saw a human soul in torment.

Jesus loved the tortured soul trapped within the wretched flesh. He had compassion for this man whose life had become infested by evil spirits. His anger was directed at demons; his love was directed at the man imprisoned by those demons.

If we want to be like Jesus, we need to love like Jesus. What was the love of Jesus like? He loved the unlovely and the unlovable. His was a compassionate love, an understanding love, an unconditional love.

Jesus crossed the Lake of Galilee for the sake of one man. He went far out of his way to touch one life, and then he left the man on the shore to give testimony to his neighbors of what God had done in his life.

Taking their fishing boat once more upon the Lake of Galilee, Jesus and the disciples sailed west toward the familiar shores of Galilee. Upon arriving, Jesus found a vast crowd lining the beach, waiting to welcome him.

As Jesus stepped out of the boat, a man rushed forward and fell down at Jesus' feet. He was a ruler of the synagogue, and his name was Jairus. Perhaps he was one of the religious leaders who had earlier opposed Jesus in the synagogue. Now, however, he desperately needed Jesus' help.

"Master, please help me!" Jairus begged. "My daughter is dying! She's only twelve! Come put your hands on her so that she will live!"

What did Jairus have to overcome in order to say those words? How much pride did he have to swallow? What if the other scribes and Pharisees heard about him begging Jesus for help? Would they strip him of his office? Put him out of the synagogue? None of that mattered to Jairus. He only cared about one thing: the life of his precious little daughter.

Jesus had a decision to make. Here was a ruler of the synagogue, one of the religious leaders who continually opposed and persecuted Jesus. What right did this man have to come to Jesus and beg for help?

Yet, this was exactly the situation Jesus had preached

about in the Sermon on the Mount. On that mountainside, he had told the people, "You've heard the old saying, 'Love your neighbor and hate your enemy.' But I say to you: love your enemies and ask God to bless those who persecute you. If you do this, then you will truly be the children of God, your Father in heaven."

> *I follow Christ. Jesus is my God, Jesus is my Spouse, Jesus is my Life, Jesus is my only Love, Jesus is my All in All.*
>
> *Jesus is my Everything.*
> Mother Teresa
> MISSIONARY

Jesus didn't hesitate for a moment. He had come to bless everyone, to love everyone—even his enemies. Just as he had shown love to the unlovable on the far shore of the Lake of Galilee, it was now time to show love to the unloving, here on the near shore.

"Take me to your daughter," Jesus said.

The Bleeding Woman

Jairus and Jesus pushed their way through a crushing, clamoring throng of people. The crowd shouted at Jesus, tugged at him, jostled and pushed him. Jairus, Jesus and the disciples could scarcely move for all the people who surrounded them.

Suddenly, Jesus stopped in his tracks. "Who touched me?" he asked.

It seemed like a ridiculous question. Obviously, dozens of people had touched him! Standing next to Jesus, Peter said incredulously, "Master, what do you mean? The way these people are crowding you—they *all* touched you!"

"Master, please," Jairus begged, placing his hand on the shoulder of Jesus. "We must hurry! My daughter . . ."

"Wait," Jesus said, scanning the faces in the crowd. "One of you touched me to receive healing—I felt healing power go out of me. Who was it?"

"Master, it was I!" said a woman's voice from somewhere behind Jesus.

Jesus turned and saw a middle-aged woman with a care-worn face. She fell at his feet, trembling. "I have been bleeding for twelve years, and I spent everything I had on doctors who couldn't help me. And then you came, and all I did was touch the hem of your robe—and my bleeding stopped at that very instant!"

It is important to understand the true depths of this woman's suffering. The bleeding she spoke of was a vaginal hemorrhage, a flow of blood that was not only painful and embarrassing, but which also made her religiously unclean. According to the Levitical law, she was cut off from Jewish society in much the same way as lepers were shunned. No one could touch her while she was bleeding, and her condition was nonstop and chronic. She couldn't even attend worship services in her synagogue. She had been cut off from her faith and her community for a dozen years. To top it off, her doctors had depleted her bank account without alleviating her suffering.

The woman had heard of the amazing powers of this healer from Nazareth. Because she was ceremonially

unclean, it would have been a violation of the Law of
Moses for her to touch Jesus. So she decided to "fudge" the
law a bit and only touch the hem of his robe. Scores of
people had bumped Jesus, grabbed Jesus and jostled Jesus,
but they had received nothing. This woman brushed the
hem of his garment with her fingertips and her faith—and
her life was forever changed.

After the woman explained what she had done and how
she had been healed, Jesus smiled. "Daughter," he said,
"your faith has healed you. Go in peace."

> *Jesus' power over death is*
> *an essential message, for*
> *we live in a dying world.*
> *We all face the in-*
> *evitability of death. We are*
> *deteriorating human beings*
> *living in a deteriorating*
> *world marked by tragedy*
> *and sorrow.*
>
> John MacArthur
> PASTOR AND AUTHOR

No sooner had Jesus said
these words when there
came a shout from the edge
of the crowd. "Jairus!" a man
called out in a distraught
voice. "Jairus! Your daughter
is dead!"

"No!" the ruler of the synagogue wailed. "No, she can't
be!"

One of the disciples put a hand on Jairus's arm. "Your
daughter is dead and the Teacher is very busy," the disciple
said. "Don't trouble him any more."

Jesus reached out, pulled Jairus closer and said, "Don't
be afraid! Believe in God and your daughter will be
healed! Now, lead me to your house."

Little Lamb, Arise!

So Jairus led Jesus and the Twelve to his home. When they arrived, they heard the wailing of mourners. Jairus staggered as if he was about to collapse. Jesus put his arm around the man's shoulder to bear him along. *Believe in God,* Jairus silently told himself. *Believe in God!* But the wailing of the mourners told him that there was no hope. His daughter was dead.

The door of the house creaked open as they approached. A woman stood in the doorway, her face drawn and pale, her eyes bleak, her cheeks hollow. She stared numbly at Jesus, and he knew that this was the girl's grieving mother. Jesus turned to his followers and said, "Peter, James and John, come into the house with me. The rest of you, wait outside."

Then Jesus went into the home, along with the three disciples, Jairus and his wife. There were mourners in the house—aunts, uncles, a grandmother, some neighbors—and they were all wailing and moaning. "Be quiet!" Jesus commanded. "The child is not dead, but merely asleep!"

For a moment, the mourners were so shocked by the words of Jesus that they forgot to mourn! Right there, in a house filled with sorrow, the mourners laughed! To them, Jesus seemed to be delirious. The child was asleep? The child was dead! Who did this stranger think he was?

"Get out of this house," Jesus said to the mourners.

The mourners stood unmoving, uncomprehending.

"Get out of this house," Jesus repeated. He then went to

the nearest ones and prodded them toward the door. The mourners protested, but out they went.

Now there was no one in the house but Jesus, the three disciples, Jairus, his wife and, of course, a twelve-year-old girl who was "merely asleep."

Jesus led the others into the room where the child lay. She appeared peaceful and beautiful in repose, just as if she were sweetly dreaming. But her chest didn't rise. Her limbs didn't stir.

Jesus bent down to her and took her soft little hand in his strong carpenter's hand. Then he spoke two Aramaic words to her. *"Talitha cumi!"* Literally, "Little lamb, arise."

The girl awoke.

The father and the mother fell to their knees, praising God. Then they hugged their bewildered daughter to themselves.

Jesus said, "Give her something to eat."

So the mother went and got the child some food while Jairus thanked Jesus profusely and tearfully.

"See that you tell no one about this," Jesus added.

Why did Jesus say that? There were many occasions when Jesus did some amazing work, then he told people, "Tell no one." When he commanded evil spirits to leave demon-possessed people, they often shouted, "You are the Son of God!" But Jesus always commanded them to be silent. When he healed the man with leprosy, he told the man not to spread the news around, but to present himself to the priests at the synagogue. Here again he says, "Tell no one." Why?

Someone once suggested that Jesus wanted to keep the little girl's resurrection quiet because he didn't want to be invited to every funeral in Palestine! That makes a lot of sense, but I think there was another reason, a deeper reason: It was not yet time for Jesus to be revealed and

> *Nails didn't hold Jesus to the cross; love did.*
> Max Lucado
> PASTOR AND AUTHOR

for his claims to be validated. Remember what he told his mother at the wedding at Cana before he turned the water into wine, "Dear woman, why are you telling me about this problem? *My time has not yet come.*"

His time for what? Chapter by chapter, we are getting closer to the answer.

The Four Loves

One of the great strengths of the English language is that it has many words to express many subtle shades of meaning. However, the English language is woefully deficient in expressing varying shades of love. Instead of having many words to express many kinds of love, we have one word that we work to death.

We use the word "love" to describe our affectionate feelings for God, parents, children, husband, wife and even a beloved pet. We use the same word to say "I love God" that we use to say "I love Chinese food." We often use the word "love" when what we really mean is lust or sex, and this misuse of the word has only served to cheapen it. By using "love" to express so many different ideas and emotions, we have emptied it of its meaning and impact.

The ancient Greeks were much wiser than we are with regard to "love". From Aristotle to the writers of the Greek New Testament, the Greeks used four specific words to express four specific and distinct kinds of love.

For an affection between unequals, such as a bond between parent and child, teacher and student, master and pet, the ancient Greeks used the word *storge* (pronounced STORE-gay). This word describes a complementary relationship in which, for example, a parent reaches down to the child to meet the child's needs, while the child reaches up to the parent for comfort and security.

The Greek word for a love between friends is *phileo,* or, "brotherly love." Philadelphia, the City of Brotherly Love, derives its name from phileo love. This kind of love is shared between equals and among friends, neighbors and coworkers. It is even expressed to strangers in the form of hospitality and cordiality. It involves a love for all people and a sense of responsibility for your neighbor's welfare.

The Greeks have another word reserved for (among other things) sexual and romantic love. That word is *eros.* To the ancient Greeks, however, eros actually went beyond sexual and romantic love and embraced a love for all things beautiful: nature, art, music, literature and ideas. Erotic love is a possessive love. If a thing is beautiful, you are attracted to it and you want to make it yours. Erotic love is exciting. It is passionate. Contrary to popular opinion, it is not the most profound and important love there is.

The ancient Greeks also created a special word for the highest of all forms of love: *agape* (pronounced ah-GAH-pay). Why is agape the highest form of love? Because agape endures. Agape lasts. Agape never fails.

Storge love is limited to unequal relationships. Philia love is based on friendly feelings, and when those feelings are strained by conflict, philia often fails. Eros love only lasts as long as beauty lasts, and when beauty fades, eros dies. Storge, philia and eros are all based on feelings and affection. Feelings change and affection fades, but agape love endures.

Why? Because agape is based on a decision in the will and not on a feeling in the emotions. Agape love is a commitment to love even when people are not lovely, lovable or loving. Agape is humble, never arrogant; accepting, never snobbish; generous and kind, never selfish. Agape does not discriminate on the basis of status, income level, skin color, language, religion or political affiliation. Agape even chooses to love opponents and enemies.

Agape love is a potent force for healing. It transforms the pain, shame and failure of human lives into forgiveness and new beginnings. The agape love of Jesus was the driving force that sent him to the cross. Jesus expressed the motivation of his life—and his death—when he said, "No one has shown greater love [agape] than by giving up his own life for his friends." Moreover, he told us that we should be like him and love like him. "This is my commandment," he said, "that you love each other in exactly the same way that I have loved you."

The love of Jesus sets the standard for our love. The agape love of Jesus demands a total commitment to loving others, a commitment that transcends mere affection and emotion. It reaches to the depths of our will. It calls us to love others even to the point of death. It cost Jesus everything to love others. If we choose to be like Jesus and love like Jesus, it will cost us everything as well.

> *God is love. Whoever lives in love lives in God, and God lives in him.*
>
> 1 John 4:16

The Love of a Hated Man

On one occasion, one of the teachers of the Law, an opponent of Jesus, approached him while he was teaching his disciples. This teacher of the Law pretended to seek wisdom from Jesus, but he was actually trying to trick Jesus into speaking heresy. He asked Jesus, "Teacher, what must I do in order to live forever in God's eternal kingdom?"

Jesus answered with a question of his own. "What is written in the Law of Moses? How do you read it, since you yourself are a teacher of the Law?"

The religious leader answered, "'You shall love the Lord your God with all your heart and with all your soul and with all your strength and with all your mind; and you shall love your neighbor as yourself.'"

"You have answered correctly," Jesus said. "If you do this, you will live forever in God's kingdom."

This religious teacher knew, however, that there was at least one part of this formula for eternal life that he had failed to keep—the part that said, "Love your neighbor as yourself." He had hatred in his heart, hatred for Jesus. He was there to trap Jesus, and he had gotten caught in his own snare! So the teacher of the Law thought quickly, grasping for a loophole.

"Define what you mean by 'neighbor,'" the religious teacher said craftily.

"Very well," Jesus said. "I shall define 'neighbor' with a story. A man was traveling by foot from Jerusalem to Jericho. On the road, he was waylaid by robbers. They beat him within an inch of his life, stripped him of his clothes and belongings, then left him beside the road, thinking him dead.

"A short time later, a priest of the Temple was walking down the road. He saw the beaten man lying naked and unconscious beside the road—but instead of helping him, the priest crossed over to the far side of the road and kept walking.

"A few minutes later, a Levite—one of the assistants of the Temple priests—came walking down the road. He saw the man lying beside the road—and he, too, crossed over to the far side and kept walking.

"Next, a Samaritan came walking down the road. . . ."

At this, an expression of distaste twisted the features of the teacher of the Law. The Samaritans, as we have previously seen, were a hated people. In this teacher's mind, there was nothing lower than a Samaritan, not even a tax collector. So as Jesus continued his story, the mental picture this religious leader had was of a miserable, contemptible and subhuman person.

"This Samaritan came to the place where the wounded man lay," Jesus went on, "and he was moved with compassion. He dressed the man's wounds with oil and wine, then placed him on his own donkey and took him to an inn. The Samaritan took care of the wounded man through the night. The next day, he gave the innkeeper money equaling two days' wages and said, 'Take good care of him. Spend whatever you must and put it on my bill. I'll settle up with you when I return.'

"You asked me to define 'neighbor'—but I'm going to let you answer your own question. You tell me—which of the three travelers proved to be a neighbor to the man who was beaten by robbers? The priest, the Levite or the Samaritan?"

The teacher of the Law eyed Jesus resentfully. "The one who showed pity on him," he said.

"In that case," Jesus said, "go and do to everyone as that Samaritan did."

How should we define "neighbor"? When we learn to love as Jesus loved, *everyone* in the human family is our neighbor.

The love of Jesus looks beyond skin color, ethnic barriers and class distinctions. The love of Jesus reaches across ideological lines and battle lines. The love of Jesus chooses to love in unlovely and unloving situations. The love of Jesus is the power that heals and transforms a wounded soul.

In his book *Mortal Lessons,* surgeon Dr. Richard Selzer draws a word sketch from his own medical experience that gives us a brief yet beautiful glimpse of the healing power of agape love:

I stand by the bed where a young woman lies, her face postoperative, her mouth twisted in palsy. A tiny twig of the facial nerve, the one to the muscles of her mouth, has been severed. She will be thus from now on. . . . To remove the tumor in her cheek, I had to cut the little nerve.

Her young husband is in the room. He stands on the opposite side of the bed, and together they seem to dwell in the evening lamplight, isolated from me, private. . . .

"Will my mouth always be like this?" she asks.

"Yes," I say, "it will. It's because the nerve was cut."

"I like it," the husband says. "It's kind of cute. . . ." He bends to kiss her crooked mouth, and I am so close I can see how he twists his own lips to accommodate hers, to show her that their kiss still works.[1]

We can never be like Jesus until we learn to love as he loved. Jesus was more than a teacher, more than a preacher. He was a healer, and the source of his healing power was love.

[1] Richard Selzer, *Mortal Lessons: Notes in the Art of Surgery* (New York: Simon & Schuster, 1976), 45–46.

CHAPTER ELEVEN

HOW TO ENDURE LIKE JESUS

Some time after Jesus raised the twelve-year-old daughter of Jairus, he journeyed once more from Galilee to Jerusalem to celebrate one of the Jewish holy days. On his way to the Temple to worship on the Sabbath, Jesus came to a pool called Bethesda, which means "house of mercy." The pool was surrounded by a five-sided enclosure of columns, and its waters were thought to have healing properties. Every day, many people with disabilities—people who were blind, lame or paralyzed—would come to the pool, hoping to find healing.

As Jesus paused in the shade of the covered colonnade that surrounded the pool, he saw a man lying on a thick cloth mat beside the pool. A large crowd surrounded the pool, yet there was something about this one man that caught Jesus' attention. So he went to the man and knelt beside him.

"Why are you here?" Jesus asked.

"I can't walk," the man said. "I've been an invalid for thirty-eight years."

"Do you *truly* want to be healed?" Jesus asked.

That may sound like a ridiculous question. Doesn't it seem obvious that the man wanted to be healed? In his position, who wouldn't?

Yet, if we reflect on this question for a moment, we realize that this is actually the most crucial question Jesus could put to this man. The truth is that many of us have impairments and disabilities, and if we were honest, we'd have to admit that we really don't want to be healed. We don't want to be healed of our sins, our addictions, our bad habits, our character flaws. We've become comfortable with these impairments of our souls, and we're not ready to give them up. True healing involves pain, hard work and honest self-appraisal. It's easier to remain disabled than to put forth that kind of effort.

If Jesus knelt beside you and me and said, "Do you want to be healed?" our honest answer might have to be, "No. I like things just the way they are. I really don't want to change."

When Jesus asked the man at the pool if he truly wanted to be healed, the man answered, "Sir, I have no one to put me into the pool. Everyone else gets into the water ahead of me."

Notice that the man didn't answer Jesus' question. He didn't say, "Yes, I want to be healed," or, "No, I don't." Instead, he expressed his hopelessness and frustration. He said, in effect, "Whether I want to be healed or not, I know it's never going to happen. Everybody crowds in ahead of me, and I can't even dip my big toe in the water."

The disabled man thought that his only chance of being healed lay in reaching the water. Clearly, he had no idea who he was talking to!

Jesus said to him, "Get up! Pick up your mat and walk."

What did the man think when he heard those words? He may have wondered, *Is this stranger crazy? I just told him I've been an invalid for thirty-eight years!* But in the very next moment, the disabled man felt strength flow into muscles that had been useless for nearly four decades. He rose up from the ground, rolled up his mat and walked.

> *When people came to Jesus, he never said, "Before I heal you, tell me what type of sin or high-risk behavior were you engaged in." He healed them, and as they were leaving, he'd tell them, "Go and sin no more."*
>
> Franklin Graham
> MISSIONARY AND EVANGELIST

Walk Where God Leads You

The healed man turned around to thank the stranger, but Jesus was gone, having disappeared into the crowd of people around the pool. So the man shrugged and continued on his way.

A group of Pharisees happened to see this man walking with his mat rolled up under his arm. "You!" the religious leaders called. "Stop right there! What do you think you're doing?"

The man, however, was so full of joy that he scarcely noticed the threatening tone in the voices of these religious leaders. "Look at what God has done for me!" he said. "I'm healed! I can walk!"

The Pharisees exchanged uneasy glances. They knew what this meant: That troublesome healer from Galilee was back in Jerusalem, and he was healing on the Sabbath again! "Look here," they said. "Don't you know that it's against God's law to carry that mat on the Sabbath?"

The man blinked in surprise. He had expected these devout religious men to share his joy. Instead, they seemed angry. "But," the man stammered, "the man who healed me said, 'Pick up your mat and walk.' So I did."

The religious leaders glared at him. "Who was this man?" they asked. "Where is he now?"

"I don't know," the healed man said. "When I turned to thank him, he was gone."

The religious leaders warned the man sternly, then let him go. The healed man continued on to the Temple to worship God and thank him for his healing mercy. He arrived at the Temple and went straight to the courts, where the collection boxes were. As he placed his offering in the collection box, he heard a voice behind him.

"You see?" said the voice. "You are well again!"

> *If you had once entered into perfect communion with Jesus or tasted a little of his intense love, you would not care anything about your own comfort or discomfort. Instead, you would rejoice in your sufferings. To truly love Jesus is to despise oneself by comparison.*
>
> Thomas à Kempis
> GERMAN MONK

The man turned and stood face-to-face with Jesus.

"Now, make sure that you do not sin any longer," Jesus said. "God has made you walk again. See that you walk where he leads you, or something worse may happen to you." With that, Jesus sent the healed man on his way.

Now, this man had no

idea of the hatred the Pharisees had for Jesus. He assumed that Jesus (who healed by God's power) and the Pharisees (who claimed to speak for God) were all on the same team. It never occurred to him that the Pharisees might actually want to destroy Jesus.

As the healed man was on his way home, he happened to see the same group of Pharisees who had questioned him before. "I saw the man who healed me!" he told them excitedly. "He was at the Temple. If you hurry, you may find him there." Perhaps he gave them a physical description. He may have even given them Jesus' name.

In any case, the Pharisees knew that it was, in fact, Jesus of Nazareth who had healed the man on the Sabbath. They decided together that, one way or another, this man had to be stopped—and *silenced.*

Jesus, Master of the Sabbath

Day after day, wherever Jesus went, the Pharisees and Temple scribes followed him, arguing with him and attacking his character. When the religious leaders accused him of performing an unlawful healing on the Sabbath, Jesus replied, "My Father is continually working, even on the Sabbath day. So I must keep working as well." This just made the scribes and Pharisees even more enraged and determined to kill him.

To the religious rulers, it was bad enough that Jesus violated the Sabbath. What made matters worse was that he spoke as if God were in some special sense his own Father, and he made himself out to be the Son of God and therefore an equal with God. To the religious leaders, Jesus was not only a preacher who eclipsed their own power and popularity, but he was also a blasphemer who placed himself on the same level with Almighty God!

On another Sabbath day, Jesus and his disciples were walking through a field of grain. As they walked, some of the disciples picked a few ripe heads of grain. They rubbed the heads of grain in their hands to separate the edible seeds from the husks and straw, then they ate the seeds.

The Pharisees saw this and were outraged. They surrounded Jesus as he and his disciples emerged from the grain field. "Look at what your disciples are doing! They are violating the Sabbath law!"

When they talked about "the Sabbath law," these rigid Pharisees were not referring to the fourth commandment that God had given to Israel through Moses. That law simply said, "Remember the Sabbath day and keep it holy. You shall work for six days and accomplish your work, but the seventh day is a Sabbath to the Lord your God, and you shall not do any work on that day."

Over the years, the scribes and Pharisees had come up with nearly forty *additional* Sabbath restrictions, and it was these *man-made* restrictions that the Pharisees referred to as the Sabbath law. According to these restrictions, it was illegal to pick heads of grain on the Sabbath, because that was the labor of harvesting. It was illegal to rub the heads of grain in your hands on the

Sabbath, because that was the labor of threshing.

Jesus replied to the Pharisees by pointing them to their own Scriptures. "Haven't you read the story of what David did when he fled from the wrath of King Saul? David and the men with him were hungry, and they went into the Temple of God. There they ate the sacred loaves of ceremonial bread—the bread that was only for the priests to eat. They broke the religious rules in order to save their strength and their lives."

> *God does not lead his children around hardship, but leads them straight through hardship. But he leads! And amidst the hardship, he is nearer to them than ever before.*
> Otto Dibelius
> THEOLOGIAN AND ANTI-NAZI
> RESISTANCE LEADER IN WWII

The Pharisees tried to shift the argument. "No man may break the rules God has established!" they said.

"The Son of Man is master even of the Sabbath," Jesus replied. "Though God gave the Sabbath commandment to the people, he cares more about the real needs of people than he cares about rigid adherence to a set of rules. You act as though people were created to be servants of the Sabbath; I tell you that God created the Sabbath to serve people, to give them a day of rest for their bodies and souls."

Jesus Creates a Scandal

On another occasion, a man who was possessed by an evil spirit was brought to Jesus. That spirit had blinded the man and left him unable to speak. There was a large crowd surrounding Jesus as he commanded the evil spirit out of the man. The people were astonished when the man's eyes opened and he began to speak, praising God for delivering him from his prison of silence and darkness.

The Pharisees in the crowd, though, grumbled to each other. "He drives demons out of people," they said, "because he is an ally of Beelzebub, the prince of demons."

Jesus knew what they were saying, so he confronted the Pharisees. "Your thinking is irrational," he said. "How can a kingdom survive if it is divided against itself? Such a kingdom would destroy itself! A house divided against itself will collapse. And if Satan drives out Satan, he is fighting against himself, destroying his own kingdom! So stop talking nonsense. If I drive out demons, I do so by the Spirit of God. Instead of attacking me, you should recognize that the kingdom of God has come among you."

The Pharisees continued to bait Jesus. "You want us to believe in you?" they said. "Then show us a miracle as proof that you are what you claim to be."

"Those who have genuine faith in God don't need a sign," Jesus replied. "Only evil people who are morally unfaithful to God demand that God prove himself with miracles. If you want a miraculous sign, then here's the only one you will be given—the sign of the prophet Jonah."

"The sign of Jonah?" the Pharisees said. "What are you talking about?"

"You remember that Jonah spent three days and three nights in the belly of the huge sea creature," Jesus said. "In the same way, the Son of Man will spend three days and three nights in the heart of the Earth."

The Pharisees looked at each other in bafflement. They were all familiar with the Old Testament story of Jonah, the reluctant prophet whom God had chosen as a messenger to the sinful city of Nineveh. Jonah didn't want to preach to Nineveh, so he booked a sea voyage in an attempt to escape from God's presence. When a storm arose, the sailors tossed Jonah overboard, hoping to appease God. Jonah ended up in the belly of a sea monster for three days and nights.

The Pharisees wondered what Jesus and Jonah had to do with each other. What was his point? They couldn't make heads or tails of it.

"The people of Nineveh will have every right to stand in judgment over all of you," Jesus continued, "because they repented when Jonah preached to them. Someone greater than Jonah is now among you, preaching repentance to you, and you reject him and his message."

This angered many of the Pharisees in the crowd, but one Pharisee sensed that there was truth in what Jesus said. He wanted to know more. He wanted to continue talking to Jesus, so he invited Jesus to his home for a meal.

Perhaps this man was Nicodemus, the Pharisee we met in chapter 5. We don't know for certain. In any case, Jesus agreed to go to the man's house and sit down at his table for a meal. In addition to Jesus, this Pharisee invited a number of his friends who were also religious leaders and dignitaries.

As they sat down to the meal, the Pharisee noticed that Jesus did not wash his hands before dinner—and the Pharisee was horrified! Understand, this was not a case of poor hygiene on the part of Jesus. The hand-washing that was customary in that culture was a ceremonial, religious cleansing rite. The Pharisee was not shocked because Jesus sat down at the table with dirty hands, but because Jesus ignored a standard religious ritual. The Pharisee asked him, "Why did you ignore the ritual hand-cleansing?"

Jesus turned to his host and said, "You Pharisees are always focused on washing the outside of the cup, yet you ignore the inside. You wash your hands, but inside you are filthy with greed, robbery, blackmail and sin! How can you be so foolish as to think that God only cares about superficial things? Didn't God, who made the outside, also make the inside? A ritual washing is only an external symbol of the cleansing that is supposed to take place on the inside. You are focused on the symbol while neglecting the reality!"

Embarrassed, the host looked around the table. His other guests were eyeing Jesus with obvious dislike. They all knew he was talking about them.

"You keep adding rules and rituals to your religion," Jesus continued, "yet you lack all sincerity when it comes to living as one of God's people! If you would dedicate your inner self to living a righteous life, caring for the poor and defenseless, expressing God's love to the people around you, then your outer self would be clean as well."

These were harsh words, especially for a dinner guest to

speak to his host! Jesus was creating a scandal. But, of course, Jesus didn't come to win a popularity contest. He came to speak the truth. So while his Pharisee host reddened, Jesus kept talking.

"You Pharisees are doomed to judgment," he said. "For you love to sit in the place of prominence at the synagogue, and you love to have people make a fuss over you in the marketplace. You are doomed, you hypocrites, because you are obsessive about the tiniest rules, even giving a tithe of your kitchen spices to the Temple treasury, yet you ignore what God really wants from you: a life of justice, mercy and faith. You are doomed, you teachers of the Law, you Pharisees, you hypocrites! You are like whitewashed tombs—so clean and beautiful on the outside, but on the inside, full of rotting corpses."

Finally, one of the scribes had heard enough. "Teacher!" he said, his fists clenched and his eyes blazing. "This is an outrage! How dare you insult us this way?"

Jesus turned to the scribe and, without missing a beat, said, "You also are doomed, you teachers of the Law, because you burden the people with backbreaking rules and rituals too heavy to bear—yet you don't even lift a

> *Consider the human disappointments Jesus endured: rejected in his home town, harassed and persecuted by the religious leaders of his nation, misunderstood by his own family, betrayed with a kiss and abandoned by all his followers. Yet through it all Jesus never complained or rebelled against God; he trusted God even on the cross.*
> John R. Cogdell
> ELECTRONICS ENGINEER
> AND EDUCATOR

finger to bear those burdens yourselves!" He said many other things, condemning the religious leaders for their hypocrisy, their faithlessness to God and the murderous hatred in their hearts.

It was not a pleasant meal for anyone. After Jesus left, the scribes and Pharisees plotted among themselves and hatched plans to catch Jesus in some word or act that they could use as a pretext for destroying him.

That Galilean Troublemaker

Following this incident, Jesus returned to Galilee in northern Israel. He decided to avoid Judea, the region around Jerusalem, for a while. He knew that the religious leaders were laying plans to kill him.

As the time approached for the Jewish Feast of Tabernacles, some of the family members of Jesus said to him, "This is no place for a man of your abilities. You should leave Galilee and go down to Judea so that your disciples there may see the works you do. If you want publicity, you shouldn't be here in a backwater place like Galilee. You should go to Jerusalem and show yourself openly."

Why did his family members give him this advice? Because they, too, saw his potential to be a political deliverer and king, but not a spiritual messiah. They encouraged him to use his miraculous powers to attain high office, so they, too, could have a place of honor. Jesus had only one family member who always believed in him for who he truly was—his mother, Mary. The rest only wanted to use him to gain their own ambitions.

"Any time is suitable for you," Jesus replied to their scornful advice. "One opportunity is as good as another for you. But I am carrying out a specific purpose, and my life is on a strict timetable—*and my time has not yet come.*"

There it is again! Once more, Jesus makes a mysterious reference to the fact that his time has not yet come. As we move deeper into the life of Jesus, we detect a growing clarity in his sense of destiny. He knows that his time is coming, but it is not yet here. His time for what? When he spoke those words, even his own relatives had no idea what he was talking about.

"You speak so easily about going to Judea, where my enemies wait for me," Jesus went on. "You have no idea what it means to be hated, because the world does not hate you. But the world hates me, because I denounce evil men, and I reveal their evil works to the whole world. So go on to Judea, if you wish, and attend the Feast of Tabernacles—but I will not go yet, because my time has not come."

So the relatives of Jesus went to Judea for the feast, and Jesus stayed behind in Galilee. After the relatives of Jesus left for Jerusalem to attend the Feast of Tabernacles, Jesus gathered some belongings and went out on the road alone. If he had traveled with the caravan, he would have been recognized for sure. This way, he could travel quickly and quietly, without anyone knowing who he was.

Meanwhile, in Jerusalem, the city was abuzz. The scribes and Pharisees kept searching for Jesus and asking each other, "Where is he? That Galilean troublemaker always comes to the feast! He must be here!"

The crowds were also stirred up over Jesus. Throughout Jerusalem, people argued. Some said, "Jesus is a great man!" Others said, "No! He's a deceiver who fills people's heads with false ideas!"

The Feast of Tabernacles was nearly over when Jesus arrived in Jerusalem. He slipped into the city, went straight to the Temple court and began to teach the people. The scribes and Pharisees found him there, surrounded by great crowds. As the religious rulers listened to him teach, they were astonished at the depth of his biblical knowledge. "How can this man know so much about the Scriptures and theology when he has had no formal education?" they asked.

Jesus heard their question. "My teaching is not my own," he said, addressing the religious leaders directly. "My teaching comes from the One who sent me. Anyone who desires to do God's pleasure will have sufficient inner light to know whether my teaching is from God or merely from my own authority. I don't speak to win honor for myself, but to bring honor to the One who sent me. Moses gave you the Ten Commandments, yet you 'teachers of the Law' are breaking the Law by plotting to kill me."

At this, several voices in the crowd shouted, "You're raving! You're talking crazy! Why do you think someone's trying to kill you?"

Jesus eyed the leaders, and they glared back at him with eyes full of hate. The rest of the crowd was divided between those who were for Jesus and those who were against him.

"You hate me because I healed a man on the Sabbath day," Jesus continued. "Yet, according to our Law, we perform the brit ritual—the rite of male circumcision—on the eighth day after the child is born, even if it falls on the Sabbath day. If it is all right to circumcise on the Sabbath day in order to keep the Law, then why do you hate me for making a body well on the Sabbath day?"

The religious leaders kept silent, because they couldn't answer the logic of Jesus. Seeing that Jesus had silenced the scribes and Pharisees, a few of the people in the crowd said, "This is the man our leaders have been looking for! The one they want to put to death! Yet he stands here, speaking openly and bluntly, and our leaders are speechless! Could it be that this man has convinced them that he truly is the Messiah?"

Others in the crowd had a different opinion. "Don't be absurd!" they said. "How could this man be the Messiah? We know where he comes from! He's nothing but a Galilean peasant, Jesus of Nazareth. When the Messiah comes, he will be a supernatural man, and no one will know where he comes from!"

"Are you so sure you know where I come from?" Jesus said, shouting to be heard over the babble of the crowd. "You think I've come of my own accord, a self-appointed teacher from Galilee. But the One who sent me is the true

Authority, and you don't even know him. I know him because I have come from his presence, and he personally sent me here."

When Jesus said this, both the religious leaders and many of the common people in the crowd became enraged. Some demanded, "Arrest him! You heard it from his own lips! He's a blasphemer!" Others in the crowd believed in him, and they said, "When the Messiah comes, will he do more miracles and signs than this man has performed? What if this man really is the Messiah?"

> *How can you be a friend of Christ if you are not willing to endure hardship? You must suffer with Christ and for Christ if you wish to reign with him.*
>
> Thomas à Kempis
> GERMAN MONK

At any time, the enemies of Jesus could have arrested him and taken him before the Sanhedrin to be tried for blasphemy. But, despite the tough talk and bitter hatred of his enemies, no one dared to even lay a hand on Jesus.

His time had not yet come.

The Conscience of One Pharisee

On the last and most celebrated day of the Feast of Tabernacles, Jesus walked through the Temple courts. He selected a colonnade that overlooked a lower courtyard where hundreds of worshipers milled about. Standing on a high place between two white marble pillars, Jesus gazed out over the people, and his heart was broken for them. They were like sheep without a shepherd. They did whatever the scribes and Pharisees told them, obeyed every pointless rule and observed every meaningless ritual. Their corrupt rulers told them that these were the acts God demanded of them.

Looking out upon the crowd, Jesus saw people who were enslaved by ignorance and imprisoned by rigid religion. They were robbed by men with long robes and pious faces whose hearts were full of greed and murder. Jesus wanted the people to know that the way to God was not a matter of rules and rituals. The way to God was through a *relationship*.

"Is anyone thirsty?" Jesus shouted. His voice echoed among the walls and columns of the vast Temple edifice. All around the courtyard below, startled faces looked up to Jesus.

"If you are thirsty," Jesus continued, "then come to me and drink! The one who trusts in me shall experience what the Scriptures have promised: 'From your innermost being shall flow a continuous stream of living water.'"

Voices shouted from the crowd below. "Who is that man?" asked one man. "What is he talking about?" Another said, "Surely, this is the prophet whom Moses promised!" Others said, "This is the Messiah, the Anointed One of God!"

Others argued, "Ridiculous! Does the Messiah come out of Galilee? Don't the Scriptures tell us that the Messiah is a descendent of King David and that he comes from Bethlehem, the village of David?"

So arguments broke out all across the crowd—arguments over who Jesus actually was. Some of the people demanded that Jesus be arrested, but no one dared to lay a hand on him.

Meanwhile, the Temple attendants burst into the meeting hall where the religious rulers were gathered. They hurriedly explained to the chief priests and Pharisees that Jesus of Nazareth was causing a commotion in the Temple courtyard outside.

The chief priests stared at the attendants in astonishment. "Why didn't you arrest the Galilean? Why didn't you bring him with you?"

The attendants looked at each other. Then one of them said, "No mere man has ever talked the way he talks!"

The Pharisees were furious. "The man is a deceiver," they raged through clenched teeth. "Have you been fooled by him, just like the ignorant rabble in the courtyard? Look at us! We are the rulers of the people! We know the Law of Moses! Have we been taken in by him? Don't let this Galilean make fools of you! Go out there and arrest the man!"

The attendants turned to do as the Pharisees ordered.

"Wait!"

The attendants stopped. Every eye in the hall turned toward one man. The speaker was a high-ranking Pharisee, a member of the Sanhedrin.

"You are all so eager to see this man convicted and

sentenced in a single breath," said the Pharisee. "Does the
Law of Moses condemn a man without hearing what he
has to say, without finding out what he has done? This
Galilean deserves to be treated justly."

The hall was silent for several seconds.

Then, a dozen angry voices erupted at once. "Why do
you defend this blasphe-
mer?" the religious rulers
shouted. "Have you been
deluded as well? Are you
also from Galilee? Is that

> *To be right with God has
> often meant to be in
> trouble with men.*
>
> A. W. Tozer
> PASTOR AND AUTHOR

why you defend him? Read the Scriptures! They will tell
you that no prophet has ever come from Galilee!"

The lone Pharisee said nothing as his colleagues
viciously berated and ridiculed him. When their rage was
finally spent, the rulers of the people filed out of the hall,
leaving their scolded brother standing alone in the meeting hall.

That lone Pharisee's name was Nicodemus.

Struck Down
but Not Destroyed

From then on, the opposition against Jesus continued to
intensify. One of the traps his enemies set for him involved
luring a woman into an adulterous relationship, catching
her in the act of adultery, then dragging her before Jesus
for judgment. We saw this incident in chapter 1.

The enemies of Jesus thought they had him trapped in a classic chess fork dilemma—he would have to side either with the law of Rome or the Law of Moses. But Jesus eluded their trap by telling his enemies, "Let the one among you who is without sin throw the first stone at her."

Did Jesus go out of his way to provoke controversy and hostility? No. He offended people, but only because the truth is often offensive. He angered people, but only because it is the nature of evil people to turn hostile when their corruption is exposed. Jesus was gentle and tender toward those who were oppressed, but to the oppressors, his words burned like a blowtorch.

Jesus comforted the afflicted and afflicted the comfortable. He never soft-pedaled his message to win friends and influence people. He never compromised the truth of who he was or why he came into the world. Again and again, his enemies tried to trick him, trap him, catch him or destroy him. Jesus never backed down or gave an inch. He was made of rugged stuff.

If we want to be like Jesus, then we need to endure like Jesus. We need to persevere under pressure as Jesus did. He boldly stood up to evil and oppression, and so should we. He dared to tell the truth, even when the truth got him into hot water, and so should we. When he saw people being exploited and mistreated, he took a stand, and so should we.

If it hasn't happened already, a time will come when you must endure like Jesus. You will see an injustice taking

place, and you will be called upon to take a costly, courageous stand. Or you will be falsely accused, attacked and
rejected. If you want to be like Jesus, then you must
endure as he did. This is never easy or pleasant.

When called upon to take a stand against evil, we
should do so in the spirit of Jesus. He stood up against
those who oppressed and exploited others, but he never
lashed out for personal vengeance. He spoke bluntly and
forcefully to the Pharisees and religious rulers, but he
never tried to hurt them. He only tried to shake them
awake so that they would recognize the truth about their
lives. Most of the Pharisees
were hardened and unwill-
ing to listen to Jesus, but
Jesus did manage to get
through to at least one
Pharisee—the man named
Nicodemus.

In just a few incidents,
we have seen the rising
level of opposition Jesus
endured, from attacks on
his character to plots

> *Comfort and prosperity
> have never enriched the
> world as adversity has
> done. Out of pain and prob-
> lems have come the sweet-
> est song, the most poignant
> poems, the most gripping
> stories. Out of suffering and
> tears have come the great-
> est spirits and the most
> blessed lives.*
> Billy Graham
> EVANGELIST AND AUTHOR

against his life. He was tried for crimes he didn't commit.
He was mocked and spat upon. He was beaten and tortured. He was nailed to a Roman cross.

Why? For doing good and opposing evil.

No one in history deserved to be more honored and
respected than Jesus of Nazareth. Yet he was treated with

contempt and put to death. If we endure like Jesus, our own battle scars will be the righteous and beautiful wounds of those who have taken a courageous stand against evil. Our wounds will be like his.

Endurance for the Race

Kipchoge "Kip" Keino is a long-distance runner from Kenya. In 1968, he represented his country in the Olympic Games in Mexico City. The world didn't know very much about the team from Kenya, except that they had an interesting quirk: The Kenyans preferred to run barefoot.

Kip Keino's first event was the five-thousand-meter race. Though he suffered from a gall-bladder infection and had trouble adjusting to the altitude in Mexico City, Keino ran courageously. Midway through the race, he faltered and collapsed with cramps. Though his coach urged him to quit, Keino got up, shook off the cramps and finished the race—as a silver medalist.

After the race, Keino suffered from a great deal of pain, and his coach advised him to sit out the fifteen-hundred-meter event a few days later. The favored runner in the fifteen-hundred-meter race was Jim Ryun, of the United States, who was one of the best milers in the history of track and field events. Keino was told that he didn't stand a chance against Ryun. Nothing, though, could keep him from that track.

The day of the race, Keino was on his way from the

hotel to the track when his taxi got stuck in traffic. He jumped out of the car and jogged the rest of the way to the stadium. By the time he arrived, he was winded, having already run over a mile before his one-mile event. He took his place at the starting line. Ryun lined up a few yards away. The gun sounded, and Keino seemed to shed his pain and weariness. He ran like the wind that blows across the Kenyan plains, and he beat Jim Ryun and won the gold medal.

Kipchoge "Kip" Keino runs with endurance, but the race he's most involved in is not measured in meters but in lives. The race Kip Keino cares about most is the *human* race. After winning the gold in Mexico City, he returned to Kenya and his job as a police officer.

Once, while on patrol, Keino came across three orphans who were living on the street and hadn't eaten in days. He took those three children into his own home and adopted them. Sometime later, he came across some more orphans. He took them home, too. People heard about Kip Keino's growing family of adopted kids, and they brought more children to him. Before long, he had turned a farm into a Christian children's home that houses nearly a hundred orphans and abandoned children.

On the track and in his life, Kip Keino knows how to endure like Jesus. When he suffers pain and obstacles, he refuses to be stopped or turned aside from his goal. He pushes past the pain, he hurdles over the opposition and he keeps on going. He ignores the advice of those who say, "Just quit. You've done all you can do." When he sees people suffering and in need, he does whatever it takes to meet that need, regardless of the cost and inconvenience.

Kip Keino is a hero in Kenya not only because he's a champion runner, but because he's a champion human being. Thousands and thousands of Kenyan boys want to be like Kip, because Kip has shown them how to endure like Jesus.

The world needs more people like Kip Keino. The world needs you. The world needs me. So let's make a commitment to be like Jesus, to endure like Jesus, to impact lives as he did, to change the world as he did. Let's get into the race, ignoring the pain and pushing past the obstacles.

There's no limit to what can be achieved by people of endurance.

CHAPTER TWELVE

HOW TO GRIEVE LIKE JESUS

John the Baptist was a rugged man who wore rugged clothes—a camel-hair coat bound by a leather belt. He ate a rugged diet— grasshoppers and wild honey. He was a simple man with a simple message: *Change your ways, and prepare to meet the man who will change the world.* John traveled in the wilderness around the River Jordan, and he baptized all who came and believed his message.

"There is someone coming after me," John told the crowds. "He is greater than I am. In fact, I'm not even worthy to untie the thongs of his sandals. I baptize you with water, but he will baptize you with the Spirit of God. I can only cleanse you outwardly, but he will cleanse you inwardly with God's own spirit."

As a result of the preaching of John the Baptist, a great spiritual awakening broke out across the land of Israel. People left their homes and jobs, and they went out into the wilderness to hear his message and be baptized. At the height of John's ministry of preaching and baptizing, Jesus came to John and was baptized, as we saw in chapter 2. That baptism marked the beginning of the public ministry of Jesus of Nazareth.

In chapter 5, we saw John's followers come to him, alarmed that the crowds had begun to forsake John and follow Jesus. John's reply was, "I've told you all along that I'm not the Messiah. I was only sent to *announce* the Messiah. If all the people follow him instead of me, then my joy is full. His reputation must grow; mine must diminish."

Even though the influence of Jesus was growing and the influence of John was diminishing, John continued his ministry of preaching and baptizing. It was during this time, as John's popularity waned, that he came to the attention of one of the most powerful men in Palestine: King Herod Antipas.

John the Baptist in Chains

Herod Antipas was the son of Herod the Great, who had built the Temple of Jerusalem and had died about two years after Jesus was born. The Herods were Jewish kings of Israel, but they had limited power and served at the pleasure of the occupation forces of Rome.

The family of Herod was a strange, dysfunctional clan. Herod the Great had married ten different wives and had children by five of them. Since royals disdain commoners, many of these half brothers and half sisters and cousins began marrying each other. Herod Antipas was married to his own niece, Herodias, who had previously been married to his half brother, Philip.

Herod had heard about John's preaching and was interested in his message of repentance. He called for John the Baptist to appear before him, and John came. This rugged man of the wilderness was not about to soft-pedal his message. Whether he spoke to peasants or kings, his message was the same: *Repent, change your ways and prepare your hearts for the Messiah.*

When John stood before Herod, he spoke bluntly. "Your Majesty," John said, "it's unlawful and indecent for you to seduce your brother's wife, alienate her from her husband and marry her. You've scandalized and disgraced the entire nation."

Herod, who had been raised in the Jewish traditions and Scriptures, knew that John spoke the truth. In fact, King Herod actually admired John's fearless stand for the truth.

Herod's wife, however, was furious with this shaggy prophet from the wilderness. Who did he think he was, judging how the royal family lived? How dare he speak openly and judgmentally about secret royal scandals and affairs? So Herod's wife demanded that Herod have John arrested. Herod, a weak-willed man, gave in to her demands. He hoped that tossing John into the dungeon would shut her up. He was wrong. No sooner was

> *From the deep inner place where love embraces all human grief, the Father reaches out to his children.*
> Henri J. M. Nouwen
> AUTHOR AND PRIEST

John chained up in the dungeon than Herod's wife started demanding John's death.

There, however, Herod drew the line. He wasn't about

to have this righteous and holy man put to death. Not only did he *not* want John's death on his conscience, but he knew enough about God to fear his divine judgment if any harm came to John the Baptist.

The Head of John the Baptist

The fateful day for John the Baptist came on King Herod's birthday. The king gave a huge banquet in his own honor, inviting all the military commanders and officials of his government. Herod's scheming wife decided to use the event to rid herself of the blunt-speaking holy man. First she waited until the food and drink of the banquet had "loosened up" the king and his guests. Then she set her plan in motion by sending her daughter out to dance. The young lady's seductive dancing pleased Herod and his guests, and the king impulsively promised the girl, "Ask anything you want, and I'll give it to you—up to half of my kingdom."

The girl went to her mother and said, "What shall I ask for?"

Herod's wife smiled in triumph, then whispered her answer to the girl.

The girl went back to King Herod and made her request: "Give me the head of John the Baptist on a platter."

Herod was stunned. The death of John the Baptist could bring nothing but judgment and destruction upon him. But what could he do? He had been tragically outmaneuvered by his scheming wife. All the dinner guests had heard him promise the girl anything she asked for, so he didn't dare refuse her. He sent an executioner to the prison, and the executioner returned with the holy man's head on a platter.

While the death of John the Baptist sounds like a scene from a Shakespearean tragedy, it is an actual historical event. You can go to modern-day Jordan and visit the ruins of Herod's castle, Machaerus, on the eastern shore of the Dead Sea. You can walk into the dungeon and see the chains in the walls where John the Baptist was held prisoner. You can walk the floor where John was beheaded, where his blood ran into the cracks between the stones.

After John the Baptist was executed, some followers of John took his body and buried it. Then they went north, to Galilee, to find Jesus and give him the news. By this time, Jesus was in the region of the Lake of Galilee. The followers of John found Jesus with his disciples, surrounded by crowds of needy people.

When the followers of John told Jesus that his friend was dead, Jesus appeared shaken. He turned to his own disciples and said, "Let's leave this place. Let's go to someplace quiet, away from these crowds, and get some rest."

Jesus and his disciples escaped the crowds and went away by themselves to a solitary place. There, Jesus grieved, wept and mourned the death of his cousin, his friend.

Jesus endured suffering

> *Religious people sometimes mishandle their own grief and the grief of others by thinking that faith and tears don't mix. . . . But grief is not a denial of faith. The shortest verse in the Bible is found in John 11:35. It states simply: "Jesus wept."*
> Haddon Robinson
> PASTOR AND AUTHOR

and loss, just as you and I do. The test of loss, the test of grief is an experience we all face sooner or later. This was not the only time Jesus was tested in this way.

The Death of Lazarus

Not long after the death of John the Baptist, something terrible happened to another close friend of Jesus. This friend, Lazarus, lived in the Judean village of Bethany, two miles east of Jerusalem. He was the brother of Mary and Martha, who were also friends and followers of Jesus. When Lazarus fell ill, his two sisters sent a message to Jesus that said, "Your friend, Lazarus, is seriously ill."

Jesus was surrounded by his disciples when the message reached him. "This illness will not end in death," he said. "God has a plan for this illness, to bring something good out of something terrible. As a result of the sickness of Lazarus, God and his Son will be greatly honored."

After receiving the message from Mary and Martha, Jesus remained in Galilee for two more days. Finally, he said to his disciples, "Let's go down to Judea."

"But Master," the disciples said, "just a short time ago, when you were in Judea, the religious leaders plotted to kill you! Why would you want to go back when the danger is still great?"

"Aren't there just twelve hours of daylight in a day?" Jesus replied. "Life is short, and I have much to do. I must work while it is still daylight. A man who walks by daylight

will not stumble, because he is able to see; the man who
stumbles is the man who has no light. I must not be
deterred from my work, just because the road ahead is
dangerous. I have to work while I have light, because just
as the daylight is short, my life is short. So let's go."

"Where in Judea are we going?" the disciples asked.

"To Bethany," Jesus said. "Our friend Lazarus has fallen
asleep. I am going there to wake him up."

The disciples, who knew that Lazarus had fallen ill, were
baffled. "But Master, if he has fallen asleep, that's good—
the sleep will help him get well."

Jesus shook his head. "You don't understand," he said.
"Lazarus is dead."

"Dead!" the disciples responded in shock.

"Yes," Jesus said, "and for your sakes, I'm glad I wasn't
there. You are going to learn something through this experience that will increase your faith. Now, come with me.
Let's go to him."

Most of the disciples still hesitated out of fear, but one,
Thomas Didymus (Thomas the Twin), said to his fellow
disciples, "Come on! Let's go with Jesus so that we can be
martyred with him!" (Remember this man, Thomas
Didymus, because we will meet him again. His personality
is marked by pessimism, but he is also a fiercely loyal follower of Jesus, willing to face danger and death for the
sake of his Master.)

Jesus and his disciples left Galilee and went south on a
journey of several days. They arrived at last at the village
of Bethany. Upon their arrival, they were told by the

townspeople that Lazarus had been placed in the tomb four days earlier. Someone ran to the house of Mary and Martha and told them that Jesus had arrived. Martha hurried out, leaving her sister behind. She met Jesus while he was still outside the village.

"Lord," Martha said, "if you had been here, my brother wouldn't have died!" She had witnessed the healings that Jesus had done for others, and she knew he would have healed her brother Lazarus. In fact, Martha's faith in Jesus was so great that, even though Lazarus was dead, she reserved hope that it was not too late. "I know that even now," she continued, "even after my brother is four days in the grave, God will give you anything you ask."

Jesus affirmed her faith. "Your brother will rise again," he said.

"I know he will rise again," Martha said, "in the final resurrection."

"I am the Resurrection and the life," Jesus replied. "Anyone who believes in me will live, even after death. And whoever lives and believes in me will never die. Do you believe this?"

"Yes, Lord," Martha replied. "I believe you are the Messiah, the Son of God, whom the Scriptures told us would come into the world."

"Where is your sister?" Jesus asked. "Would you bring her?"

Martha went back to the house and called to her sister, "Mary! The Master is here! He's asking for you!"

When Mary heard this, she left the house and hurried to

see Jesus. He was still at the place where Martha had met him, just outside the village of Bethany. When Mary arrived and saw Jesus, she fell weeping at his feet. "Lord," she said, "if you had been here, my brother wouldn't have died."

By this time, a crowd of mourners and townspeople had gathered, many of them weeping openly. Some of these people were followers of Jesus, and some, as we shall soon see, were opponents of Jesus. All of them, friends and foes alike, wondered what Jesus would do next.

Seeing the great sorrow of Mary, Martha and the other mourners, Jesus was overcome with grief. It was as if he absorbed the pain and sorrow of everyone around him. He groaned within himself and became filled with anguish—and anger. The Gospel account tells us that his body shook with *rage*—a rage against Death. Jesus was *angry* because this bitter enemy, Death, had snatched away his friend, Lazarus, and had stricken these beloved sisters with grief.

"Where have you buried Lazarus?" Jesus asked.

"Come and see," the people replied.

As they led Jesus to the tomb of Lazarus, he wept openly. The people who watched him were impressed by how intensely Jesus grieved. Here was a man whom many viewed as the promised Messiah. They saw him as beyond the

> *Grief is a tidal wave that overtakes you, smashes down upon you with unimaginable force, sweeps you up into darkness, where you tumble and crash against unidentifiable surfaces, only to be thrown out on an unknown beach, bruised, reshaped.*
>
> Stephanie Ericsson
> GRIEF COUNSELOR AND AUTHOR

reach of normal human pain and suffering. He had healed and comforted so many people. Yet, here he was, in deep sorrow over the death of Lazarus.

Some said, "We had no idea how deeply Jesus cared about Lazarus." Others said, "He opened the eyes of the blind. Couldn't he have prevented Lazarus from dying?"

Lazarus, Come Out!

Jesus arrived at the tomb. It was a cave dug out of a hillside, with a large circular stone over the mouth. There were many tombs dug into the hillside. Some were old and worn by time and the elements, but the stone that covered the tomb of Lazarus looked new and freshly cut. Still weeping, still shaking with grief and rage, Jesus said, "Roll the stone away."

Martha stepped in front of Jesus. "But, Lord," she said, horrified at what he had commanded. "By this time, the body will be badly decomposed—he's been in the grave four days!"

"Martha," Jesus said, "didn't I tell you that if you believed, you would see the wonder of God's power?"

With that, Martha was reminded of what she had said to Jesus earlier: *I know that even now, God will give you anything you ask.* She stepped out of Jesus' way.

The people rolled the stone away, and the mouth of the tomb stood open. It was as dark inside as death itself.

Standing in front of the tomb, Jesus turned his eyes heavenward and said, "Father, thank you for hearing me.

Now these people will know that you have truly sent me."

The people around the tomb looked at each other and at Jesus. What was he going to do?

Jesus shouted, and his voice echoed across that graveyard: "Lazarus, come out!"

For a moment, no one breathed.

Then, a pale form appeared out of the darkness of the tomb. It was the form of a man, his body wrapped in strips of linen burial cloth.

Jesus told the people who stood around the tomb, "Go to him, take off his grave cloths and set him free."

> *Jesus, the Lord of Life, has conquered death. He calls us out of the tomb of a dead world to join him in life.*
> Joseph Pellegrino
> PRIEST

A Miracle of Life and a Scheme of Death

Lazarus had died, and now he lived again. Many of those who witnessed the miracle were so amazed that they immediately put their faith in Jesus.

Of course, there were also some whose hearts were so hardened by unbelief that they would never accept the claims of Jesus, even after seeing a dead man walk out of the tomb. They ran to the enemies of Jesus, the Pharisees and other religious rulers, and told them what Jesus had done. The Pharisees got together with the high priests and convened a meeting of the ruling council, the Sanhedrin.

No sooner had the meeting begun when the shouting began.

"We've been trying to silence this troublemaker from Nazareth," one of them said. "We've tried to discredit him and show him up as a fraud, but what have we accomplished? Nothing! Everything we do to destroy his reputation only makes his popularity grow!"

"If we let him go on like this," another said, "the whole nation will soon be following him! And then what? The Roman army will come in, remove us from power and destroy the nation of Israel!"

Finally, the high priest, Caiaphas, stood and said, "Don't you know anything at all? It is time we face facts: It is better that one man die as a sacrifice for the people than that the whole nation be destroyed. It's time we get serious about dealing with this man, Jesus of Nazareth."

With that, the religious leaders intensified their effort to take the life of Jesus. They knew that Jesus always showed up in Jerusalem for the Passover festival, so they put out the word that anyone who saw Jesus should report his presence to the authorities.

> *No one ever told me that grief felt so like fear. I am not afraid, but the sensation is like being afraid. The same fluttering in the stomach, the same restlessness, the yawning. I keep on swallowing.*
>
> C. S. Lewis
> SCHOLAR, NOVELIST
> AND LAY THEOLOGIAN

As the Passover festival approached, the leaders of the people kept an eye out for him, especially in the area around the Temple. "What do you think?" they asked each other. "Will he dare to show himself at the Passover festival this year?"

Jesus, of course, knew that these men were waiting for him, and he wasn't anywhere near Jerusalem. Instead, he and his disciples had withdrawn to the remote desert village of Ephraim.

Even so, Jesus wasn't hiding from a confrontation with his enemies. He was simply planning and awaiting the right time for his return. When the Passover festival arrived, Jesus would be in Jerusalem, and he would boldly confront his enemies face-to-face.

A Man of Sorrows and Acquainted with Grief

Even while the moment of his own death approached, Jesus was forced to deal with the death of two close friends, John the Baptist and Lazarus of Bethany. Sooner or later, grief comes to us all. Yet, we can take comfort in knowing that Jesus went before us, enduring it all, identifying with us, drinking that pain into his own soul and entering fully into our experience.

How should we deal with the sorrow that is an inevitable part of life? How can we learn to grieve like Jesus?

I believe a lesson from nature may give us some insight. There is a species of bean plant that is native to the hot, dry foothills of the American Southwest and northern Mexico. This bean plant—the tepary bean or *Phaseolus acutifolius*—is one of the most drought-resistant, heat-resistant food crops known to humanity. Tepary beans not only survive but *flourish* in harsh climates that would destroy other crops. Tepary plants can produce flowers and bean pods in extreme desert heat, even if there is only one rainfall during the entire year. The plant's leaves remain green even in the 115-degree heat of a desert in July.

Tepary beans have what it takes to withstand withering adversity. How do they do it? The answer is in their roots.

The seed of the tepary bean sends its roots *deep* in search of moisture, often six feet or more into the soil. If we want to have the endurance of the tepary bean, then we must send our roots deep into the soil of God, just as Jesus did.

He had his roots deep in the soil of prayer. He maintained a deep and daily connection with God the Father.

He had his roots deep in the soil of Scripture. He knew great quantities of Scripture by memory, and those words of comfort from the Psalms and from other Scripture passages were never far from his mind.

He had his roots deep in the soil of relationships. He was close to his disciples and to friends like Mary and Martha. There were always people in his life, people he could lean on and talk to, people who helped him work through his grief.

By observing the grief of Jesus, we find a number of principles for enduring grief as Jesus did. Those principles include:

1. *Grief is inevitable.* We often wonder *if* we will have to endure a trial of loss, but that's the wrong question. The only question we should ask ourselves is, *when* suffering comes, *how* will I respond?

   Our unwillingness to accept the inevitability of grief is one of the reasons we often feel that loss is so unfair. In one sense, it *is* unfair. It is never fair when we lose someone we love. There is never a good time to experience grief. In another sense, though, grief is a universal and inevitable part of the human condition. When loss comes into our lives, when someone we love is taken from us, we are not experiencing anything but what all people experience at one time or another. Grief is inevitable.

2. *Grief is painful.* Jesus suffered greatly when he lost a friend, and he didn't try to hide or suppress his grief. He wept. He groaned within. He raged against the pain of grief. Jesus expressed his pain and his emotions with complete honesty.

   It is important to notice the sequence of events in the story of Jesus and the death of Lazarus. First, Jesus received word that Lazarus was sick and he said, "This illness will not end in death." Then, he delayed for two days before going to Bethany. When he finally arrived in Bethany, he told Martha, "Your brother will rise again." In short, *Jesus knew all along that Lazarus would rise again!*

   Why, then, did he weep? Why did he rage against

the loss of Lazarus when he knew that Lazarus would rise again? I believe Jesus grieved and wept because he understood that death is an enemy. He knew the pain and grief that Mary and Martha felt. He knew what Lazarus had gone through as he slipped into the shadow of death. He knew, too, that death was stalking him and would claim him within a matter of weeks. Even though Lazarus would rise again, Jesus grasped the awful reality of death and loss. Grief is painful, and the experience of loss is about the closest thing to unbearable suffering we are ever called to endure.

You may experience grief as an actual, physical pain. You may feel pain in your chest, stomach or back. Your skin may become acutely sensitive. That is not imaginary pain; it is the part your body plays in feeling your loss. That experience of physical pain will pass, but it will take time for you to heal and for the pain to subside.

3. *Grief is baffling.* Death is a mystery. When we lose someone we love, the loss often stuns and shocks us, sending us reeling. We wonder why God allowed it to happen. We wonder if God is in control, and if he really knows what he is doing. During a trial of grief, the world seems as if it no longer makes sense. Loss is one of the most baffling and perplexing of all human experiences.

Denial is often a part of grief. "I don't believe it!

This must be a bad dream! This can't be happening!"
At times, you may turn to say something to your
loved one—then remember that he or she is gone.
There will be times when you feel that the loss
hasn't happened, and then it hits you with a sicken-
ing blow that, yes, this is real, you will never see this
person again in this life. It takes time to adjust to the
bafflement of grief, but in time, you *will* adjust.

4. *Grief is a process.* Every process requires time. No
   one gets over grief quickly. Jesus didn't, and you
   won't, either. When Jesus learned that John the
   Baptist had been executed, he took his disciples
   away from the crowds to a remote place. He knew he
   had a process of grief ahead of him, and he needed
   time to mourn.

   Grief is an intensely personal experience. No two
   people grieve in exactly the same way. No one can
   tell you how you should grieve. As you go through
   the grief process, it may be best for you to talk about
   your feelings—or be silent; to weep—or sit quietly;
   to feel sad—or feel angry. You must go through the
   process in your own time and in your own way.

   As you grieve, take care of your physical needs.
   Make sure you get plenty of rest, food and sleep.
   Don't neglect regular visits to your doctor. Seek out
   caring people who will understand the feelings of
   loss you are going through. Find trusted friends or
   relatives you can be honest with.

Don't expect the pain of your loss to ever completely go away. People who say that time heals all wounds don't know what they're talking about. Time does enable you to gain new insights and a new perspective, but the sense of loss never completely goes away. That doesn't mean you won't experience joy and happiness again, because you will. In time, you will begin enjoying the present instead of dwelling on memories of the past. You won't ever forget your loss—you wouldn't want to. But you will adjust to it, and the memories of your loved one will inspire you and carry you through the rest of your days.

5. *Grief can be a purposeful experience.* One of the worst aspects of a loss is that it seems so pointless and purposeless. In time, however, you will gain a perspective on your loss that will enable you to say, "I can see how God can use even this to produce something good."

What are some of the good things that God can bring out of a terrible experience such as grief? First, we know that grief and loss can often increase our capacity to comfort others. The experience of grief gives us an extra dimension of empathy that we can use to help other people.

Second, we know that an experience of grief and loss can often lead us to a deeper relationship with God. A trial of suffering can drive us deeper into prayer and into the Scriptures for strength and support. As we learn to rely more completely on God, we grow in faith.

Third, we know that suffering and grief can often produce the character of Jesus in us. We know that Jesus suffered grief, loss, pain and hardship in his life. When we suffer these same experiences, we learn to identify with him and to build his character traits into our lives. The result is that we become more and more like Jesus.

As the Old Testament prophet Isaiah once wrote, Jesus was "a man of sorrows, acquainted with grief." Jesus understands our pain, because he has entered into our pain. He has endured suffering and sorrow *for* us and *with* us. We can be like Jesus because *he chose to be like us* and endured the sorrow and loss that is common to us all.

CHAPTER THIRTEEN

HOW TO LEAD LIKE JESUS

In the third and final year of Jesus' ministry, his disciples sensed in him a new and growing sense of urgency. It was as if he knew his time was growing short and there were still too many unfinished tasks, too many broken lives in need of his touch. Jesus kept up a vigorous pace, walking from town to town, village to village, teaching in the synagogues, preaching the good news of the kingdom of heaven. Everywhere Jesus and his disciples went, he was besieged by crowds of needy, searching people.

So many wounded souls. So many broken and diseased bodies. So many blind eyes and deaf ears. The look of anguish in their faces haunted Jesus, troubled his sleep and broke his heart. "Like sheep without a shepherd," his disciples often heard him say.

One day, as Jesus and the Twelve walked toward a Galilean town, they passed a wheat field. A breeze rippled the field of grain, so that it shimmered like pale gold. "Master," said one of the disciples, "look at that field! It is ripe and ready for harvest."

"No," Jesus said, pointing down the road, toward the

279

pale brown houses of the town before them. "The harvest is there, where the people are. The harvest is plentiful— but there are all too few laborers for the fields. Pray and ask the Lord of the Harvest to send forth more laborers into his harvest field."

Arriving in the town, Jesus preached the message of the kingdom, cured many diseases and opened many blind eyes. When Jesus and the Twelve moved on, they left the road and went up on a hill.

"I have a task for you," Jesus told them. "I am going to give you power to work in my name. You shall have authority to drive out unclean spirits. You shall have authority over diseases and disabilities. I want you to go to the lost sheep of the house of Israel. Preach as you have seen me preach— tell everyone you meet that the kingdom of heaven is among them. Cure the sick, raise the dead, cleanse the lepers, drive out demons. I give you this power freely and without cost, so do not take money from anyone. And take no provisions with you. As you go, grateful people will give you food and lodging. When you enter someone's house, give your blessing to the household. Be wise, for I am sending you out as sheep among wolves."

The disciples looked at each other with worried expressions. They had seen the opposition Jesus had encountered, and they knew that some of Jesus' enemies were plotting his death. "What about the danger?" one of them asked. "What about those who want to kill you—and us as well?"

"Aren't two little sparrows sold for a penny?" Jesus said.

"Yet, not one of them falls to the ground without your Father's notice. Don't be afraid. You are more valuable to the Father than many sparrows. So I tell you, my friends, do not be afraid of evil men; they can kill the body, but after that they can do no more harm

> *I am an historian, I am not a believer, but I must confess as an historian that this penniless preacher from Nazareth is irrevocably the very center of history. Jesus Christ is easily the most dominant figure in all history.*
> H. G. Wells
> HISTORIAN AND NOVELIST

to you. Whoever would save his mortal life will lose his eternal life; but whoever loses his mortal life for my sake will live forever."

With this challenge, Jesus sent the Twelve out. They went from town to town, from village to village, preaching the good news and healing people wherever they went, just as they had been taught by the Master.

What was Jesus doing in sending the Twelve out to preach and heal? He was practicing *leadership*.

The Leadership Style of Jesus

Leadership is the ability to work through other people to achieve a vision or goal. The vision of Jesus was something he called "the kingdom of heaven." The people he chose to fulfill his vision were the Twelve Apostles—twelve men of untested ability from a variety of backgrounds. One of them, Matthew, was a social outcast. At

least four—Peter, Andrew, James and John—were fisher-
men with little education. At least one of them, Simon the
Zealot, was an agitator in an extremist political party.
There wasn't one impressive resumé in the bunch.

If you wanted to change the world, are these the twelve
people *you* would have chosen? I can tell you that if I
were conducting the job interviews, few of those men
would have made the first cut.

But Jesus was a visionary leader. He looked at these twelve
underachievers and saw something that you and I probably
would have missed. He saw men who would one day
become a powerful force for change in the world. Then he
proceeded to pour his life into them.

He walked with them, talked with them, encouraged
them, challenged them and mentored them. He dragged
them out of their comfort zones and threw them into sink-
or-swim situations. He took this diverse group of backgrounds, temperaments and personality types, and he
placed them in the crucible of human need and opposition. In the process, he molded them into an unstoppable
force for spiritual and social transformation.

Jesus invested a great deal of time in one particular disciple, the man we now know as Peter. When Jesus first met
him, his name was Simon. Jesus said to him, "You are
Simon, the son of Jonah—but from now on you will be
called Peter." The Greek name "Peter" means "The Rock."

But when you read the story of Simon Peter, you find he
was anything *but* a rock. He was unstable and unreliable. Jesus
constantly had to reprimand Peter for his impulsiveness.

Just hours before Jesus went to the cross, Simon Peter denied Jesus three times. Some rock!

Yet, that's exactly how Jesus wanted Peter to see himself—as a walking Rock of Gibraltar. That is the vision Jesus set before Peter, and in time, Peter actually began to conform to that vision of himself. He ultimately became the rock Jesus foresaw him to be. Jesus never settled for what a person *was;* he focused on what a person could *become.* When people came to Jesus, they went away *changed.*

Change is what leaders are all about. They turn visions into reality through people. Leaders accomplish goals and realize visions by influencing, training, inspiring, empowering and motivating others. Jesus pioneered a model of leadership that has since become the benchmark for how leadership should be done. His model of leadership includes these three characteristics:

1. *Mentoring.* A mentor is a wise and trusted teacher who molds lives through close, one-on-one teaching relationships. Jesus spent large amounts of time with the Twelve Apostles, both as a group and as individuals. He used that time to build relationships and communicate his vision to them. Through this intense relationship-building experience, he was able to impart to them such crucial but intangible character traits as faith, courage, obedience, integrity and humility.

2. *Training and coaching.* Jesus worked closely with the Twelve to build their confidence and their skills.

He stimulated thinking by asking open-ended questions. He placed them in challenging situations where they could stretch themselves and develop talents and uncover abilities they didn't even know they had. He listened to them and answered their questions. He demonstrated enthusiasm for their successes, helped them learn from their failures and showed them that he believed in them.

3. *Delegating.* In the early stages of his ministry, Jesus did *everything.* He did all the preaching, teaching, healing and driving out demons by himself. He worked and the disciples watched. In the middle stages of his ministry, Jesus involved the disciples in the ministry and gave them hands-on experience. They learned by doing, by making mistakes, and by doing it better the next time.

As the Twelve grew in understanding and experience, Jesus gradually transferred more responsibility to their shoulders. In the process, Jesus gave us a model for leading by delegating. Here's how his model of leadership works: First, Jesus says to the disciples, "I'll work; you watch." Next, as he involves them in his ministry, he says to them, "I'll work; you help." Then, he shifts even more responsibility to their shoulders, saying, "You work; I'll help." Finally, he entrusts the work completely to the Twelve, saying, "You work; I'll watch."

When Jesus sent the Twelve out to minister in his

name, he had been working with them for nearly three years. He called them together and commissioned them with full authority to do the same work he had been doing. He sent them into the world to preach, to heal and to battle evil. He delegated his full authority to the Twelve.

Delegating is the essence of leadership. Jesus was one man, but through his disciples he reproduced himself twelve times over. He didn't simply clone himself. He invested himself in their diversity. He produced a team of individuals that represented a rainbow of backgrounds and abilities, a broad spectrum of colorful human personalities to shine God's light into a darkened world.

When Jesus delegated his ministry to the Twelve, he made an amazing promise to them. "I tell you the truth, those who have faith in me will do what I have been doing. In fact, they will do even greater things than I have done, because I am going to the Father." Jesus knew that his time was short and that he wouldn't be there to personally lead them by the hand. He had to wean them of their dependence upon him. He had to build their confidence and enable them to stand on their own two feet.

So Jesus poured himself into the Twelve. One of them would later betray him, but the rest would be loyal to him until death. Those faithful eleven would pour their lives into more people, and those people would pour their lives into still more people. Generations later, that process is still going on.

Two thousand years have come and gone, and the leadership model of Jesus continues to multiply followers. Day after day, more and more people are choosing to follow Jesus and be like Jesus. I am one of these twenty-first-century disciples of Jesus, and so is every person who chooses to be like Jesus after accepting him as their savior. Through this simple leadership model, Jesus was able to use twelve men to transform the world.

That is what it means to lead like Jesus. That is why Jesus sent the Twelve out in his name to preach the message of the kingdom, to cure diseases, to open blind eyes. That is why he gave them his authority over unclean spirits and disease.

When the Twelve returned to Jesus and excitedly told him all they had done, they felt they had conquered the world. They had no idea that they had barely scratched the surface of what Jesus had planned for them. He had merely given them a taste of the awesome ministry that would one day be theirs.

> *One encounter with Jesus Christ is enough to change you, instantly, forever.*
> Luis Palau
> EVANGELIST AND AUTHOR

"Come with me," Jesus told them. "There is much more that I have to show you." So, together they set off for the fishing village of Bethsaida, on the northeastern edge of the Lake of Galilee.

Five Loaves and Two Fish

The crowds learned where Jesus was staying and followed him to Bethsaida. There were so many people there that the little village couldn't hold them all, so Jesus led the people out to the broad plain along the shore of the lake. There, throughout the day, he healed those who needed healing, and he explained to them the kingdom of heaven.

Finally, as the afternoon shadows were lengthening and Jesus was becoming visibly weary, the Twelve Apostles approached him. "Master," one of them said, "send the crowd away. Let them find food and lodging in the surrounding villages."

"No," Jesus said, looking at the crowds. He saw that the people were hungry, but this hunger was a soul-deep hunger that only he could satisfy. "No, we won't send them away. They shall stay, and you shall feed them."

"What?" the astonished disciples said. "We *can't* feed them! We have no food!"

"There must be three or four thousand people here!" Simon Peter said.

"I see more than five thousand men alone," Jesus said. "Plus the women and children."

Philip groaned. "Eight months' wages wouldn't buy enough bread to give each of them a bite!" he said.

"How much food do we have?" Jesus asked.

Andrew, the brother of Simon Peter, brought a boy forward. The boy had a basket in his hand. "This boy," Andrew said, "has five small loaves of barley bread and two small salted fish. That's all we have."

"It will do," Jesus said.

The disciples' jaws dropped. They didn't know where to begin to answer such an absurd statement.

"Go out among the people," Jesus continued. "Have them sit down in groups of fifty." Still wondering if their teacher had lost his mind, the disciples reluctantly did as Jesus told them. Soon, all the people were seated on the grassy plain beside the lakeshore.

Jesus took the five barley loaves and two small fish, and he looked up toward the sky. He gave thanks to the Father, then he broke the bread and fishes and gave the pieces to the disciples to distribute to the crowd.

The Twelve distributed the food to each group of fifty, then returned to Jesus for more food. Jesus kept breaking pieces of bread and dried fish, and the disciples kept distributing. Finally, all the people had eaten and none were hungry.

When the meal was over, Jesus said to the Twelve, "Gather the leftovers. Don't let any food be wasted." So the disciples collected twelve baskets of uneaten pieces of barley bread and salted fish.

> *I'm a Jew. I consider myself an agnostic. But I believe Jesus Christ is the most influential person who ever lived.*
>
> Larry King
> TALK-SHOW HOST

A sense of awe came over the entire crowd. Some whispered to each other, "This man is surely the Prophet promised by Moses! Let's make him our king! A man who can feed us all can surely lead us to victory over the Romans!"

When Jesus knew that the people were planning to make him their king—even against his will—he told his disciples to take a boat and cross to the other side of the lake without him. Then he slipped away from the crowd and withdrew to the mountains to pray. As his disciples set off across the Lake of Galilee, even they didn't know where Jesus had gone.

The "Ghost" upon the Lake

Long past midnight, the disciples struggled to make headway in their boat. They had to tack across the wind and pursue a zigzag course, and this slowed their progress considerably. By four or five in the morning, the disciples were still far from shore.

There was a full moon over the lake. Though the winds lashed at the sail and the waves pounded the hull, the air was crisp and clear. The disciples could see the horizon in all directions.

The men in the boat rubbed their eyes in disbelief! The gray, moonlit shape of a man was coming toward them— *and he was walking on the water.*

The disciples shouted hysterically, "It's a ghost!" A dozen hearts hammered in fright.

"Take courage!" the approaching figure shouted from the lake. "I am here! Don't be afraid!"

Simon Peter clutched the rail and peered through the darkness toward the man on the water. It sounded like the voice of Jesus! "Master!" shouted Peter, wanting to believe despite his doubt and terror. "If it is really you, tell me to come to you on the water!"

"Come to me!"

Without hesitating, Peter vaulted over the side of the boat. His feet touched the water—and the water held him up! Just like the Master, Peter could walk on the water as if it were dry land! Step by step, Peter walked upon the surface of the lake, keeping his eyes on Jesus. It was an exhilarating feeling! He had never experienced anything like it.

Then, out of the corner of his eye, he saw a wave bearing down on him. He took his eyes off of Jesus and looked at the wave—and he sank.

"Master!" he called before his head went under. "Save me!"

The next instant, Simon Peter felt a strong hand reach down to him through the surging waves and lift him out of the water. "How small your faith is," Jesus said. "After all you have seen, why didn't you trust me?"

Jesus helped Peter into the boat, then he climbed in as well. At that moment, the winds died down. Before long, they reached the shore at Gennesaret. There, Jesus preached about the kingdom and healed many people.

In the space of a few weeks, the disciples had been sent out with power to do the same works their Master and Leader had done. They had watched him do the impossible, feeding a crowd of thousands with nothing more than a basket of bread and dried fish. Then they had seen him do something even more impossible—walking on the surface of the Lake of Galilee. Though

> *When he said, "Follow me and I will make you fishers of men," Jesus transformed the disciples from people who worked for themselves to people who were part of a larger team.*
>
> Laurie Beth Jones
> AUTHOR AND MANAGEMENT EXPERT

they didn't realize it then, they were learning powerful, life-changing lessons in leadership from the greatest leader of all time.

And there were even more profound leadership lessons still to come.

The Bread of Life

From Gennesaret, Jesus and the disciples returned to his adopted hometown of Capernaum. On the Sabbath day, Jesus went to the synagogue in Capernaum to preach. The crowd found out where he was and came to hear him. Many of those in the crowd had been miraculously fed at the feeding of the five thousand. These were the people who had wanted to make Jesus their king, but he had disappointed them by slipping away into the mountains.

The crowd streamed into the synagogue, interrupting Jesus as he spoke. Standing in front of the congregation, Jesus waited as the noisy crowd streamed into the synagogue, filling every inch of floor space between the stone columns. The people pushed and jostled each other, trying to get as close to Jesus as they could. "Teacher!" the people called out. "We found you! Where have you been?"

"I tell you the truth," Jesus solemnly said to them. "You have been searching for me because I provided bread for your bellies. How tragic that you are not interested in bread for your souls! Stop chasing after food that perishes, and search instead for food that endures and satisfies eternally."

Some of the people asked, "How can we work the miraculous works of God, as you and your disciples have done?"

"The only work God asks you to do," Jesus answered, "is to place your trust in the one whom he has sent."

The people knew that Jesus was talking about himself. "What miraculous sign will you perform now so that we will believe in you? When Moses led our ancestors through the wilderness, God gave them bread out of heaven to eat. What will you do for us?"

"I tell you the truth," Jesus answered, "the bread Moses gave your ancestors in the wilderness was not the bread from heaven that I'm talking about. God the Father has given you the true bread of heaven, which is he who comes down from heaven and gives life to the world."

"Master," said the people, "give us this bread all the time!"

"I am the bread of life," Jesus said. "If you come to me, you will never be hungry. If you trust in me, you will never thirst. You should know this by now. Yet, even though you have seen me, you still don't believe in me. All those whom my Father gives me will come to me, and the one who comes to me will be welcomed and will never be rejected. I have come here to accomplish the plan of the One who sent me, not my own plans. And it is the will of the Father that I will not lose any souls he has given me, but I will give them all new life and raise them up at the end of human history."

The synagogue echoed with angry whispers. Some of the people were angry with Jesus because he had refused to produce another miracle on demand, and because he now claimed to be "bread from heaven." They said to each other, "Who does he think he is? Isn't this Jesus, the son of Joseph the carpenter? We know his parents and that he came from the village of Nazareth. How can he claim to come straight from heaven?"

"Why do you grumble among yourselves and speak against me this way?" Jesus asked. "I tell you the truth, I am the living bread, the bread that gives life. Yes, your ancestors ate so-called 'heavenly bread' in the wilderness—and yet they all eventually died. All physical food is temporary at best. But I am the living bread from heaven. Eat of this bread, and you will live forever. The bread I give for the life of the human race is my own body."

"What nonsense!" some of the people said. "How can he give his own body to be eaten?"

"I tell you the truth," Jesus said, "unless you eat the body of the Son of Man and drink his blood, you will die. If you feed on me, you possess eternal life, for I will raise you up from the dead on the last day of human history."

After Jesus finished speaking, a large group of his follow-ers, including the Twelve Apostles, gathered outside in the courtyard of the synagogue. In low tones, they discussed among themselves the strange things Jesus had just said.

"Everything the teacher said today was hard to under-stand," said one follower.

"It was downright offensive!" said another. "All this talk of eating his body and drinking his blood!"

"How could anyone accept such teaching?" said one of the Twelve, Judas Iscariot. "How does he expect to win fol-lowers with such a message?"

"So, you think the message today was offensive?" said a familiar voice. Everyone turned and saw Jesus approach-ing. Some wondered guiltily how much he had heard.

"You're upset because of my message today?" Jesus con-tinued. "You're shocked and scandalized? What would you think if you saw the Son of Man ascend to the place he came from? The words I have spoken to you are spirit and life, yet some of you still do not believe in me." With that, Jesus locked his gaze on the face of Judas.

Judas looked away.

"This is why I said," Jesus continued, "that no one can come to me unless the Father permits it."

Some of those who had been following Jesus shook their heads in disgust. "I believed in you," one of them said, "because you preached about the coming kingdom. I thought you would remove the Roman boot from our necks and make Israel free and powerful once more. But after hearing your message today, I think I've been following a madman." He turned and walked away.

Jesus looked around at the scores of other followers. One by one, people turned their backs on Jesus and walked away. Soon, there was no one left but Jesus and the twelve men of his inner circle. An air of gloom and depression hung over them.

"What about you?" Jesus said, looking at the faces of the Twelve Apostles. "Do you also want to leave me?"

There was a long moment of silence.

Then, Peter spoke up. "Master," he said, "to whom shall we go? You have the message of eternal life."

Jesus nodded. "That is why I have chosen you twelve men," he said,

> *Leading like Jesus is not a technique. It is a transformation of the heart.*
> James W. Rueb
> PASTOR

"because I know that you are faithful and loyal—all of you except one." His eyes scanned the faces of the Twelve, and only briefly lingered on the face of Judas.

"And that one," Jesus said, "is a devil."

Feeding the Gentiles

From Capernaum, Jesus and the Twelve journeyed around northern Israel and across Syria. He preached and healed from the Mediterranean coastal towns of Tyre and Sidon to the inland region of Decapolis. Though his ministry was primarily among the Jewish people in the region, he also delivered the daughter of a Syrian woman from possession by a demon.

From Syria, Jesus and the Twelve journeyed south to Decapolis, along the eastern shore of the Lake of Galilee. They were met by multitudes of people who knew of his fame. Jesus camped in the hills and healed many people.

After three days of preaching and healing in the Gentile region of Decapolis, Jesus called his disciples around him and said, "My heart breaks for these people. They have been with me for three days now, and they have nothing left to eat. If I send them away, they'll faint from hunger on the way. We must feed them."

The disciples looked at Jesus in dismay. "There must be four thousand men alone," they said, "plus all the women and children! Where will we get enough bread to feed such a crowd? We're miles from the nearest town."

Jesus' heart sank. Just a few weeks earlier, he had fed an even greater crowd of five thousand people, and it had been accomplished with only five barley loaves and two salted fish. The disciples had been there and had seen it all. What's more, they had seen him walk on water. They had seen healings and the deliverance of many people from evil spirits. They had been sent out with power to heal. Now, here they were, facing a situation almost identical to one they had faced before—and where was their faith? Hadn't these disciples learned anything in the three years they had been with him?

Jesus sighed deeply. "How much food do you have?" he asked.

"Seven loaves of bread," one of the disciples replied, "and a few small fish."

"Tell the people to sit on the ground," Jesus said.

The disciples did as Jesus said. Then Jesus took the bread and the fish. He gave

> *Jesus, the most lowly of all men, the despised, beyond comparison, of the despised Jewish nation, has ascended the world's throne to become the Great King of the whole Earth.*
> Kaufmann Kohler
> RABBI

thanks to the Father then broke the bread and fish into pieces and passed it out to the disciples. Just as before, the bread was distributed, the people ate their fill, and there even were leftovers—seven large baskets of broken pieces of bread and fish.

Do You Still Not Understand?

Jesus and the disciples then sailed west, toward Galilee. The disciples had forgotten to bring food for the trip, and there was only one loaf of bread for thirteen men. As they sailed west, Jesus stood in the boat and solemnly said to them, "I want you to understand the danger you are facing. Be always on guard against the yeast of the Pharisees and the yeast of Herod and the Herodians."

Later, when the disciples were sitting among themselves at the stern of the boat, they discussed what Jesus had said. "What does he mean?" asked one disciple. "What's this about the 'yeast' of the Pharisees and the 'yeast' of Herod?"

"Yeast is for making bread," said another. "Maybe he's

unhappy with us because we forgot to bring enough bread for the journey."

"Are you truly so dense?"

Startled, the disciples turned and saw Jesus standing over them. The Master shook his head in disgust. "How can you sit there and say such things? I talk to you of spiritual reality, and you say, 'It is because we forgot to bring bread.' How long have we been together, and yet you still do not understand the simplest matters? You have eyes, yet you see nothing I have shown you! You have ears, yet you hear nothing I have told you! Don't you remember any of the things I have done in your presence?"

"Master," one of the disciples said, "we have seen and heard so many things. What do you mean?"

"When I broke the five loaves for the five thousand people, how many small baskets of leftover pieces did you gather?"

The disciples answered, "Twelve."

"And when I broke the seven loaves for the four thousand people, how many large baskets of leftover pieces did you gather?"

The disciples answered, "Seven."

"Do you still not understand?" Jesus asked them.

The disciples looked back at him, not understanding.

Shaking his head, Jesus gazed out over the Lake of

> *Leadership isn't creating gifts in people. It's recognizing giftedness, then nurturing and developing it and giving it focus and direction.*
> Al Mawhinney
> THEOLOGIAN AND
> SEMINARY PROFESSOR

Galilee. "After all you have seen and heard," he said again, "do you still not understand?"

In the Same Boat

If you and I were in that boat, would we have understood? I doubt it.

It's clear that Jesus was trying to get something vitally important across to his disciples. The point he was making had something to do with the two mass feedings—the feeding of the five thousand in Galilee and the feeding of the four thousand in the Gentile region of Decapolis. There is also something significant in the number of baskets of leftovers that were gathered after each feeding—twelve in the first case, seven in the second. Jesus specifically asked the disciples to recall those numbers and when they answered, he said, "Do you still not understand?"

What was Jesus trying to tell them?

Many people have heard this story without pondering the significance of the two mass feedings. Some people mistakenly assume they are merely differing accounts of the same event. However, two Gospels, Matthew and Mark, contain both feedings, and when Jesus talks to his disciples in the boat, he reminds them of *both,* making it clear that these were, in fact, two separate events.

In each case, Jesus multiplied a small amount of bread and fish in order to feed a multitude of people. The first time, he performed this miracle among the Jewish people in Galilee. The second time, he performed this miracle among the non-Jewish people, the Gentiles, of Decapolis. Clearly, there were significant lessons Jesus wanted his disciples to learn from these two feedings. Following are three lessons I see from these events:

1. *When confronted with a need, use whatever is available to meet that need—then leave the results to God.* Our tendency when we see a staggering need is to throw up our hands and say, "The problem is too big. My resources are too small. Why even try?" But Jesus tells us, in effect, "Okay, you can't adopt every abandoned child in the world, but can you adopt just one? You can't reach out to every lonely widow in the world, but could you talk to the widow next door? You can't shelter every homeless family in the world, but could you volunteer with Habitat for Humanity and help build one house for one family?"

   Offer your limited supply of resources to God, let him bless it and break it and distribute it—and then watch it multiply.

2. *Focus on spiritual reality, not mundane matters such as food.* The disciples had seen Jesus feed five thousand people with five loaves of bread and some fish. They had seen him feed four thousand people with seven loaves of bread and some fish. Now, the thirteen men are on a boat in the middle of the Lake of Galilee with one loaf of bread between them, and

they think Jesus is upset with them for not bringing enough bread! Certainly, they should have known that one loaf of bread in the hands of Jesus would feed thirteen—or thirteen thousand!

A lack of bread was not the problem. The problem was a lack of spiritual understanding. Instead of thinking about food, the disciples should have been thinking about what Jesus was telling them when he spoke of the "yeast" of the Pharisees and of Herod.

The disciples actually made a rather bizarre leap in their thinking when they heard Jesus talking about "yeast." They thought, "Well, yeast has something to do with bread, so maybe Jesus is rebuking us for failing to bring enough bread."

What was Jesus actually talking about?

The "yeast of the Pharisees" referred to the self-righteous pride that blinded the religious rulers to the truth. The Pharisees believed that God cared about rules and rituals, but Jesus tried to tell them that God was interested in relationships. The Pharisees believed that God cared about outward appearances, and Jesus tried to tell them that God cared about the inner reality. Jesus warned the disciples not to fall into the same trap as the Pharisees, or they, too, would end up in spiritual darkness.

So what was the "yeast of Herod"? Herod was a spineless king who served as a toady to the Roman oppressors. He was so weak-willed and cowardly that he gave in to the whim of his vengeful wife and ordered John the Baptist executed. Herod knew that he was doing an evil thing, but he lacked the intestinal fortitude to stand up to his vindictive wife. The "yeast of Herod" was the willingness to take the path of least resistance—to do what is easy or popular instead of what is right. Herod chose the easy path, and he, too, ended up in spiritual darkness.

Jesus wanted his disciples to understand the truth that he demonstrated when he was tempted by Satan in the wilderness. "Human beings cannot live by bread alone, but must live by every word that comes from God's own mouth." He wanted to lift the disciples' minds from mundane matters such as food. He wanted them to move from physical hunger to spiritual satisfaction.

3. *God's resources are perfect and complete.* As the disciples struggled to understand what Jesus was telling them, he asked them a couple of questions that seem, at first glance, to make no sense. He asked how many baskets of leftover bread and fish were gathered after the feeding of the five thousand. The disciples answered, "Twelve." Jesus asked how many baskets were gathered after the feeding of the four thousand. The disciples answered, "Seven." Then, as if the significance of those two numbers was staring the disciples in the face, Jesus said, "Do you still not understand?"

What did Jesus mean? What is the significance of twelve and seven? The number twelve may be significant because it relates to the feeding in the Jewish region of Galilee in northern Israel. Throughout the Old and New Testaments, the number twelve is used as a symbol of the twelve tribes of Israel.

What about the number seven? The seven baskets were gathered after the feeding in the Gentile region of Decapolis. The number seven is used in the Bible as a symbol of perfection or completion. It may be that Jesus was telling his disciples that these two miraculous feedings signified that Jesus had come first to the house of Israel, then ultimately and completely to the entire world, including the non-Jewish world.

Whether God is at work among the Jewish people or in the non-Jewish world, his resources are more than adequate to any need. God loves all people with an extravagant love, and he gives us what we need in abundant, overflowing ways. With God, we never have just enough to get by. Through prayer, we have total access to his unimaginable resources.

Does this mean that God guarantees us an overflowing abundance of wealth and material possessions? If that is your interpretation of these feedings, then you have missed the point as completely as the disciples did. Jesus is trying to direct our attention to God's *spiritual* resources. He wants us to understand that God's resources are more than adequate to supply all of our *spiritual* needs. We may not have all the material things we *want,* but through God we can have all the spiritual things we need.

"You have eyes, yet you see nothing I have shown you! You have ears, yet you hear nothing I have told you!" Throughout the Gospels, Jesus says words like these to his own disciples. Again and again, he tries to get them to look beyond the superficial and to see the profound and invisible realities of spiritual truth. He wants to heal our spiritual blindness and open our eyes to see the unseen realities of God.

"Don't you remember anything that I have done in your presence?" Again and again, Jesus has done amazing things in the presence of the disciples— miracles of healing, of power over evil spirits, of walking on water, of stretching meager resources into a banquet for thousands. Yet the disciples continually forget the meaning of what they have seen. They easily lose sight of the power and goodness of God.

> *Leadership is a matter of having people look at you and gain confidence by seeing how you react. If you're in control, they're in control.*
>
> Tom Landry
> NFL COACH

You and I are in the same boat with those disciples, and the question Jesus put to them is as valid today as it was two thousand years ago. "Do you still not understand?"

Who Do You Say I Am?

Jesus and the disciples beached their boat at the village of Bethsaida. From there, they went to the Roman town of Caesarea Philippi. As they walked along the road, Jesus asked his disciples, "Who do the people say I am?"

"Some say you're John the Baptist," said one, "returned from the dead."

"I've heard some call you the resurrected prophet Elijah," said another.

"Some say you're one of the other prophets from long ago," said another. "Isaiah, perhaps, or Jeremiah."

Jesus stopped in his tracks and looked at his disciples. "And what about you?" he said. "Who do *you* say I am?"

Simon Peter spoke up boldly. "You are the Messiah," he said, "the Son of the living God."

Jesus smiled. "You are greatly blessed, Simon, son of Jonah, for this truth was not revealed to you by any human being, but by my Father in heaven. This is why I named you Peter, the Rock, for upon this rock I will build my fellowship of believers. And that great fellowship will storm the gates of Hell, and Hell will not be able to stand against it. The keys of the kingdom of heaven will belong to you, and anything you bind on Earth will be bound in heaven, and anything you release on Earth will be released in heaven."

A look of awe was on every face that looked at Jesus. They were certain it was true: They were walking alongside the long-awaited Messiah himself.

"Make sure you tell no one about this," Jesus said, "for my time has not yet come. The Son of Man must suffer many things, and be rejected by the elders, priests, scribes and rulers of the people. He must be killed. . . ."

At this, a dozen faces registered shock and dismay.

". . . and on the third day, he shall be raised to life."

"No, Master!"

All eyes turned to Simon Peter. The rugged fisherman grabbed Jesus by the arm and pulled him aside, away from the others.

"Master, no!" Simon Peter said again. "May it never be so! The Messiah cannot die! Just let your enemies try to arrest you! I won't let them! I swear by . . ."

"Get behind me, Satan!" Jesus shouted, pulling away from Peter's grasp.

Startled, Peter backed away from Jesus.

"You speak out of human folly," Jesus said, "and without any understanding of God's eternal plan!" He turned to the rest of the disciples. "Listen to me, all of you! If you would follow me, then you must disown yourselves and your own interests. If you want to save your life, then I guarantee you will lose it; but if you give up your life for my sake, you will have eternal life in the kingdom of heaven."

The disciples looked at Jesus with bewildered faces. "But what is the kingdom?" one of them asked. "Why do you talk about dying? We thought we would reign with you in your kingdom. But sometimes it sounds as if there won't be any kingdom!"

"I tell you the truth," Jesus replied, looking from face to

face. "Some of you standing here with me will not taste death until you have seen the kingdom of God with your own eyes."

> *All leadership is influence.*
> John C. Maxwell
> AUTHOR AND SPEAKER

That promise would be fulfilled just eight days later.

A Blinding Glimpse of the Kingdom

Jesus and the Twelve went to Caesarea Philippi, where Jesus preached and healed. After that, Jesus took Peter, James and John with him and left the other disciples to carry on the work of the ministry in the town. The four men journeyed north, to Mount Hermon, the highest peak of the Anti-Lebanon range. Eight days after Peter boldly professed Jesus as the Messiah, they were high on its slopes. There, Jesus knelt and began to pray. The three disciples, weary from the climb, rested a short distance away.

As Jesus prayed, the three disciples were astonished to see an amazing change come over him. His face and clothing shone with a brilliant white light. As the disciples watched, two men appeared out of nowhere—and they, too, were clothed in a blinding white light. No introduction was needed. Somehow the three disciples knew who the two men were: Moses and Elijah.

Moses, of course, was the greatest of all Hebrew prophets, the man who led the people of Israel out of bondage in Egypt and who received the Ten Commandments from God on Mount Sinai. Elijah was the prophet who had battled idolatry and stood up to the wicked King Ahab and his queen, Jezebel. At the end of his earthly life, Elijah did not die but was carried bodily to heaven in a whirlwind.

Jesus stood and talked with Moses and Elijah. Peter, James and John listened in awe and astonishment, scarcely comprehending the conversation. They grasped only that the discussion had to do with the "departure" of Jesus, which was soon to be "fulfilled" in the city of Jerusalem. What did it all mean? Where was Jesus going?

"Master!" Peter shouted.

Jesus turned and looked at the impetuous disciple.

"Master, this is wonderful!" Peter continued, babbling excitedly, almost delirious with joy. "How can we thank you for allowing us to see this? I know what! We shall make three tents, one for you, one for Moses and one for Elijah!" The tents Peter had in mind were temporary houses of worship. Peter was overcome with religious wonder and awe.

Just then, a cloud of light billowed over them, and a voice said, "This is my Son, whom I love. All that he does pleases me. Listen to him and do what he says." At the sound of that voice, Peter, James and John fell on their faces, quaking in fear.

Seconds passed. Peter jumped when he felt a touch on his shoulder. He looked up and saw Jesus, but the Master's face and clothing no longer shone with light. "Get up," Jesus said gently, "and don't be afraid." Jesus touched the other disciples and said, "We must go."

Peter, James and John looked all around. There was no one with them but Jesus. Moses and Elijah, the two greatest men in Israel's history, had disappeared.

As the four men started down the slope of Mount Hermon, Jesus ordered the disciples to tell no one what they had seen until after the Son of Man had arisen from among the dead. The three disciples didn't dare question Jesus as to what he meant.

Jesus had promised that some of his disciples would not die until they had seen the kingdom of God with their own eyes. Peter, James and John had caught a bril-

> *A very important part of leadership is lifting people up and making them realize they can be better than they are.*
>
> Richard J. Munro
> BUSINESS EXECUTIVE

liant, blinding glimpse of the kingdom, just as Jesus promised. But they also knew that before the kingdom arrived in full, something terrible was going to happen.

Approaching Darkness

Jesus showed us how one leader can change the world. He began with a bold vision that he put up in lights for all to see—a shining vision of God's kingdom on Earth. Then he chose twelve people and entrusted his vision to them. He built close, tightly bonded relationships with them and mentored them. He trained them, coached them and delegated his authority to them to minister in his name.

Jesus knew they would fail and make mistakes, but he

unleashed them and transferred increasing amounts of responsibility to their shoulders. He knew he could not do it all, especially in view of the short time he had left. So he poured his life into them and multiplied himself through them.

Jesus fed a crowd in northern Israel to demonstrate to his disciples what his ministry was all about: spiritual bread for hungry souls. The feeding of the five thousand was not, as some would suppose, just a flashy display of miraculous power. It was symbolic of what Jesus had come to do for the nation of Israel. The second feeding of four thousand people took that same message of living bread beyond the borders of Israel and into the world at large.

As a leader, Jesus walked on water. You may think, *How can I lead like Jesus? I can swim, but I can't walk on water!* It's a mistake, however, to think that the point of this miracle was just to show off the power of Jesus. The theme of that event was *faith.* Jesus did something unthinkable, then he called Peter out of the boat and commanded him to do the unthinkable as well.

If you are a leader, there are things you do every day that your followers probably consider impossible to imitate: You envision the future, think creatively, initiate action, take charge, motivate, inspire, mentor, empower, communicate, manage conflict, remain calm under pressure, handle multiple tasks, exude confidence, demonstrate management skills, demonstrate sales skills and more. To the people around you, the leadership abilities that are natural to you look like "walking on water" to them. Your job as a leader is to call people out of the safety of the boat and urge them to take a step of faith. Get them out on the water and tell them to *start walking!*

Jesus, the ultimate leader, taught his disciples that if they would dare the unthinkable, they could achieve the impossible—as long as they kept their eyes on him. Peter didn't sink until he took his eyes off of Jesus and started looking at his circumstances. As long as he kept looking to Jesus, there was no limit to what he could do. So it is with you and me.

Above all, Jesus tried to prepare his followers for the fact that he would not always be there holding their hands. Jesus knew that the goal of leadership is not to produce childlike dependents, but mature, confident, dependable disciples. So Jesus did amazing things in their presence, then he told his followers that they would achieve even greater things. He wanted his followers to understand that, with God's power flowing through them, they were going to change the world.

Finally, he took three of his closest disciples upon Mount Hermon, where he gave them a glimpse of the incredible glory that lay ahead of them—the culmination of God's plan for the human race, a plan that led through such men as Moses and Elijah, as well as through Peter, James and John.

Jesus knew that a time was soon approaching when he would gather his disciples in an upper room in Jerusalem. He would bid them farewell, and they would feel lost and without hope. One of them would slip away from that room and sell the life of Jesus for thirty pieces of silver. But the eleven who stayed with Jesus would change the course of history.

The work of Jesus remains unfinished. He is still calling men and women who are willing to follow him and become his next "inner circle" of leaders-in-training. The world is crying out for change and for people who are willing to lead like Jesus.

Are you ready to lead?

CHAPTER FOURTEEN

HOW TO FOCUS LIKE JESUS

s Jesus led his disciples from Galilee down toward Jerusalem, he knew he would never walk that road again. He was going to Jerusalem to die. Though he had told the disciples what would happen to him there, they either didn't understand it or didn't accept it.

At some point in the journey, Jesus and the disciples crossed the Jordan and spent time in the region of Perea. They paused for a while in one of the little villages east of the Jordan River, and people brought their children and babies to Jesus to be blessed. At first, the disciples tried to keep the children back. "The Teacher is busy," they said. "He doesn't have time for children!"

When Jesus saw what his disciples were doing, he scolded them. "Let the little children come to me," he said. "Don't hinder them, for the kingdom of God belongs to children and to

> *The rich young man was reluctant to follow Jesus because the cost of following was the death of his will. In fact, every command of Jesus is a call to die.... But we do not want to die.*
>
> Dietrich Bonhoeffer
> THEOLOGIAN AND AUTHOR

people with childlike faith." With that, Jesus took the children in his arms, and he blessed them.

As Jesus and the disciples were leaving the village, the townspeople followed him and begged him to stay with them a little longer. But Jesus couldn't stay. His life was on a fixed timetable. He had an appointment in Jerusalem.

A Wealthy Young Man

When Jesus reached the edge of town, a young man ran up to him and knelt in the dust at his feet. This young man came from a rich and powerful family, and he had grown up accustomed to luxury. "Good teacher," the young man said. "What do I have to do to receive eternal life?"

"Why do you call me 'good'?" Jesus asked. "There is no one who is perfectly good except God alone. You know the commandments of God: Do not commit adultery. Do not murder. Do not steal. Do not speak falsely or defraud others. Honor your father and mother.'"

"I have faithfully kept all of the commandments since I was a boy," the young man said.

When Jesus heard the sincerity in the young man's voice, he was touched. "That's fine," Jesus replied. "There's just one thing you haven't done: Let go of your fondness for luxury and security. Go and sell everything you have, and give the proceeds to the needy. Then you will have lasting treasure stored up in heaven. Once you have done that, come and follow me."

The young man's face sagged, because he was very rich, and he enjoyed his prestige and his possessions. "I can't do that," he said. He turned his back on Jesus and sadly went home to his possessions and his empty life.

As Jesus watched the young man depart, he said to his disciples, "It is so hard for the rich to enter the kingdom of God! In fact, it is easier for a camel to pass through the eye of a sewing needle than for a rich man to enter God's kingdom."

The townspeople who heard this could hardly believe their ears. After all, it was the rich who gave the largest offerings at the Temple. Couldn't all their money help to purchase eternal life? "If it's hard for the rich to enter God's kingdom," the people asked, "then who can be saved?"

"With human beings, eternal life is impossible," Jesus said. "But with God, all things are possible."

"Master," Peter said, "we have left everything to follow you."

"I tell you the truth," Jesus answered. "There are those who have left all for my sake—they've given up home, possessions and even family. Yet, they will receive a hundred times over what they have given up, both in this life and in the life to come. Many who are first now will then be last; many who are last now will then be first. Come along. We must go to Jerusalem."

So they went south, crossed over the Jordan River and continued down the road toward Jerusalem. As they walked, Jesus again tried to impress upon his followers what was going to happen in the near future.

"You must understand," Jesus said, "that when we get to

> *Jesus promised his disciples three things: that they would be entirely fearless, absurdly happy, and that they would get into trouble.*
>
> W. Russell Maltby
> MINISTER AND AUTHOR

Jerusalem, the Son of Man will be handed over to the chief priests and scribes of the Temple. They will conspire against him, condemn him, and sentence him to death. Then they will turn him over to the Gentiles for execution. The Gentiles will humiliate him, spit on him, flog him and execute him. But on the third day, the Son of Man will rise again."

The disciples listened to Jesus and tried to understand what he was saying to them, but the meaning of his words was a mystery to them. Even though Jesus was telling them as plainly as he could that he was about to suffer and die in Jerusalem, the disciples couldn't comprehend it.

Healings in Jericho

On the way to Jerusalem, Jesus and the disciples came to the ancient town of Jericho. At the edge of town, a blind man named Bartimaeus sat by the side of the road, begging. When he heard a crowd gathering in front of him, Bartimaeus asked, "What's happening? Who's coming?"

"It's Jesus of Nazareth!" someone told him. "He's coming to Jericho!"

Jesus of Nazareth! Bartimaeus had heard of this wonder-worker who had healed lepers and given sight to the blind. Now, this amazing man was coming his way!

"Jesus, son of David!" the blind man shouted from the back of the crowd. "Take pity on me! Have mercy on me!"

His shouts annoyed the people in the front of the crowd. "Shut up!" they snapped.

This just made Bartimaeus even more frantic. "Son of David!" he shrieked at the top of his lungs. "Take pity on me! Have mercy on me!"

When Jesus heard Bartimaeus, he stopped in the middle of the road. "Bring that man to me," he said to his disciples. They went into the crowd, pulled the blind man to his feet and led him to Jesus.

"What do you want me to do for you?" Jesus asked.

"Master," Bartimaeus said, "I want to see!"

"Then you shall receive your sight," Jesus said. "Your faith in God has healed you."

In an instant, the man could see. He joined the procession that was following Jesus through the town. As he went, he praised God for the gift of his sight.

Continuing through Jericho, surrounded by crowds, Jesus and the disciples passed a sycamore tree beside the road. Jesus looked up and saw a man sitting in the tree. Jesus called to the man and told him to come down. The man scrambled out of the tree.

His name was Zacchaeus, and he was a chief tax collector—a Jewish man who reported directly to the Romans and who had other tax collectors working under him. He was a short man, which is why he had to climb a tree to see Jesus. The crowd hated tax collectors, and they refused to let Zacchaeus move to the front for a better view.

Once Zacchaeus was down from the tree, Jesus said to him, "Show me where you live. I'm staying with you tonight." The tax collector's face brightened, and he welcomed Jesus to his house. The people in the crowd, however, were displeased. "The Galilean is a poor judge of character!" they said. "He's staying tonight in the house of a sinner—a low-down tax collector!"

As Zacchaeus led Jesus to his house, he said, "Look, Master! Right here and now, I am giving half of everything I own to the poor! And if I have cheated anyone while collecting taxes from them, I will pay back four times what I stole."

> *I am drawn to Jesus, irresistibly, because he positioned himself as the dividing point of life—my life. . . . According to Jesus, what I think about him and how I respond will determine my destiny for all eternity.*
>
> Philip Yancey
> AUTHOR AND JOURNALIST

Jesus smiled. "You are a true son of Abraham. The Son of Man has come to seek and to save the lost—and today, salvation has come to this house." Then Jesus entered the house of Zacchaeus, and he ate with him and spent the night as his guest.

Triumph in the Shadow of Tragedy

From Jericho, Jesus and the disciples continued on to the town of Bethany, located at the southeastern foot of the Mount of Olives, about two miles east of Jerusalem. Three of Jesus' closest friends—Mary, Martha and Lazarus—lived in Bethany. It was there, in Bethany, that Jesus had raised Lazarus from the dead.

Mary and Martha fixed a sumptuous dinner in honor of Jesus. As Jesus and the disciples sat at the table with Lazarus, Mary knelt before Jesus and lavished a large amount of rare perfumed oil on the feet of Jesus. As she dried his feet with her hair, the rich fragrance of the perfume filled the house.

The disciples watched Mary's act of devotion with astonishment, and one of the Twelve, Judas Iscariot, was indignant. "That perfume could have been sold for a full day's wages!" he said. Then, perhaps as an afterthought, he added, "The money could have been given to the poor!"

Mary heard what Judas said. Her eyes filled with hurt.

"Leave her alone," Jesus said. "She has kept that perfume in a safe place so that she could use it in preparation for my burial. There are always poor people around you. If you sincerely want to help the poor, you can do so at any time. But you will not always have me with you."

As this was taking place inside the house, a large crowd gathered outside. Some had come because they believed in Jesus and were eager to see him. Others had come from Jerusalem as agents of the religious rulers. The rulers wanted to kill Jesus—and they wanted to kill Lazarus, too. After Jesus had called Lazarus from the tomb, hundreds of people began believing in Jesus. The rulers were determined to stamp out faith in Jesus, no matter whom they had to kill.

The next day, Jesus and his disciples set off for Jerusalem. On the road, as they approached the little village of Bethphage, Jesus took two of his disciples aside and told them, "Go into Bethphage. As you enter the village, you will see a donkey's colt tied to a post—a colt that has never been ridden before. Untie it and bring it to me. If anyone asks why you are untying the colt, just say, 'The Master has need of it.'"

So the two disciples did as Jesus told them. A short time later, they returned with the donkey colt. The disciples threw some cloaks over its back. A huge crowd gathered as Jesus climbed onto the donkey. One of the disciples tugged on the rope of the donkey's halter, and the animal started forward.

The people who stood watching knew what this moment meant. For centuries, the Jewish people had been waiting for the arrival of the Messiah. The prophet Zechariah had promised that he would come in a very specific way:

> Be glad, daughter of Zion! Shout for joy, daughter of Jerusalem! Look! Your king comes to you. He is righteous and victorious, yet gentle and humble. See! He comes riding on a donkey—on a colt, the foal of a donkey. And God will remove the battle chariot from Ephraim, and the warhorse from Jerusalem. The bow of war shall be broken. Your king shall speak the word, and the nations shall be at peace. His kingdom shall stretch from the Mediterranean Sea to every other sea, and from the River Euphrates to the ends of the Earth!

So when the people saw Jesus riding on a young donkey, they believed they were witnessing the arrival of the

Messiah. They were overjoyed, because they just knew that Jesus had come to overthrow the Romans, to remove the enemy battle chariots from their land and to drive the enemy warhorses out of the holy city of Jerusalem. The Messiah had come! Peace was at hand! Liberation was just around the corner!

The people cheered and ran ahead of Jesus. Some spread their garments on the road for the donkey to walk upon. Others cut palm fronds from the trees and spread them across the path. Jesus rode the donkey from Bethany, along the road that wound around the foot of the Mount of Olives and down the gentle slope toward the city of Jerusalem.

As Jesus rode that two-mile stretch of road, hundreds of people jammed the wayside. They shouted and cheered and praised God for the miracles that Jesus had done and for the political miracle they thought he was about to do. All along the road, people shouted, "Blessed is the king who comes in the name of the Lord! Peace in heaven and glorious splendor in the highest!"

But there were some along that road who did not share the enthusiasm of the crowd. "Teacher!" the Pharisees shouted to Jesus as he rode by. "Tell your followers to stop this noise and nonsense!"

"If the people kept silent," Jesus replied, "the stones themselves would shout aloud!"

Soon, the donkey brought Jesus within sight of the walls of the holy city, and he wept out loud. "Jerusalem!" he cried out as tears rolled down his face. "If only you had known on this day what would bring you peace—but now it is hidden from your eyes!"

The cheering died on both sides of the road as the people realized that their Messiah was weeping and shouting in apparent grief. What was he upset about? Everyone around him was celebrating, yet Jesus himself seemed to be in mourning!

"A time is coming," Jesus continued, "when your enemies will surround you and storm you from all sides! They will dash you against the ground within your walls, both you and your children! They will not leave one stone upon another, because you did not recognize the time of God's visitation among you!"

A stunned silence hung over the crowd.

Jesus nodded to the disciple who led the animal, and the disciple urged the donkey forward. They continued plodding down the road toward the city. As they approached the city gate, crowds came out, cheering and shouting. Jesus rode the donkey through the city gate and into the narrow streets. On every side, people appeared in doorways and windows, wondering what the commotion was about.

"What's happening?" the people shouted. "Who is that?"

> *This idea of dying to self and "taking up your cross" is one of the hardest concepts in the Christian faith to understand. But it is hard not because it is complicated. It is hard because it is so difficult to accept. We try to complicate it precisely because we know intuitively what it means, and we do not like the idea. No one likes to die.*
>
> John Fischer
> SINGER-SONGWRITER AND AUTHOR

From the crowd in the streets came answering shouts. "It's Jesus, the Prophet from Nazareth, in Galilee!"

The religious rulers, seeing how the crowds cheered for Jesus, grumbled and complained to each other. "What can we do about this man? Every scheme we try only makes him more popular! Look! The whole world is following after him!"

This happened on Sunday, the first day of the final week of the life of Jesus. It was a day of triumph, but tragedy was close at hand.

The Time Has Come

Throughout the story of Jesus, we have heard him talk about his life as if it were on a timetable. When his mother, Mary, coaxed him into changing water into wine at the wedding at Cana, he answered her, "Dear woman, why are you telling me about this problem? *My time has not yet come.*"

When he commanded demons out of people, and they shouted, "You are the Son of God!" Jesus told them to be silent—*because his time had not yet come.* When Jesus raised the twelve-year-old daughter of Jairus from death to life, he told the girl's parents, "See that you tell no one about this." Why? *Because his time had not yet come.*

When family members sarcastically urged him to go to Jerusalem and perform miracles where the whole world could see, Jesus replied, "Any time is suitable for you, but my life is on a timetable—*and my time has not yet come.*" After the feeding of the five thousand, when the people wanted to make Jesus their king, he slipped away and escaped to the mountains—*because his time had not yet come.*

When Peter, speaking for all the disciples, told Jesus, "You are the Messiah, the Son of the living God," Jesus told the disciples to tell no one about this—*because his time had not yet come.* As Peter, James and John walked back down from the mountain after seeing Jesus shining with glory and standing with Moses and Elijah, Jesus again told them to tell no one—*because his time had not yet come.*

Now, just days before the Crucifixion, we see Jesus riding into Jerusalem, receiving the shouts, cheers and songs of the people. When the Pharisees tell him to silence his disciples, Jesus refuses to do so. No longer does he say, "Tell no one." No longer does he avoid the limelight. No longer does he slip away from the crowds. Now he openly receives the praise of the people.

Why? *Because his time has finally come!*

How did Jesus know when his time had come? Where did he get this fine-tuned sense of his own destiny? The answer to this question is nothing less than astounding.

On one occasion, when Jesus was debating with the scribes and Pharisees, he told them, "You carefully study the Scriptures because you think you will find the secret of eternal life there. Yet you fail to understand: *These Scriptures are prophecies about me!* So you refuse to come to me to receive eternal life."

This is a bold and shocking statement. Jesus was telling the religious rulers that the Old Testament was a vast, detailed prophecy concerning his own appearance on the stage of history. As you read these words, you may accept the claim Jesus makes, or you may be skeptical. Whether you believe

> *God gave the prophecies, not to gratify men's curiosity by enabling them to foreknow things, but so that after they were fulfilled, they might be interpreted by the event, and God's own providence, not the interpreter's, be thereby manifested to the world.*
> Sir Isaac Newton
> SCIENTIST AND MATHEMATICIAN

Jesus or not, this is the claim he made for himself: The Old Testament Scriptures are all about Jesus of Nazareth.

The most shocking aspect of the claim Jesus makes, though, is the eerily precise way the Old Testament prophecies actually do appear to be fulfilled by Jesus.

An Ancient Calculation

We saw how the triumphant entry of Jesus into Jerusalem was connected to a passage from the Old Testament's Book of Zechariah. But the entry was hardly remarkable. Jesus could have easily arranged with a friend in Bethphage, the owner of the young donkey, to have the animal ready for his arrival. In this way, Jesus could have easily made it *appear* that he was coming in fulfillment of the prophecy. The crowds were already worked up about Jesus being the promised Messiah. Seeing him ride the donkey into Jerusalem would only confirm what the people wanted to believe. There is not necessarily anything miraculous in such a "fulfillment" of prophecy.

What few people realize, though, is that the triumphant entry of Jesus is also tied to *another* passage of Old Testament Scripture, and this connection is absolutely startling. That passage is found in the Book of Daniel, which was written centuries before Jesus was born. In this ancient book, the prophet Daniel was reading from another book of Hebrew Scripture, the Book of Jeremiah, and he began praying for his people, who were held captive in Babylon. As Daniel prayed, the angel Gabriel suddenly appeared and said, "Daniel, I have come at this time to give you wisdom and understanding. The moment you began to pray, an answer was given. I have come to tell you the answer because you are greatly loved by God. So consider this message and interpret the vision."

Gabriel proceeded to give Daniel a mathematically precise prophecy, saying, "Seventy sevens [of years, or 490 years] are established for your people and your holy city Jerusalem to bring an end to the violation of God's law, to put an end to evil, to purge away sinfulness, to bring about everlasting righteousness, to fulfill the vision and prophecy, and to anoint the most holy. Know, therefore, and understand that from the issuing of the decree to restore and rebuild Jerusalem until the Anointed One [the Messiah], the ruler, comes, there will be seven sevens [of years, or 49 years], and sixty-two sevens [of years, or 434 years]."

That may seem confusing at first glance, but the mathematically determined time frame that Gabriel gave Daniel was actually quite simple. The calendars of the ancient Jewish and Babylonian cultures used a 360-day year. Gabriel told Daniel that from the time the Medo-Persian king issued a decree to rebuild Jerusalem until the Messiah would appear would be a specific period of time, "seven sevens [of years, or 49 years], and sixty-two sevens [of years, or 434 years]." Add 434 and 49, and you get 483 years. Multiply 483 years by 360 days in the ancient calendar, and you get a total of 173,880 days.

Now, here's where it gets very interesting. Historians have determined the exact date when the Medo-Persian king, Artaxerxes Longimanus, issued the decree to rebuild Jerusalem: March 14, 445 B.C. If you count 173,880 days past that date, you arrive at Sunday, April 6, A.D. 32. We know that Jesus entered Jerusalem as king on the Sunday prior to the fourth Passover following the fifteenth year of the reign of Tiberius Caesar (this can be reliably determined by comparing secular historical sources with the date given in Luke 3:1). We also know that the date of that particular Sunday was April 6, A.D. 32.

So there can be no doubt: The Messiah's arrival as king was set to take place at a particular moment in time—*right to the very day.* When that moment came, Jesus was riding a donkey's colt into Jerusalem. He was there in that place, on that day, *because his time had finally come.*

You'll recall that, as we saw in chapter 1, when Jesus was only twelve years old, he was missing for three days until his mother Mary found him in the courts of the Temple at Jerusalem. The boy Jesus talked to the priests and scribes, asked them questions and discussed the Jewish Scriptures. The priests and scribes were astonished at the depth of his understanding. What passages of Scripture were they discussing?

We can't know for sure, of course, but I strongly suspect that the young Jesus was talking to the priests and scribes about the mathematically precise prophecy of the Messiah in Daniel 9, as well as other Old Testament prophecies of the Messiah. For example, they may have also discussed Psalm 22, which contains an eerily precise description of Roman crucifixion—even though it was written centuries before that fiendish torture device was even invented. Psalm 22:19 is astonishingly specific: "They pierced my hands and my feet." They may have also discussed Isaiah 53. Though it was written about seven centuries before the birth of Jesus, it reads like a brief but exact synopsis of the life and death of Jesus.

In all, there are an estimated *three hundred* Old Testament prophecies relating to the coming of the Messiah, and they stretch from Genesis to Malachi, from the beginning to the end of the Old Testament. Jesus fulfilled them all with uncanny precision. These are the Scriptures that Jesus probably spent three whole days discussing with the learned men in the Temple.

It is important to note that the prophecy in Daniel 9 speaks of much more than the promise of a coming Messiah. It also speaks of a troubled and turbulent time that will come after the Messiah arrives in Jerusalem as king. The prophecy goes on to say that Jerusalem "will be rebuilt with streets and a trench during troubled times. After the sixty-two sevens, the Anointed One [Messiah] will be cut off [killed] and will have nothing."

This is an unmistakable reference to the Crucifixion.

The Daniel 9 prophecy goes on to say, "And the people of another ruler who is to come will destroy the city and the sanctuary. The end of the city shall come like a flood, and even to the end there shall be war."

Compare those words with the doom that Jesus himself pronounced upon Jerusalem as he approached the city. "A time is coming," he said, "when your enemies will surround you and storm you from all sides! They will dash you against the ground within your walls, both you and your children! They will not leave one stone upon another, because you did not recognize the time of God's visitation among you!"

As both Daniel and Jesus predicted, "the city and the sanctuary" were destroyed thirty-eight years after Jesus entered the city riding on the colt of a donkey. This happened when Roman legions under the command of Titus Vespasian laid siege to Jerusalem in A.D. 70. The Romans were "the people of another ruler" as the Daniel prophecy stated, and the enemies of the Jewish people, as Jesus stated.

You may recall from chapter 11 that when Jesus was preaching at the Temple during the Feast of Tabernacles, the scribes and Pharisees were astonished at the depth of his knowledge of the Hebrew Scriptures. "How can this man know so much about the Scriptures and theology when he has never studied?" they asked. Jesus truly did have an encyclopedic knowledge of the Scriptures, including all the prophecies of the Messiah. Drawing upon that knowledge, he was able to calculate exactly when the Messiah should come riding into Jerusalem on the back of a young donkey.

For three years, he carefully avoided the premature acclaim of the crowds and any attempts by the people to make him their king. Why? Because he had done the calculations, and he knew that his time had not yet come. Only on the one special day, precisely 173,880 days after a certain Gentile king issued a certain proclamation, could Jesus present himself as the rightful king and Messiah of Israel.

> *Jesus was able to strike a balance between showing compassion and staying focused on his mission.*
> Mary Maxwell
> MISSIONARY

The Focus of Jesus

Jesus was a man with an unerring sense of purpose and an intense focus on his mission in life. This sense of purpose was instilled in him from his earliest years by his mother, Mary. The Gospel of Luke tells us that before Jesus was born, she was visited by the angel Gabriel—the same angel who visited the Old Testament prophet Daniel and gave him the timetable of the appearance of the Messiah.

Gabriel told Mary, "You will become pregnant and you will give birth to a son. You shall call him Jesus. He will be great and will be called the Son of the Most High God. The Lord will give him the throne of his father David, and he will reign over the descendants of Jacob forever. His kingdom will go on forever, without end."

This was the vision Mary had for her son as he was growing up, and this was undoubtedly part of the reason that Jesus saw himself as a man on a mission from God. Throughout his life, he prepared himself for that mission and focused on that mission. He didn't let anything deter or deflect him from the work God had called him to do.

Now we begin to see why Jesus sometimes spent an entire night in prayer. He was committed to his purpose and focused on his mission. He was following a life plan that had been set down for him long before he was born. So he spent a great amount of time in communion with the One who had originated that plan and who had commissioned him for that purpose. He wanted to know God's strategy every step of the way. Jesus spent an enormous amount of time in prayer so that he could renew his inner focus.

The example of Jesus confronts us with a question: How much time do you and I spend in prayer? How much time do we spend getting to know God's strategy for our lives so that we can renew our focus on our life's mission?

Jesus knew that his life was on a timetable. Throughout his life, he knew that he had an appointment with destiny.

He knew he had to arrive in Jerusalem at a specific moment in human history, and he didn't let anything deflect him from that appointment.

At the same time, he knew that part of his mission (as he told Zacchaeus in Jericho) was "to seek and to save the lost." Though he was focused on his destiny, he was not a slave to the clock or to the calendar. He was never so focused on his timetable that he lost sight of his real purpose: to seek, to save, to preach and teach, to heal and rescue, to serve, to mentor and make disciples, to show God's love and compassion, to draw people to himself and point the way to the kingdom of heaven.

So even as he was on the road from Galilee to Jerusalem, knowing that he was going there to die at an appointed time, he was focused not on himself or his schedule. He took time to hold children in his arms and bless them. He took time to call a wealthy young man to himself, and he grieved when the young man was unable to let go of his earthly riches. He took time to talk to his disciples and prepare them for the horrors that lay ahead—the arrest, trial, torture and execution of their Master. He paused in Jericho to heal blind Bartimaeus and dine with the tax collector, Zacchaeus. Wherever he went, he remained focused on the needs of the people he met along the way.

Because Jesus had an intense focus on his mission in life, he possessed a serene confidence in his own identity. He was totally comfortable in his own skin. People could attack him, slander him, oppose him, threaten him, scheme against him and try to move him off his course, but his confidence was never shaken and his identity was never in doubt. As he once told a group of Pharisees who tried to entrap him, "I know where I came from and I know where I am going." He had come from God the Father, and he was returning to God the Father. In between, he had a mission to carry out, and nothing could keep him from it.

When Jesus told his disciples about his impending death, his close friend, Peter, took him aside and said, "No, the Messiah cannot die!" Jesus responded with harsh words. "Get behind me, Satan!" Jesus knew his mission. If he wasn't going to let his *enemies* stop him, he certainly wasn't going to let his *friends* keep him from his mission.

What is the mission God has given you to do? Your mission in life is not just your job (though it may involve your career). It is not just your volunteer work (though it may involve that, too). Your mission in life is nothing less than your reason for existing, the reason God made you, the unique purpose he called you to fulfill.

You are irreplaceable to God. There is no other person in the world who can fulfill your purpose but you. God placed you here so that you can know him and have a relationship with him. He also placed you here with a mission to love and serve the people around you. Your mission in life—your unique calling from God—involves the way you live out your love for God and your love for other people. As someone once put it, your mission in life is the place where your deep gladness in God meets the deep hunger and need of the world. Your purpose in life is to glorify

God by obeying his calling and his will for your life.

Do you have the same intense focus on your calling, on God's plan for your life, that Jesus had? Are you pursuing God's strategy for your life with laserlike focus and intensity? Has God called you to teach needy children in the inner city? Then focus on God's plan for your life. Has God given you a unique message to speak to the world? Has he called you to write a book that will change thousands of lives? Then focus on that mission with an intensity worthy of Jesus himself. Are you a young person struggling to maintain your moral and sexual purity in a world that has lost its standards? Don't let anyone pull you from your focus—not your enemies, not your friends. Focus on God's plan for your life.

Jesus was able to focus with intensity because he knew the irreplaceable value of a single moment. He never "killed time," because he knew that time was precious. A single moment, once passed, would never come again. That's why, when his disciples urged him to stay out of Judea because of the danger there, Jesus replied, "Life is short, and I have a lot of work to do. I must work while it is still daylight."

> *The focus of Jesus' life was to stay perfectly attuned to his Father's voice. He was determined to live every moment in harmony with the Father's will.*
> Jennifer Kennedy Dean
> NONPROFIT ORGANIZATION
> EXECUTIVE

Jesus made the maximum use of the time God had given him. He was focused on effective time management. Because of his keen focus on working hard and working wisely, he was able to reach the end of his brief span of thirty-three years and say, "Mission accomplished." Just hours before the cross, Jesus prayed to the Father. "I have honored you on Earth by accomplishing the mission you gave me." When you and I reach the end of our lives, will we be able to face God and make the same statement?

Jesus the Marathon Runner

A marathon is a foot race of 26.2 miles. The first marathon I ever ran was the 1996 Disney Marathon, in Orlando, Florida. Since then, I have run twenty-six marathons, in such cities as Boston, Chicago, New York and Washington, D.C. I have found that the single most important ability needed to run a marathon is not strong legs or strong arches or powerful lungs. Those are important, certainly, but the single most important capacity for a marathon runner is found right between the ears: It's the ability to *focus*.

When the starter's pistol fires and you start the race, the finish line seems an eternity away. The first few miles are not too bad, but when your body starts to scream "Stop!" and your lungs begin to strain and you realize that you have only gone a quarter of the distance to the finish line, you have to reach down inside yourself and call upon depths of stamina and endurance, character and courage that you never imagined you had.

You reach the halfway mark and all you want to do is stop, rest and perhaps even die—anything to stop the pain and nightmarish suffering. At the same time, your intense focus is saying, "You haven't come this far for nothing. You're halfway there! Come on! Let's go!" You have to keep telling yourself, "Focus! Focus! The goal! The goal!" at every milestone, with every step, with every painful, ragged breath, because your heart, your lungs, your muscles, your feet, your spine are all screaming, "Stop!"

When you finally do reach the end of the race, though, you feel an overwhelming sense of euphoria. "Yes! I've accomplished my mission! I've finished my course! I've kept my focus all the way to the finish line!" It's a feeling you can't imagine until you have experienced it.

Jesus was a marathon runner in the race of life. From his earliest years, he maintained an intense focus throughout his life. As a twelve-year-old boy, he already had a deep, impressive mastery of theology and biblical prophecy, because he was focused on reading and studying the Scriptures. From the beginning of his three-year ministry, he was intent on the timetable that God had set for him and on the work he had to do. He pushed through pain, exhaustion, opposition, persecution and even the well-meaning distractions of his friends.

Jesus had a keen sense of the timetable of his life. He had an appointment to keep, and he made sure he did not arrive too early or too late. Again and again, he said, "My time has not come." But when the time finally *did* come, he was right where he was supposed to be and doing exactly what he was born to do.

Jesus maintained his focus, and he accomplished his mission.

If you want to be like Jesus, you must run the race as he did, focus as he did and always keep your eye and your mind on the finish line. Don't let anything distract you, discourage you, dissuade you or deflect you from your goal. If you maintain your focus in life, you'll find out how incredibly good it feels to reach the end of your race and say, just as Jesus said, "God, I have honored you on Earth by accomplishing the mission you gave me."

CHAPTER FIFTEEN

HOW TO BE COURAGEOUS LIKE JESUS

**A**fter his triumphant entry into Jerusalem, Jesus dismounted from the young donkey and walked through the city streets, accompanied by his disciples. As they went, the cheers of the crowd echoed in the canyons between the stone-walled buildings. Jesus did not wait to receive the acclamation of the crowds. He had a job to do. He had done it once before, at the beginning of his three-year ministry. Now, as the end approached, he would do it again.

Up ahead, towering over the city, was the massive structure of the Temple, the House of God. As the disciples hurried to keep up, Jesus climbed the steps of the Temple Mount. Entering the enclosure of the Temple, he looked around, eyes flashing. He had cleansed God's house once before, but Caiaphas, the corrupt high priest, had reopened the Temple for commercial exploitation. Again, the courtyard was lined with booths, tables, cages and pens. All around the courtyard, greedy men were hawking sacrificial animals. The Temple courts reeked of animal waste and rang with the clinking sound of coins changing hands.

Jesus stormed through the courtyard, overturning tables and benches, driving out the merchants and moneychangers. "It is written," he shouted, quoting the prophets Isaiah and Jeremiah, "'My house will be called a house of prayer,' but you have made it a 'den of thieves.'"

Jesus also did something that he had not done the first time he cleansed the Temple: He stopped the Temple priests from carrying utensils of worship through the courtyard. He not only halted the corrupt *financial* activity in the Temple, as he did at the first cleansing. This time he also interrupted the *religious* activity of the Temple. He brought the rituals and ceremonies of the Temple to a grinding halt.

What were those rituals and ceremonies? The priests and Levites would bind sacrificial animals on the altars, slit their throats and allow the blood to flow out. There, they sprinkled the blood on the altar of incense. The animal carcasses on the altars would be cut up, and certain parts would be ritually burned as sacrifices. The unburned parts were set aside as food for the priests and other Temple workers.

So, from sunrise to sunset, there was continuous traffic of priests carrying basins of blood and other ceremonial utensils back and forth across the Temple courtyard. Jesus halted all of that traffic and shut down the religious activity of the Temple.

After cleansing the Temple, Jesus sat down in one of the great column-lined porches and began to teach. Many of the common people who had come to worship sat at his feet and hung on his every word. At the edge of the crowd, the priests, scribes and other rulers of the people watched and grumbled among themselves, discussing how to get Jesus out of their way. They wanted to seize him on the spot, but the people were clearly on the side of Jesus. The rulers dared not move against him—not yet.

As word spread through the city, the blind and sick were brought to Jesus at the Temple, and he healed them. As all of this was going on, there were children chanting in the Temple courts, "We praise you! Save us, blessed Son of David!"

The religious rulers heard this and were beside themselves with rage. They went to Jesus and said, "Do you hear what the children are chanting about you? Why do you let this go on?"

> *Jesus has many lovers of his heavenly kingdom, but few bearers of his cross.*
> Thomas à Kempis
> GERMAN MONK

"Have you not read in the Psalms," Jesus said, "'From the lips of children and infants God has ordained praise'?"

The rulers turned and left in a huff.

Jesus continued teaching and healing until evening, then he and his disciples left the city of Jerusalem and returned to Bethany, where he spent the night.

Jesus Defies His Persecutors

During the week that followed Jesus' entry into the city, he went to Jerusalem daily, where he taught the people in the Temple courtyard. Then, every evening, he would return to Bethany, where he spent the night.

One day while he was teaching, the Temple priests interrupted him. "What right do you have to do the things you've been doing?" they asked. "Who gave you the authority to clear the merchants from the Temple? Who gave you the authority to teach and heal in the holy place?"

"I have a question for you," Jesus said. "If you answer my question, then I will be glad to answer yours and tell you by what authority I do these things."

The priests eyed Jesus warily. "What is your question?"

"My question is about the baptism of John the Baptist," Jesus said. "Tell me—where did it come from? Was his baptism of God? Or was it merely a man-made ritual without any meaning?"

The priests huddled together and discussed the question among themselves. "If we say John's baptism was of God, then he will ask, 'Then why didn't you believe him?' But if we say that John's baptism was nothing but a man-made ritual, we will anger the crowd, for they all believe John was a prophet sent from God."

Finally, the priests turned to Jesus and said, "We don't know."

"In that case," Jesus said, "I won't tell you by what authority I do these things."

The priests glared at him but could not argue with his answer. Jesus had eluded their trap, just as he had done so many times before.

Jesus told them a story to make a point. "There was a

man who had two sons. He told the first son, 'Go work in the vineyard today.' The first son said, 'No, I won't,' but he later changed his mind and did as his father told him to do. The father then told his second son the same thing. The second son said, 'Yes, sir, I'll do as you say,' but he later changed his mind and didn't go. Which of the two sons did what pleased the father?"

"The first son," answered the priests.

"Exactly," Jesus said. "You say 'yes' to God with your words, but your actions say 'no.' I tell you the truth, the tax collectors and prostitutes are entering God's kingdom ahead of you. John the Baptist came to show you the way of righteousness. He called you to repent, but you did not believe him. The tax collectors and prostitutes believed him, and that is why they repented and are being saved. But even after you saw sinners turn their lives around, you did not repent and believe him."

The priests were outraged by the tough, confrontational words of Jesus, but before they could think of an answer, Jesus turned to the people around him and began telling another story. "A landowner planted a vineyard," he said, "and he rented it to some tenants. The tenants promised to take care of the vineyard while the landowner went to another country for a long time. When the harvest season came, the landowner sent one of his servants to the tenants to collect a portion of the grapes from the vineyard, which was the agreed-upon rent payment. But the tenants beat the servant and kicked him off the property, sending him away empty-handed.

"The landowner sent another servant to collect the rent, but the tenants beat him as well, then insulted him and sent him away empty-handed. The landowner sent a third servant, and the tenants treated him even worse, wounding him and tossing him bodily from the vineyard. Finally, the landowner said, 'What shall I do? I know! I will send my own son, whom I dearly love. They mistreated the servants, but they will certainly respect my son.'

"But when the tenants saw the landowner's son, they discussed among themselves what they should do. 'This is the heir of the landowner!' they said. 'Let's kill him, and his inheritance will be ours!' So they drove the landowner's son out of the vineyard, and they murdered him. What will the owner of the vineyard do to the wicked tenants? He will come and destroy those tenants and give the vineyard to others."

The priests and scribes who heard the story knew exactly who the "tenants" in that story symbolized. Jesus was talking about *them!* The servants in the story were the Old Testament prophets who had been persecuted in times past for speaking the truth. And the landowner's son? Clearly, Jesus spoke of himself.

So the priests and scribes discussed the matter among themselves. They searched for some pretext on which to arrest Jesus, because he had told this story against them. However, they could find no way of getting to Jesus as long as he was surrounded by a crowd of followers.

Then the religious rulers seized upon the idea of sending spies who could pretend to be sincere seekers of the truth. The spies would question Jesus in an attempt to trap him in his own words.

"Teacher," the spies said, making a show of great respect, "we know that you are a man of complete integrity. We have seen that you teach God's ways according to what is true, and that you never show favoritism to people because of their position. So please tell us your opinion on a very important question: Is it morally right to pay taxes to Caesar or not?"

Jesus, however, wasn't taken in by the smooth talk and flattery. "You hypocrites!" he said sharply. "Why are you trying to trap me?"

The spies blinked in surprise. How did he know their secret intentions?

"Bring me a coin that is used for paying the tax to Caesar," Jesus said. One of the spies reached into his money bag and pulled out a Roman coin, a denarius, and handed it to Jesus.

Jesus held up the coin for all to see. "Whose portrait do you see on the coin? And whose inscription is stamped on it?"

"Caesar's," the spies replied.

"Then pay to Caesar what belongs to Caesar," Jesus said, "and give to God what belongs to God."

The spies were astonished at the brilliance of Jesus' answer. Unable to trap him in his own words, his enemies were silenced.

Just then, a man spoke up from the edge of the crowd. He was an old scribe, a learned teacher of the Law of Moses, and he had heard the entire exchange between

Jesus and the spies. He stepped forward to ask a question of his own. "Teacher," the old man said, "of all the commandments in the Law, which is the most important?"

Jesus said, "The most important commandment is this: 'Hear, O Israel, the Lord our God, the Lord is one. You shall love the Lord your God with all your heart, and with all your soul, and with all your mind, and with all your strength.' The second most important commandment is this: 'Love your neighbor as you love yourself.' Everything the Scriptures say about how to please God is based on these two commandments."

"You have answered well, teacher," the old scribe replied. "You are correct in saying that God is one and that there is no other but him. To love God with all your heart, with all your understanding and with all your strength, and to love your neighbor as yourself, is more important to God than making many burnt offerings and sacrifices."

> *Am I not in command of your circumstances? Be strong and courageous. Do not be frightened and do not be discouraged.*
> Joshua 1:9

Jesus smiled. "You," he said, "are not far from the kingdom of God."

From then on, the enemies of Jesus didn't dare to ask him any more questions.

Speaking Truth to Power

Elie Wiesel was born in 1928 in Romania. He grew up in a warm and nurturing world of family, community and the Jewish religion. His world was abruptly destroyed during World War II when the Nazis deported his entire village to the prison camps. Though Wiesel survived the horrors of Auschwitz, Buna, Buchenwald and Gleiwitz, the concentration camps burned his youthful faith in God to ashes. In his first book, *Night,* Wiesel recorded this reflection on what the Holocaust did to his soul:

> Never shall I forget that night, the first night in camp, which has turned my life into one long night, seven times cursed and seven times sealed. Never shall I forget that smoke. Never shall I forget the little faces of the children, whose bodies I saw turned into wreaths of smoke beneath a silent blue sky.
> Never shall I forget those flames which consumed my faith forever.
> Never shall I forget that nocturnal silence which deprived me, for all eternity, of the desire to live. Never shall I forget those moments which murdered my God and my soul and turned my dreams to dust. Never shall I forget these things, even if I am condemned to live as long as God Himself. Never.[1]

Wiesel devoted the rest of his life to making sure that the world would never forget—and never repeat—the unspeakable crimes of the Holocaust. He once defined his mission in life as "to bear witness and speak truth to power."

[1] Elie Wiesel, *Night* (New York: Avon Books, 1958), 44.

That, in fact, was the life mission of Jesus. He bore witness to the truth, and he spoke truth to power. He afflicted power. He irritated power. He exposed the corruption of powerful men. He dared to speak the truth, even though he knew that speaking truth to power would win him no awards, no acclaim, no prizes. In fact, it would only bring him the agonies of the cross.

Where does that kind of courage come from? More to the point, what is courage?

I believe *courage* is made up of two ingredients: *fear* and *faith.* Someone once defined courage as "fear that has said its prayers." Courage is not the absence of fear. Courage is the faith to act in spite of your fears. Courage cannot exist without fear. You cannot be courageous until you are first afraid.

If you think Jesus had no fear as he faced opposition, persecution and crucifixion, then you do not know Jesus. The same Jesus who dared to speak truth to power in the Temple courtyard also sweat blood as he prayed to his Father just hours before the cross, "My Father, if there is any way possible, please let this cup be taken from me."

Jesus faced his fears and overcame them in exactly the same way that you and I must overcome our fears: through *faith* in God. Jesus was no more eager to go through torture and death than you or I would be. He recoiled in horror at the prospect of being separated from his heavenly Father during those three fateful hours when he cried out, "My God, my God, why have you forsaken me?"

Yet, he knew what he had to do in order to accomplish

his mission in life. Once, when he was trying to prepare his disciples for his approaching death, he explained to them the kind of death he was going to die. "When I am lifted up from the Earth," he said, referring to the cross, "I will draw all people to myself." That was his purpose in coming to Earth, and he had *faith*—absolute trust and confidence—that God the Father would carry him through even that dark abyss of torture, death and separation.

If you want to be like Jesus, you must learn to have courage like Jesus. You must learn to let your faith master your fears so that you can accomplish the plan that God has for your life.

Dietrich Bonhoeffer was a German theologian in Berlin in the 1930s. He was appalled by Adolf Hitler and the Nazi message of anti-Jewish hate. He was even more appalled to see anti-Semitism infect his own church, as Christians of Jewish descent were barred from holding high church office.

In 1934, Bonhoeffer and other courageous Christian leaders founded the "Confessing Church" to oppose anti-Semitism and Nazism in Germany. Three years later, the Gestapo (the Nazi Secret State Police) closed the seminary where Bonhoeffer taught. Many of Bonhoeffer's students were arrested and sent to prison. Bonhoeffer continued to teach and preach, traveling secretly from town to town, speaking out against Nazism and hate.

In 1939, Bonhoeffer left Germany to teach at Union Theological Seminary in the United States, but within days, he had a change of heart. He wrote his friend

Reinhold Niebuhr and confessed, "I made a mistake in coming to America. . . . I shall have no right to take part in the restoration of Christian life in Germany after the war unless I share the trials of this time with my people." He resigned his teaching post, returned to Germany and became actively involved in the German resistance.

Later that same year, Germany invaded Poland. As Hitler's war machine rumbled through Europe, Bonhoeffer devoted himself to Operation Seven, a secret group that helped German Jews escape to Switzerland. At the same time, he joined a plot to assassinate Adolf Hitler. This was a difficult decision for Bonhoeffer, because he had been a devout pacifist all his life. Yet, he couldn't escape the conclusion that the death of Hitler would save the lives of millions of people.

His involvement with Operation Seven was discovered by the Gestapo, and Bonhoeffer was arrested in April 1943. On July 20, 1944, while he was in prison, Colonel Claus von Stauffenberg, a secret member of the resistance, left a suitcase bomb in Hitler's offices at Wolf's Lair fortress in East Prussia. The bomb exploded, but Hitler escaped, shaken but unharmed. Von Stauffenberg was executed, and Bonhoeffer's role in the plot was discovered.

The Gestapo transferred Bonhoeffer to Buchenwald and later to the concentration camp at Flossenburg. He was hanged on April 9, 1945—just three weeks before the end of the war—at the age of thirty-nine. A German doctor who watched Bonhoeffer die said that he went to the gallows "brave and composed. . . . I have hardly ever seen a man die so entirely submissive to the will of God."

Dietrich Bonhoeffer dared like Jesus and he died like Jesus. He spoke truth to power. His faith conquered his fear of death, and he paid the ultimate price of sacrificing his life for others. That is a fine and fitting epitaph for anyone.

If you want to live a life of meaning, if you want to die a meaningful death, then you must dare to be like Jesus. Don't avoid danger and fear—live bravely, live boldly!

You and I have the same source of courage available to us that Jesus drew upon—complete trust and confidence in the sovereign power of God. As the Psalmist wrote centuries before Jesus was born, "Even though I walk through the valley of the shadow of death, I will not fear what evil may do to me, because you, God, are right beside me."

Jesus walked through the valley of the shadow of death. He spoke truth to power. He set his feet on the road to the cross and he refused to let anyone or anything keep him from his destiny: "When I am lifted up from the Earth, I will draw all people to myself."

If you want to be like Jesus, then you must be courageous like Jesus. You must master your fear with *faith*.

CHAPTER SIXTEEN

HOW TO SERVE LIKE JESUS

When Jesus wasn't teaching and healing in the Temple courtyards, he spent time with the Twelve trying to prepare them for what was about to happen. "The Passover is coming soon," he told them. "That's when the Son of Man will be handed over to be crucified."

Eleven of the disciples were apparently in denial and refused to grasp what Jesus was telling them, but one of the Twelve understood clearly what Jesus was saying. His name was Judas Iscariot. He had followed Jesus for three years and was a trusted member of the inner circle. He was the treasurer of the group, the keeper of the money bag. He was well-liked by the other disciples.

Judas, though, was not what he seemed to be. He had his own reasons for following Jesus. He was a man of intense ambition. He expected to gain prominence, wealth and prestige as one of the right-hand men of King Jesus when the Romans were overthrown and the "kingdom of heaven" came into power.

Judas had watched in excitement as Jesus entered Jerusalem to the cheers of thousands. Then Judas had listened in growing disappointment and frustration as Jesus talked about his approaching trial and execution. What kind of talk was that? What kind of leader was Jesus? Did the man have a death wish?

Finally, Judas could take no more of such talk from Jesus. The "kingdom" Jesus talked about was a mirage. Judas saw that there was not going to be a revolt against the Romans, there was not going to be a new kingdom and he was not going to have a high position in the Messiah's new government. Jesus, it seemed, was nothing but an impractical dreamer, and Judas decided he'd had enough of impractical dreams. These were hard times, and a man had to look out for Number One. It was time for Judas to cash in his chips and get out of the game.

So Judas began to make his plans.

At that same time, the chief priests and the elders of the people were gathered together in the lavish palace of Caiaphas, the high priest of the Temple. There was only one item on their agenda: how to arrest and destroy Jesus.

The trial and execution of Jesus of Nazareth had to be handled with extreme care. The Galilean had to be taken at a time and place where there were no crowds, or there would be a riot among the people. A riot would bring the Roman armies down upon them, and the religious rulers couldn't afford that. They only held power as long as the Romans permitted it. This Galilean had to be eliminated before the Romans cracked down.

As the religious rulers debated, a servant brought a man into the meeting hall of the palace of Caiaphas. Many who were gathered there recognized the man, for they had seen him in the company of Jesus. He was one of the Twelve who followed the Galilean everywhere.

The man's name was Judas Iscariot.

"What are you willing to pay me," the false disciple asked, "if I were to hand Jesus over to you?"

One of the priests counted out thirty silver coins—the price of betrayal—and placed them in front of Judas.

"We can't arrest him in the streets or at the Temple," said one of the religious rulers. "We can't arrest him anyplace where there are crowds."

> *He came for the sick and not the well, for the unrighteous and not the righteous. And to those who betrayed him—especially the disciples, who forsook him at his time of greatest need—he responded like a lovesick father.*
>
> Philip Yancey
> AUTHOR AND JOURNALIST

"I know where he goes to be alone," Judas said. "You can arrest him there. It will be dark and quiet—no crowds. You can take him and do whatever you want with him."

So Judas concluded his business, then he left the palace and rejoined the disciples in Bethany. Soon, very soon, an opportunity would come for him to earn his blood money.

The Last Seder

On the first day of the Passover feast, the disciples asked Jesus where they should make preparations to celebrate the Passover. Jesus gave them the name of a man in

Jerusalem. "Go to the man," he said, "and tell him, 'The Teacher says that his appointed time is near, and he wishes to celebrate the Passover with his disciples at your house.'"

So the disciples did as Jesus told them. They found the man Jesus told them about, and he showed the disciples to a large upstairs room in his house. There, the disciples made preparations for the *seder,* the Passover meal.

That evening, Jesus and the Twelve gathered together in the upper room. An unblemished lamb was slaughtered, and the carcass was roasted. One of the disciples read the Haggadah, the story of the Jewish Exodus from slavery in Egypt. The candles were lit. The wine was blessed.

Next was the ritual washing of hands, commemorating the words of the Psalmist: "Who may stand in the holy place of God? He who has clean hands and a pure heart." Of all the men who were gathered there, only Jesus noticed the flicker of emotion in the eyes of Judas as he took part in this ritual.

In the Middle Eastern manner, Jesus and the disciples reclined at a low table. Each man took a sprig of parsley, a bitter herb, and dipped it in a bowl of salt water. The herb served as a reminder of the bitterness the Israelites experienced as slaves in Egypt. The salt water symbolized the tears of their suffering. They ate unleavened bread, which symbolized the fact that the Israelites left Egypt in such haste that there was no time for leavened bread, which takes time to rise.

Next, the roast lamb was served. The lamb symbolized (as John the Baptist had called Jesus), "the lamb of God, who takes away the sin of the world." As they ate, Jesus said to them, "My friends, I have been looking forward to eating this Passover meal with you before I go through my final suffering. I will not eat the Passover meal again until everything it symbolizes is fulfilled in my Father's kingdom."

It should have been a festive and joyous *seder,* but this Passover lamb was eaten solemnly and quietly. After the lamb, Jesus raised the unleavened bread and gave thanks to the Father. Then, looking into the eyes of his friends—and his betrayer—Jesus broke the bread and passed it to his disciples. "Take this bread and eat," he told them. "It represents my body, which is broken for you. Do this in remembrance of me."

Then Jesus lifted a cup of wine, the Cup of Redemption, and he gave thanks and offered it to his disciples. As they passed the cup from man to man, Jesus said, "This cup represents my blood—the blood of God's new promise, my own lifeblood poured out to redeem many people. I tell you the truth, I will not drink again of the fruit of the vine until the day when I drink the new and superior wine of my Father's eternal kingdom."

> *Jesus kneels down and gazes upon the darkest acts of our lives. But rather than recoil in horror, he reaches out in kindness and says, "I can clean that if you want." And from the basin of his grace, he scoops a palm full of mercy and washes our sin.*
>
> Max Lucado
> PASTOR AND AUTHOR

The Fellowship of
the Basin and Towel

Jesus' mention of the kingdom stirred up an old dispute among the disciples: Who among them would be the greatest and most powerful leader (next to Jesus) in the coming political kingdom? It was less than a week after Jesus' triumphant entry into Jerusalem, and the cheering of the crowds was still fresh in their ears. They didn't understand why Jesus kept talking about his approaching suffering and death, but obviously, it couldn't mean very much, since he was still planning to reign over the coming "kingdom of heaven."

Only one of the Twelve really heard, understood and believed Jesus when he talked about his suffering and death, and that was Judas. The false disciple knew that it was true, because he himself was going to *make* it so. Judas had lost all faith in the "kingdom of heaven." Let those eleven fools believe! Let them brag about being the greatest in the coming kingdom! Judas knew there would be no kingdom. He was a practical man. He had already made his profit on the life of Jesus. It was a paltry thirty silver coins, but it was better than nothing.

As the eleven disciples bragged to each other about being the greatest in the coming kingdom, Jesus sat sadly and listened. He had spent three years pouring his life into these men, and still they understood so little. Yet he loved them. They were his friends. They were the ones he would leave behind to carry out this revolution of love he had come to set into motion upon the Earth. Soon, he would leave this world and go to the Father, but there was still one thing he could do for his friends, one last lesson he could teach them.

None of the boastful, contentious disciples noticed as Jesus quietly got up from the table. No one looked his way as he removed his outer robe, laid it aside and wrapped a towel around his waist. He poured water into a basin, then he took the basin and towel to the nearest of the Twelve. Without a word, using water from the basin, he washed that disciple's feet and dried them with the towel.

The arguing and boasting faded to a dead silence as the disciples saw what their Master was doing. Jesus went on to the next disciple in line and washed his feet; then the next; and the next.

He came at last to Simon Peter. The rugged fisherman's voice shook as he said, "Master, you aren't going to wash my feet, are you?"

"You don't understand what I'm doing," Jesus said, "but later you will understand."

"No!" Peter said. "You shall never wash my feet!"

"Unless I cleanse you," Jesus said, "you can have no part with me."

"Then, Master," Peter said, "don't just wash my feet, but my hands and head as well!"

Jesus smiled at his impetuous friend. "Someone who has already had a bath needs only to wash his feet to be completely clean," and Jesus washed and dried the feet of Peter.

"Now, you are clean," Jesus said, as he finished drying Peter's feet, "though not every one of you."

Judas avoided Jesus' eye.

Jesus set the basin and towel aside, then put his outer robe back on and returned to his place at the table. "Do you understand what I have just done for you?" he asked. "You call me 'Teacher' and 'Master,' and that is correct, for that is who I am. Now that I, your Master and Teacher, have washed your feet, you must follow my example and wash one another's feet. I have shown you this example so that you would be like me—a servant to others. I tell you the truth, no servant is greater than his master. If you would call me Master, then you must do as I have done."

The shamefaced men around the table nodded silently.

"You know how arrogant the kings of the Gentiles are," Jesus continued, evoking the mental image of the Caesars of Rome, the Pharaohs of Egypt and the ancient kings of Babylon and Assyria. "They love to shout orders and boss people around. They enjoy having people praise them and tell them how wonderful they are. Is that what you had in mind when you argued about your place in the kingdom? Is that how you want to treat people—as slaves and underlings? Is that how you want to be treated—as a conceited Gentile master?

"My friends, you are not to be like that. Instead, the greatest among you must become like the least. The one who rules must become like the one who serves. You call me Master and Teacher, yet I am among you as one who serves, as one who washes feet.

"You are the ones who have stood by me through all the opposition and persecution of these past three years. Now, I give you a kingdom, just as my Father has given me. It is not an earthly political kingdom. It is something more grand and

> *Jesus measured greatness in terms of service, not status.*
> Rick Warren
> PASTOR AND AUTHOR

lofty than you can imagine. In that kingdom, you will eat and drink at my table, and you will sit on thrones, judging the twelve tribes of Israel."

Desertion, Denial, Betrayal

Then Jesus turned to Peter. "Simon, Simon," he said with a deep note of sadness in his voice, "Satan has demanded permission that all twelve of you be given over to him so that he might sift you like so much grain. This very night, you will all desert me. You will be afraid to be caught anywhere near me."

"Master, no," the disciples said. "We will never desert you!"

"You will," Jesus said. "Every one of you. As it is written by the prophet Zechariah, 'Strike the shepherd and the sheep will scatter.' But after I have risen, I will go to Galilee and meet you there."

"Even if all the rest desert you," Peter said fiercely, "I never will."

"Oh, Peter," Jesus said sadly. "I have prayed especially for you, that your own faith may not fail during this time of testing. You *will* desert me, just like the rest. But when you have returned and regained your faith, I want you to strengthen and establish your brothers."

"Master," Peter answered boldly, "I'm ready to follow you anywhere—to prison, even to death!"

Jesus' voice choked with emotion. "Peter," he said, "before the rooster crows at dawn, you will deny even knowing me."

"Master, no!" Peter protested in shock. "It will never be so!"

"Yes, Peter, it will happen just as I have told you," Jesus said. "You will deny me—three times."

Peter could not believe what Jesus was telling him. *Me, deny the Master?* thought Peter. *Impossible!* All around him, the other disciples insisted that they would never desert Jesus, even if they had to die for him.

"I tell you the truth," Jesus continued, addressing all twelve men, "one of you will betray me—one who has shared this meal with me. It will take place just as the Scriptures foretold: 'Even my own trusted friend, who ate of my bread at my own table, has turned against me.'"

The disciples were shocked and saddened. One by one, they said, "You don't think I'm the one, do you?" and "Master, I would never betray you!" Even Judas claimed to be innocent.

"It is one of the Twelve," Jesus answered. "The Son of Man will be delivered, just as the Scriptures have said, but how tragic for the one who betrays the Son of Man! It would be better for that man had he not been born."

The two disciples who were placed on either side of

Jesus were John and Judas Iscariot. Simon Peter motioned to John, urging him to ask Jesus who the betrayer was. So John leaned close to Jesus and whispered, "Master, who is going to betray you?"

Jesus held a piece of unleavened bread in his hand. "It is the one," he said, "to whom I give this bread," and he passed the piece of bread to the man next to him. Judas, unaware of the conversation between John and Jesus, took the bread, and his eyes met those of the Master.

"What you intend to do," Jesus told him, "do quickly."

Shaken, Judas rose, hurriedly left the table and went out into the night. Because Judas was the treasurer for the group, everyone around the table assumed that Jesus had sent him on some errand. Of the disciples, only Peter and John knew the truth.

Sadness and depression hung over the room like a storm cloud. The disciples could not understand these two conflicting predictions Jesus had made so many times: He was going to suffer and die, and they were going to be with him in his kingdom. Those were mutually exclusive concepts, and the disciples could not see how both could be true. The only thing they could understand was that Jesus was telling them that something terrible was about to happen—desertion, denial, betrayal, and the suffering and death of the Master. It seemed like the end of everything.

Jesus could see what his disciples were thinking and feeling. "My friends," he said, "don't be depressed, don't lose hope. You trust in God, don't you? Trust also in me. In my Father's house are many rooms. I'm going there to prepare a place for you, and then I am coming back to take you with me, so we can always be together. You know the place I'm going, don't you?"

"Master, we don't know where you're going," said Thomas Didymus (Thomas the Twin), the fiercely loyal but ever-pessimistic disciple. "How can we know the way, so we can follow you there?"

"I am the way," Jesus said, "and the truth and the life. No one comes to the Father except through me. If you know me, you know the Father."

"Master," said Philip, "just show us the Father and we will be satisfied."

"Philip," Jesus said, "after all the time I have been with you, do you still not know me? I tell you the truth, if you have seen me, you have seen the Father. I am in the Father and the Father is in me. When I speak and act, it is the Father living in me, doing his work through me. And I tell you the truth, anyone who trusts in me will do the works I've been doing and even greater works, because I am going to the Father. After I have gone, all you have to do is pray in my name, and I will do it."

Then, after Jesus had encouraged and comforted his disciples, they stood together and sang the *Great Hallel*, a hymn from the Psalms:

> Oh, give thanks to the Lord, for he is good.
> For his love endures forever.
> Oh, give thanks to the God of gods.
> For his love endures forever.

Oh, give thanks to the Lord of lords:
For his love endures forever.

Once they had finished singing, they left the upper room and went out into the city streets. They walked out of Jerusalem by the Golden Gate at the eastern wall, and they descended into the Kidron Valley. Before them rose the gentle

> *Thousands of books have been written on leadership, but few on servanthood. Everyone wants to lead; no one wants to be a servant.*
> Rick Warren
> PASTOR AND AUTHOR

slope of the Mount of Olives. On that mountainside was the place where Jesus was taking them.

That place was called Gethsemane.

The Principle of the Second Mile

To most people, there is no role in life that is lower, more demeaned or more humiliating than the role of a servant. Many people aspire to be leaders, managers and bosses. Few aspire to be servants. By the standards of the world, bosses are the greatest, most honored, worthiest people in our society. By God's standards, the greatest of all are those who serve.

When Jesus laid aside his robe, took up the towel and basin and began washing feet, he did something that was as shocking in his day as it would be in ours. In the time of Jesus, washing other people's feet was not just the job of a servant, but of the *lowest order* of servant. The average peasant wouldn't stoop so low. Jesus, however, shed all pride and dignity to give his disciples a lesson in servanthood.

The moment Jesus set that basin in front of the first disciple and began washing the first pair of feet, every trace of celebration vanished from the Passover feast. Men who had been bragging about their own greatness were stunned into silence. Laughter died. Faces reddened with embarrassment. It was an electric moment that was charged with dramatic energy.

But Jesus didn't wash feet only to make an impression on twelve men some two thousand years ago. He was also setting an example for you and me and all who want to be like Jesus.

This is one of the most profound questions in this entire book: *Who* does Jesus want you to serve?

Are there people in your family whose feet you need to wash? Are there people at your place of worship? People in your office or your neighborhood? Are there children in your neighborhood, children with "dirty feet" who really need a servant who will love them, read to them, help them with their math, hug them and tell them someone cares? Are there people with "dirty feet" at the homeless shelter or on the street corner who need a servant like you? Are there people with "dirty feet" at a hospital or an old folks' home near you?

What are some of the *other ways* you can be a servant? Can you make coffee? Set up folding chairs? Clean bathrooms? Make sandwiches and ladle soup? Saw lumber and hammer nails?

Are you in a leadership position in your church, company or organization? Good. So am I. That means you and I have a lot of opportunities to be servants! You certainly wouldn't claim to be a greater leader than Jesus, would you? Neither do I. So if serving others and washing feet was good enough for Jesus, it's good enough for you and me.

> *I've learned from personal experience that what Jesus taught me was true: that the greatest sense of fulfillment we can find here on Earth comes not from fame or fortune but from serving and doing things for other people.*
>
> Deloris Jordan
> MOTHER OF MICHAEL JORDAN

Another principle Jesus taught us about servanthood is that his servants go above and beyond the call of duty. "Good enough" is never good enough. I call this the Principle of the Second Mile. It comes from the Sermon on the Mount, where Jesus said, "If someone forces you to walk one mile, be willing to go an extra mile with him."

This was a reference to a common practice of the Roman oppressors. Soldiers of Rome had a right called "impressment"—the power to force civilians in occupied lands to carry their military baggage for a maximum distance of one mile. A Jewish farmer could be minding his own business, planting his field, and a Roman soldier could come along, saddle him with a heavy pack and force him to carry it down the road. This was one of many reasons the Jewish people hated the Roman occupation.

Jesus was saying, "If that soldier orders you to go one mile with him, then you volunteer to go two. Show him your servant's heart. Don't do just enough, do twice as much, and do it without complaining!" Understand, too, that the Principle of the Second Mile doesn't just double a servant's commitment to servanthood. It quadruples it! If a farmer has to leave his field and walk two miles down the road instead of one, then he also has to walk two miles back before he can return to his own work—a four-mile round-trip.

> *In prayer we meet Christ, and in him all human suffering. In service we meet people, and in them the suffering Christ.*
> Henri J. M. Nouwen
> AUTHOR AND PRIEST

Imagine how we would change the world if we would do everything with an attitude of servanthood, going the extra mile, and doing everything with uncompromising excellence. Imagine the impact we would have on our bosses, our employees, our customers, our neighbors and our family members if we would practice the Principle of the Second Mile in everything we do!

Leading Through Serving

No leader in human history ever had more right to be called "great" than Jesus of Nazareth. Yet, no leader was ever more humble. He willingly laid aside his power, his authority and his rights along with his robe when he knelt down to wash the feet of his disciples. Jesus invented a form of leadership that the world had never known before. It's called *servant leadership.*

The humble servant leadership of Jesus rivets our attention and compels our admiration. We all know leaders who are nothing but bosses. Arrogant and self-important, they dominate people and think that the world revolves around them. But, as John Stott, the great Anglican author and preacher, once said, "Leaders have power, but power is safe only in the hands of those who humble themselves to serve." Only leaders who serve should serve as leaders. If you don't grasp servanthood, you don't grasp leadership.

Servant leaders do not always wind up in the corner office or at the head of the parade. In fact, servant leaders sometimes find themselves nailed to a cross. That, of course, is the example Jesus set, so it is the example we must follow. The greatest leader who ever lived took his towel and his basin and stooped to wash the feet of eleven followers and one traitor. Through his example of servanthood, a world was transformed.

There is another side to the servanthood equation. Not only must we be willing to wash the feet of others, we must also allow others to wash *our* feet. When Jesus reached the place where Peter sat, the rugged fisherman refused to be served. "No!" he said in his pride. "You shall never wash my feet!" Jesus replied, "Unless I cleanse you, you can have no part with me."

A true servant is humble enough to serve—and humble enough to be served. When Jesus impressed this fact on Peter, the impulsive fisherman replied, "Don't just wash my feet, but my hands and head as well!" Swinging from one extreme to the other, Peter suddenly wanted to be washed from head to toe!

Jesus, however, made it clear that only his "feet" were dirty, and at this point it becomes clear that Jesus was speaking symbolically. The cleansing that Jesus pictures for us is not a washing of the body but a washing of the soul. Jesus told Peter that his whole being, his entire soul, was clean. "Someone who has already had a bath needs only to wash his feet to be completely clean."

Peter had been bathed and cleansed by his faith in Jesus. Only his feet were dirty. When Peter walked in sandals on dusty roads, his feet got dirty, and so it is with all of us. In our daily "walk," our souls accumulate "dirt" and "dust" from the thoughtless actions, the momentary sins, the individual acts of lust or coveting or gossip that we commit from day to day. Even if we have been bathed and baptized by God, we still need to have our "feet" washed on a continual, daily basis. That was what Jesus was telling Peter.

"Now, you are clean," Jesus said when he had finished washing the disciples' feet, "though not every one of you." Jesus had washed the feet of all the disciples, but they were not all "clean." One of them was dirty, even though his feet had been washed. Judas, the betrayer, was filthy from the inside out.

There is a powerful irony embedded in this story. Jesus didn't just wash the feet of his disciples, his friends, his followers. He also washed the feet of Judas, the betrayer.

Jesus knew that Judas had sold him out, yet he didn't hesitate to be a servant even to a traitor.

What went through the mind of Judas as Jesus bent down to wash his feet? Did he feel shame? Was there even a flicker of remorse, or did Judas only feel contempt for Jesus—a man Judas had followed and believed in, a man who had turned out to be such a disappointment to Judas? We don't know.

But there is a much deeper question for you and me in this story. The question is: Who is the

> *Your attitude should be the same as the attitude of Jesus the Messiah. Though he existed in the form of God, he didn't consider equality with God something to hold onto. Instead, he emptied himself and took the form of a servant. And being made in the shape of a man, he humbled himself by becoming obedient to the point of death—even death on a cross.*
>
> Philippians 2:5-8

"Judas" in your life? Who is the person whose knife is in your back, who has betrayed you and sold you out?

And how would Jesus ask you to serve your Judas?

Carpenter, Preacher, Healer, Servant

The island of Molokai, part of the Hawaiian chain, is a paradise today, but in the mid-nineteenth century it was a place of misery, disease and death. That was when a terrifying epidemic of leprosy broke out in the Hawaiian

Islands. In those days, there was no cure for this disfiguring, fast-spreading disease, so the Hawaiian government rounded up leprosy victims, separated them from their family and friends and quarantined them on the island of Molokai.

The ships with their human cargo would anchor offshore, and the lepers were forced overboard to either swim to the rocky shore or drown. Those who survived lived in caves or in shacks made of leaves and branches. The lepers huddled together, condemned and without hope. An occasional supply ship would toss crates of food into the water, which the currents would wash ashore for the lepers to retrieve, but the government provided no shelter or drinking water.

Seven years after the leper colony on Molokai was founded, a Belgian priest, Father Damien de Veuster, volunteered to serve there. He arrived in 1873 only thirty-three years old, and he lived among the lepers. Skilled in carpentry and medicine, he helped the lepers build decent houses, treated their degenerating bodies and buried their dead.

One night in 1885, as he was preparing for bed, Father Damien filled a basin with boiling water so he could wash his feet. He had a pitcher of cold water nearby, and he intended to mix the cold and hot water to a comfortable temperature, but he forgot the cold water. He put his feet in the boiling water—but he felt no pain.

When he realized his mistake, he knew he had contracted leprosy, a nerve-destroying disease that robs its victims of sensation. After twelve years of serving lepers, Father Damien had become a leper himself. The next Sunday morning, Father Damien stood before his congregation and began his sermon with the words, "We lepers . . ."

Father Damien lived like Jesus and served like Jesus. Just like the Master himself, Father Damien was a carpenter, a preacher, a healer and a servant—above all, he was a servant. He went to people who were castaways and without hope, and he took their disease into himself. In 1889, at the age of forty-nine, he died like Jesus—he laid down his life for his friends.

That is what it means to serve like Jesus. It's not easy to be a servant to others, but that is the example Jesus left us—the example of the basin and the towel. If you cannot *serve* like Jesus, you cannot be like Jesus.

Who is he calling you to serve today?

CHAPTER SEVENTEEN

HOW TO DIE LIKE JESUS

fter his last meal with the Twelve, Jesus led them out of the city and down into the Kidron Valley. "Just as the Father has loved me, I have loved you," Jesus told them as they walked. "So remain in my love after I leave you. Obey what I have told you—especially this command: Love each other. There is no more profound way to show your love for others than to lay down your life for them. So love each other as I have loved you."

There was a sense of urgency as he spoke, as if he had much to say and little time in which to say it. "I am sending you out to change the world. If the world hates you, remember that it hated me first. You don't belong to this world—I have selected you out of it. You will be hated and persecuted, as I have been. A day will come when people will think that killing you is a service to God—they will hate you because they do not know the Father, nor do they know me. Soon, I will be taken from you. Then, after a while, you will see me again."

When Jesus said this, the disciples whispered to each other, "What does he mean?"

Jesus heard them and said, "I can't explain it to you in detail. I can only tell you that you will grieve for me, but your grief will turn to joy, a joy that can never be taken from you. Don't try to understand it now. Just believe me when I tell you that I came from the Father and now I must return to the Father. But when I am gone, you can pray in my name, and the Father will answer you because he loves you, and because you have loved and trusted in me."

"We believe you know all things," said one of the disciples.

"And we trust you," said another. "We know you came from God."

> *He died not for men, but for each man. If each man had been the only man made, he would have done no less.*
>
> **C. S. Lewis**
> SCHOLAR, NOVELIST AND
> LAY THEOLOGIAN

"You believe and trust me now," Jesus said sadly, "but soon you will be scattered. I needed to tell you these things so that you would be at peace with yourselves when these things come to pass. This world is full of trouble, but don't be discouraged. I have overcome the world."

Abba! Daddy!

Then Jesus looked toward heaven and said, "Father! The time has come! You have given me authority over all people so that I might give eternal life to everyone you have given me. Eternal life is to know you, the one true

God, and Jesus the Messiah, whom you have sent. I have honored you on Earth by accomplishing the mission you gave me. Now, Father, as I return to your presence, honor me with the splendor I had before the world existed.

"I pray for these followers you gave to me, who have obeyed your commands. I am leaving this world, but they must remain in it. As you sent me into this world, I have sent them. The world hates them; the Evil One is determined to destroy them. Father, protect them by your power. I am not praying for these followers only, but for all who will one day trust in me as a result of their message. May they be unified with each other and with us. Let their unity be a witness to the world of your reality and your love."

When Jesus finished praying, he led his disciples across the Kidron Brook and up the eastern slope of the Kidron Valley, toward the Garden of Gethsemane. They entered the garden with its ancient olive grove, and Jesus told his disciples, "Stay here while I go over there and pray."

He took Peter, James and John with him to a grassy clearing surrounded by olive trees. "My soul is breaking under a load of sorrow," Jesus told them. "Stay here, pray for me—and keep watch." The three disciples had seen Jesus in many different moods—joyful, peaceful, sorrowful, angry—but never had they seen him in such agony.

Jesus went off alone, about a stone's throw away from his three friends, and he fell to his knees. In the shadows and stillness of the garden, he looked up at the stars and poured out his anguished heart to the Father.

"Abba!" he shouted in Aramaic. In English, it would be like saying, "Daddy!" At that moment, Jesus was not making a formal request of his Father, but an intimate plea to his "Daddy" in heaven. *"Abba!"* Jesus prayed. "All things are possible for you! Please let this cup be taken from me!"

He waited. The night sky was silent.

He continued praying, imploring his Father again and again as time seemed to stand still. Must he drink this cup? Wasn't there any other way to accomplish the Father's will? His anguish was so great that the sweat ran down his brow and fell upon the ground like drops of blood. His suffocating sense of horror was so intense that an angel appeared beside him to strengthen him.

This long, intense, emotional prayer of Jesus was not just a conversation with God. It was a fierce *battle*—his human desire to escape the horror of the cross and the separation from the Father that horror would entail versus his spiritual desire to obey his Father and fulfill his purpose on Earth.

"Father, please—let this cup be taken from me!" he prayed once more. And then he closed with these words: "Yet, let it not be as I will, but as you will." As he spoke those words of submission, the battle was won, and the angel left him.

Weary and exhausted, feeling as though a dagger was lodged in the core of his being, he rose to his feet. He trudged through the shadow-wrapped garden to the place where he had left his three closest friends to keep watch. When he saw Peter, James and John, his heart sank. They were all sprawled on the ground! While he had been ago-nizing in prayer, his friends had slept! A horrible feeling of abandonment and loneliness closed in around him.

"Simon!" he called in a wounded voice. "How can you sleep? Couldn't you keep watch with me for just one hour? Stay alert! Pray that you do not fall to temptation!"

Peter stirred, then jumped to his feet, looking at Jesus with shame in his startled eyes. The rugged fisherman started to apolo-gize, but Jesus gripped his

> *Fear not that your life shall come to an end, but rather fear that it shall never have a beginning.*
> Cardinal John Henry Newman
> UNIVERSITY RECTOR AND
> CHURCH LEADER

shoulder and said, "It's all right. The spirit is willing, but the body is weak. But be alert, now, and pray for me!"

Then Jesus went away and prayed again.

The Kiss of Betrayal

The Garden of Gethsemane was Jesus' favorite place of retreat and prayer. Judas Iscariot knew the place well. He also knew that Jesus would go there after the Passover supper. He had arranged a signal. The guards would arrest the man he greeted with a kiss. Judas entered the garden leading a group of priests, elders, servants and Temple guards. The enemies of Jesus carried torches, clubs and swords.

As Jesus prayed, he heard the heavy sound of footsteps coming up the hillside. He heard voices and saw the flicker of a torchlight shining through the trees. He got up and ran to the three disciples. Again, they were asleep!

"Get up!" Jesus said. "The hour has arrived!"

Peter, James and John opened their eyes and scrambled to their feet. They looked around and saw the approaching lights and heard the voices. Then they looked at Jesus. Why didn't he try to escape? Amazingly, he walked straight toward the threatening crowd!

Then, they saw the familiar face at the front of the crowd, his features glimmering in the torchlight. It was Judas Iscariot.

"Who do you want?" Jesus said in a bold voice.

"Jesus of Nazareth," someone in the crowd replied.

"I am," Jesus said. An astonishing thing happened when he said that. Judas and all of the priests, elders, servants and guards stumbled backward! Some fell to the ground, along with their torches and weapons.

In the language of Jesus, the words "I am" were actually a single Hebrew word, *Ehyeh*. In Exodus 3, when God spoke to Moses out of the burning bush, God identified himself by saying, "*Ehyeh Asher Ehyeh*. I am that I am." When Jesus identified himself with that same divine name, his enemies fell back.

The other disciples crept forward out of the deep shadows of the olive grove and were horrified by what they saw. On one side of the clearing stood Jesus, backed by Peter, James and John. On the other side stood a group of Temple officials and sword-carrying guards picking themselves up off the ground. Then, to their astonishment, the disciples saw Judas step forward from the crowd.

Suddenly, the disciples understood what Jesus had tried to tell them: "One of you will betray me." But Judas, the treasurer, the most trusted man of all the Twelve! They had never suspected him.

"Teacher," Judas said, and he kissed Jesus. After submitting to the kiss of betrayal, Jesus looked the traitor in the eye and said, "Judas, my friend, do you betray the Son of Man—with a kiss?"

Judas met the eyes of Jesus for a moment, then he turned away.

Jesus faced the hostile crowd. "I'm the one you want," he said. "Let these others go."

"Master," Simon Peter shouted, "they will never take you!" Peter reached beneath his cloak, pulled out a sword and rushed at Jesus' enemies, swinging and slashing, his sword glittering in the torchlight.

The Temple officials and guards had not expected such a ferocious attack. Shouting and cursing, they fell back as Peter waded in among them, his eyes blazing with rage, his deadly sword slicing through the air. He was not just trying to scare off the crowd—he wanted to kill. He aimed his sword at the neck of the nearest man, a servant of the high priest, and he put all his strength into a vicious, slashing sword stroke.

The servant saw Peter's blade arc toward him, and he knew that the enraged disciple was trying to decapitate him! The servant stumbled backward, and the sword missed his neck, slicing through his ear instead. Blood spurted from the man's ear as he fell with a scream, clutching his head.

"No more violence!" Jesus shouted to Peter. "Put away your sword! Shall I not drink the cup the Father has given me?" Jesus knelt down beside the servant, touched his split and bleeding ear and healed him. Then Jesus stood and faced the priests and elders.

"Am I leading a revolt," Jesus asked boldly, "that you come against me with clubs and swords? Every day this week, I have stood openly in the Temple courtyard. You could have taken me at any time. But no, you strike at midnight, so that the darkness of the night will hide the darkness of your deeds."

> *The valley of the shadow of death holds no darkness for the child of God. There must be light, or else there could be no shadow. Jesus is the light. He has overcome death.*
>
> Dwight L. Moody
> EVANGELIST AND EDUCATOR

The guards rushed forward and seized Jesus.

Instantly, the disciples panicked and scattered. Not one of them looked back to see what was happening to their Master. They dashed down the hill, running among the trees, their hearts pounding. They had no thought but to save their own skins.

A Trumped-Up "Trial"

The Temple guards bound Jesus and led him back to Jerusalem. He was taken first to the house of Annas, the head of the priestly family. Jesus stood before Annas with his hands bound and his legs shackled.

"Tell us," Annas said. "What have you been teaching the people about yourself?"

"I taught in synagogues or at the Temple," Jesus replied. "I taught openly, in broad daylight, in front of crowds. I said nothing in secret. So why do you question me in secret? Ask those who heard me, and they will tell you what I said."

Annas shifted uncomfortably in his robes. He was annoyed that Jesus drew attention to the secrecy of this preliminary hearing—secret trials were a violation of Jewish law. So were trials that took place after sundown. An official reached out and slapped Jesus across the face, accusing him of disrespect.

"If I said anything wrong," Jesus answered calmly, his face stinging, "then prove me wrong. If I spoke the truth, then why did you strike me?"

Annas did not want to question Jesus anymore, especially since the entire proceeding was illegal and politically dangerous. When word reached the streets that Jesus of Nazareth had been arrested and tried at midnight by the Temple rulers, there was no telling how the people might react. So Annas sent Jesus to his son-in-law, Caiaphas, the corrupt high priest of the Temple. Maybe Caiaphas could find a way to entrap the Galilean with his own words.

A "trial" was convened at well past midnight in the splendid palace of Caiaphas. All the chief priests, elders and scribes came together and sat around the hall. Jesus stood in the center of the hall, surrounded by his enemies, his hands still bound. As the religious rulers glared at the troublesome preacher, they knew that they desperately needed to accomplish two things.

First, they had to trump up a charge that would make the common people turn against Jesus. This would not be easy, because the people loved Jesus, and many had been healed and helped by him. The only accusation that would turn all the people against him was a charge of blasphemy, the act of speaking against God or claiming equality with God.

> *We understand the prophecies of the Bible only when we see the events happen.*
>
> Blaise Pascal
> MATHEMATICIAN, SCIENTIST
> AND PHILOSOPHER

Second, the religious rulers had to trump up a charge that would motivate the Romans to execute Jesus. Why did the religious leaders need to convince the Roman government? Why couldn't they execute Jesus themselves? Herein lies a fascinating piece of Jewish history.

The Shiloh Prophecy

Before the land of Israel had come under the control of the Roman Empire, all authority over religious, civil and criminal law was vested in the Sanhedrin. The Sanhedrin was the ruling council of the Jewish nation and consisted of seventy-two members. When Israel was an independent nation, the Sanhedrin had the power to impose capital punishment under the Law of Moses. Sixty years before the birth of Jesus, however, Israel was conquered by the Roman general Pompey. Even under Roman rule, the Jewish Sanhedrin was allowed to maintain authority over legal matters, including capital punishment, for a number of decades. This was primarily because they had a king, Herod, who was considered, as a descendant of Esau, to be half-Jewish. They still considered themselves under Jewish rule.

Then, in A.D. 6 or 7, Caesar Augustus removed King Herod Archelaus (son of Herod the Great) as king of Judea and sent him into exile. Caesar then appointed a procurator (a Roman governor) to exercise authority on behalf of Rome. The procurator was named Coponius. One of the first official acts of Coponius was to strip the Sanhedrin of much of its power, including the power of the death penalty.

Why is this significant? For two reasons. First, it meant that the Pharisees, scribes and rulers of the Sanhedrin, had no legal way to put Jesus to death. Only the Romans could execute criminals. In order to kill Jesus, the religious rulers would have to convince the Roman government that Jesus was guilty of a capital crime. That wouldn't be easy—the religious rulers all knew he was innocent.

Second, the Sanhedrin's loss of the power of capital punishment was significant because of an Old Testament prophecy of the Messiah. In Genesis 49, Jacob, the father of the nation of Israel, was on his deathbed. He called his sons together to bless them. "Gather around me," he said, "and I shall tell you what will happen to you in the future." He then prophesied over each of his sons.

When Jacob came to his fourth son, Judah, he gave him a prophecy concerning the coming of the Messiah. "The scepter will not depart from Judah," Jacob said, "nor the ruler's staff from between his feet, until Shiloh comes. And unto him shall be the gathering of the people." These strange-sounding words actually had very clear meaning to the ancient Jewish scribes. The scepter and the ruler's staff referred to the sovereignty of Israel and the right to enforce the Law of Moses, including the power of the death sentence. "Shiloh" was another name for the Messiah, and "Judah" referred not only to Jacob's fourth son, but to the entire southern kingdom of Israel.

So when the Roman procurator, Coponius, stripped Israel of its national sovereignty and the power of capital punishment, Jewish society was shaken to its roots. The scepter had been taken away from Judah—but where was the Messiah?

This question dismayed the religious leaders of Israel. In the *Babylonian Talmud,* Rabbi Rachman observed, "When the members of the Sanhedrin found themselves deprived of the right over life and death, a general consternation took possession of them. They covered their heads with ashes, and their bodies with sackcloth, exclaiming, 'Woe unto us, for the scepter has departed from Judah, and the Messiah has not come!'"

Yet, at that same time the leaders of Israel were in despair and mourning, a Jewish boy was growing up in the tiny village of Nazareth. His Hebrew name was Y'shua, but he is more famous today as Jesus. If the ancient prophecy of Jacob was true, then when the scepter departed from Judah, Messiah had in fact come—but no one knew it!

Messiah would not be revealed until he rode into Jerusalem on a young donkey one Sunday in April in A.D. 32.

Here, we see another piece of the puzzle of Old Testament prophecy fitting into place. If the Sanhedrin had the power to enforce the Law of Moses and put Jesus to death themselves, they would not have used a cross and some iron nails, as the Romans did. They would have simply taken Jesus outside the city walls and stoned him to death.

That, however, is not what Old Testament prophecy said about the death of the Messiah. In Psalm 22, his death was described in terms that only fit death by crucifixion, even though crucifixion had not even been devised when these words of Psalm 22 were written: "They pierced my hands and my feet." In order for those words to be fulfilled, Messiah had to die by crucifixion, not stoning.

So Caiaphas and the Sanhedrin had to rely on the Roman government in order to put the troublesome Galilean to death. That meant they had to find some way to portray Jesus as a threat to Roman rule.

> "See, here are the wood and the fire," Isaac said, "but where is the lamb for the burnt sacrifice?" "My son," Abraham answered, "God himself will provide the lamb for the burnt sacrifice."
> Genesis 22:7-8

A Lamb to the Slaughter

Because Caiaphas and the Sanhedrin couldn't find any authentic evidence against Jesus, they brought in a series of "witnesses" to give perjured testimony. The problem with lying witnesses is that it is hard to get their statements to agree. Some of the "witnesses" against Jesus not only contradicted each other, but they contradicted themselves.

As the "trial" dragged on through the night, Caiaphas became increasingly frustrated. He could hardly afford to let the prosecution of Jesus be seen as the utter farce it was. So Caiaphas stood up and tried to goad Jesus into incriminating himself. Under Jewish law, the high priest was to protect and defend the accused.

"Aren't you going to answer these charges?" the high priest demanded. "What about the testimony against you? What do you have to say for yourself?"

Jesus remained silent. That, of course, was his right. He was not required by law to testify either for or against himself.

The silence of Jesus also fulfilled an Old Testament prophecy about the promised Messiah. Isaiah 53 is a well-known messianic passage. Verse 7 says that the Messiah would be "persecuted—yet when he was attacked, he did not speak in his own defense. He was led like a lamb to the slaughter, and as a sheep is silent before its shearers, he did not open his mouth."

The composed silence of Jesus only made Caiaphas lose

his own composure. The high priest fumed. "I demand," he snarled, "that you tell us under oath and swear by the living God—are you the Messiah, the Son of God?"

Jesus answered Caiaphas with the same word he used when the men with clubs and torches came to arrest him in the Garden of Gethsemane, "*Ehyeh*—I am." Then he added, "And the day will come when you will see the Son of Man sitting at God's right hand, and he will come against you in judgment from the clouds."

In that instant, Caiaphas must have felt that the tables had turned. This upstart Galilean was talking as if *he* were sitting in judgment of the high priest instead of the other way around! It was as if Jesus of Nazareth could somehow look into the heart of Caiaphas and see all the hatred, murder and corruption he hid inside—and Caiaphas felt naked and exposed.

"Enough!" Caiaphas shrieked. "I won't hear any more! He has spoken blasphemy! You all heard it! Why call any other witnesses? Decide his fate now!"

"Death!" the other priests and elders shouted. "He deserves death!" Some of the Temple guards and officials spit at him. One of the officials placed a blindfold on Jesus, then the guards slapped him in the face and hit him with their closed fists. "Prophesy to us, if you are truly the Messiah!" they shouted. "Tell us who hit you!"

Jesus absorbed the blows and the insults and did not

> *Peter had boasted of more love to Jesus than the rest; and Peter had failed more than all.*
>
> John Nelson Darby
> BIBLE SCHOLAR

respond. He knew where all of this was leading, and he made no attempt to avoid his destiny.

The Three Denials

Meanwhile, Simon Peter lurked in the darkened court-yard of the high priest's palace, looking through the windows and listening to everything that went on inside. Though he had given up any hope of rescuing the Master, he couldn't stay away. He had to find out what fate the religious rulers had planned for Jesus.

There were Temple guards in the courtyard, and Peter nervously sat down among them, warming himself at a fire. The back of his neck tingled with fear. He silently prayed that no one would recognize him as a follower of Jesus.

"You're one of them," said a voice behind him.

Peter turned and saw one of the servant girls of the high priest. His heart jumped with panic.

"You were with that Galilean, the one they call Jesus," the girl said accusingly.

"I don't know what you're talking about," Peter said. Then he stood up, went to the archway in the courtyard wall and tried to lose himself in the shadows.

But the obnoxious servant girl refused to mind her own business! "I tell you, he's one of them!" she said to the Temple guards, pointing in Peter's direction.

Cold sweat beaded up on Peter's brow. "I tell you, I don't know who you're talking about!"

Two of the Temple guards got up from their place beside the fire and walked toward Peter. "You certainly sound like one of them," said one, eyeing Peter closely. "Your accent is Galilean."

"Yes," said the other, "you look like the man in the olive grove—the one who struck down the servant of the high priest! I'm sure of it. You're a follower of this man, Jesus."

At that, Peter swore a horrible oath and called down curses on himself. "I swear to you on my own soul," he said, "that I never heard of this man you're talking about!"

As Peter said this, the first faint glimmer of light was appearing in the eastern sky. Somewhere, a rooster crowed.

> *So Judas kissed his master, and cried, "All hail!" whereas he meant all harm.*
> William Shakespeare
> PLAYWRIGHT

Then Peter remembered the words Jesus had said to him in the upper room. "Peter, before the rooster crows at dawn, you will deny me—three times."

Peter turned and staggered out of the courtyard, weeping bitterly, wishing he was man enough to unsheathe the sword at his side and fall on it.

The Traitor's Remorse

The "trial" of Jesus was held in the house of Caiaphas, even though it was illegal for the Sanhedrin to convene a religious trial outside of the Temple grounds. It was against the law for a defendant to be convicted and sentenced to death solely on his own confession, yet that was precisely what Caiaphas did. It was illegal to mistreat and abuse a defendant and treat him as a criminal before he had been properly found guilty, yet Jesus was blindfolded, beaten and spat upon.

Everything that was done to Jesus was a violation of the law, but none of that mattered now. The end justified the means. Jesus had to be silenced at any price.

In the hours after midnight, Jesus was taken out of the hall while the Sanhedrin discussed his fate. They had gotten what they wanted from Jesus—a "confession," though Jesus hadn't actually admitted wrongdoing. He had, though, made a statement in the presence of many witnesses, a statement in which he had placed himself on the same level as God. It was blasphemy, pure and simple!

Best of all, his statement could be used against him in two ways. First, the members of the Sanhedrin would tell the people of Jerusalem that Jesus of Nazareth was a blasphemer who was deserving of death.

Second, the blasphemy of Jesus could be turned around and used as proof of the crime of sedition—an attempt to incite a rebellion against Rome. He had claimed to be the Messiah, the long-promised king of Israel, the Son of God who had come to liberate Israel from foreign domination. Claiming to be a king was a crime against the king of Rome, Tiberius Caesar, and penalty for that crime was death. The Romans would deal with Jesus in the Roman fashion—with a wooden cross and iron nails.

At daybreak, Caiaphas and the Sanhedrin had Jesus

brought back before them. The midnight proceedings were technically illegal, so they decided to dot the "i's" and cross the "t's" as soon as the sun came up.

"If you are truly the Messiah," they said, "tell us once more."

"If I said 'yes,'" Jesus answered, "you wouldn't believe me. If I asked you what you mean by that question, you wouldn't answer me. So, I will only say this from now on: The Son of Man will be seated at the right hand of God."

"Then," the members of the council said, "you are claiming to be the Son of God, are you not?"

Jesus answered, "You are correct in saying that I am."

The members of the council exchanged satisfied glances. "We don't need to hear any other testimony. We have heard the proof from his own lips."

The Temple guards led Jesus away with orders to lead him to the house of the Roman procurator, Pontius Pilate, at the Antonia Fortress.

As Jesus was led through the streets of Jerusalem, a man stood in the shadows, watching the procession. This man had followed Jesus for three years. He had seen all the miracles and healings and he had heard wonderful words from the lips of Jesus. Now, he watched as Jesus was led through the streets, a condemned prisoner. The man in the shadows clutched in his hand a bag of thirty silver coins, the price of betrayal.

As the procession passed him by, the man left his shadowy hiding place and slipped into the courtyard of the palace of Caiaphas. He entered the palace and found a number of priests and elders still sitting at their tables, discussing the trial that had just ended. The religious leaders fell silent as the man entered with his bag of money.

"What do you want?" asked one of the elders.

"I have condemned my own soul!" Judas Iscariot shouted. "I have betrayed innocent blood!"

"What is that to us?" said one of the priests.

"He was the only truly good man I've ever known," Judas said, "and I've destroyed him."

> *But what is truth? 'Twas Pilate's question put/To Truth itself, that deigned him no reply.*
> William Cowper
> POET

"You were paid well," the priest said. "Take your money and get out!"

Judas turned and left the palace of Caiaphas. He went to the Temple and flung the bag of silver coins into the courtyard. The bag flew open, and the coins jingled across the pavement.

Then, Judas Iscariot turned and went outside of Jerusalem to the southern bluff of the valley of Hinnom. There, he threw a rope over the limb of a tree and hanged himself.

What Is Truth?

The Temple officials and guards led Jesus to the Antonia Fortress and the house of Pontius Pilate. The religious rulers refused to enter the house of a Gentile, because that would have made them ceremonially unclean. So Pilate came out onto a portico overlooking the courtyard to see what they wanted at this hour of the morning.

The religious rulers thrust Jesus forward so that Pilate could see him. "This man, Jesus," they said, "is an enemy of Rome."

Pilate looked Jesus up and down. "Oh?" he said. "What are his crimes?" The Roman governor viewed the religious officials with both amusement and contempt. He had heard vague rumors of this Jesus, and he knew that the religious leaders envied him because of his popularity with the crowds.

"If this man were not guilty of crimes," the religious leaders answered, "we would not have brought him to you for judgment."

Pilate was unimpressed. "Take him away," he said. "Judge him by your own law."

"Our law says he deserves to die," the rulers said, "but Rome will not allow us to execute criminals."

"What does Rome care about your law?" Pilate asked.

"We tell you, this man is an enemy of Rome!" the rulers answered. "He is guilty of sedition! He tells the people not to pay taxes to Caesar! He claims to be the Messiah—the king of the Jewish people."

Pilate sighed. He knew a little bit about the Jewish people and their Messiah legend. Though Rome could easily put down any Jewish rebellion, this Messiah talk was dangerous. It wasn't good to have someone running around claiming to possess supernatural powers and getting the people stirred up.

Pilate went inside and told one of his aides to bring Jesus to him. When Jesus was brought before him, still bound, Pilate asked him, "Are you the king of the Jews?"

"Is it your own idea to ask me that?" Jesus said. "Or did other people put that idea in your mind?"

Pilate chuckled. "Do I look Jewish to you? I'm a Roman. What do such matters have to do with me? Your own people, your high priests—they're the ones who turned you over to me for judgment."

"I am indeed a king," Jesus said, "but my kingdom is not of this world."

Pilate frowned, not sure what to make of Jesus or his answer. "You do claim to be a king, then?"

"You are correct in calling me a king," Jesus said. "I reign over the realm of truth. I came into the world as a witness to the ultimate truth. Everyone who believes in the truth recognizes that my message is truth."

Pilate shook his head. "What is truth?" he said, expecting no answer.

Jesus said nothing.

Pilate tried a different tack. "What did you do to make them hate you so?"

Still, Jesus made no answer.

"Didn't you hear the charges they leveled at you?"

No answer.

Pilate was amazed. "Won't you make any attempt to defend yourself against their accusations?"

No answer.

Pilate left Jesus and walked back onto his portico

overlooking the crowd. "I have questioned this man, and I find no basis for any criminal charge against him."

"Haven't you heard?" the religious leaders asked. "He has gone all over Judea, stirring up trouble with his disloyal teachings! He started in Galilee, and he's spreading his treasonous ideas all the way to Jerusalem!"

Pilate's eyebrows raised. "He's a Galilean, is he? In that case, I can do nothing with him. Galilee is under the jurisdiction of Herod Antipas. I shall send him to King Herod for judgment."

The religious leaders were beside themselves with frustration. This was not getting them anywhere!

Pilate went back inside, smiling at his good fortune. Herod was normally at his castle, Machaerus, on the eastern shore of the Dead Sea, but he happened to be in Jerusalem for the Passover. All Pilate had to do was hand this so-called "King of the Jews" over to the real Jewish king, Herod Antipas, and this Jesus would no longer be Pilate's problem.

> *A man who was completely innocent offered himself as a sacrifice for the good of others—including his enemies—and became the ransom of the world. It was an act of moral and spiritual perfection.*
> Mahatma Gandhi
> PHILOSOPHER AND
> HINDU SPIRITUAL LEADER

So Pilate sent Jesus to Herod and supposed that would be the end of the matter. Pilate could not have been more mistaken.

Crucify Him! Crucify Him!

The chief priests and scribes led Jesus to the lavishly furnished palace of Herod. Jesus was brought before Herod, the man who had beheaded his friend John the Baptist. King Herod was surprised and happy to finally meet Jesus of Nazareth. Like the curiosity seekers who followed Jesus from town to town, Herod was eager to see Jesus perform some sort of miracle.

However, Jesus disappointed the king. Not only did he refuse to perform any miracles, but he also refused to answer a single question Herod put to him. Finally, Herod's curiosity turned to contempt. He ordered his soldiers to dress Jesus in a courtly robe—the purple robe of a king. Herod and his soldiers jeered at Jesus, ridiculing his claim to be the Messiah. When Herod grew tired of mocking Jesus, he sent him back to Pontius Pilate. As the soldiers marched him back, a growing mob of people followed.

Pilate was sitting in the judgment seat when he received a message that Herod was returning Jesus of Nazareth to him for judgment. As he was reading that message, another note came to him, this time from his own wife. "Have nothing to do with that innocent Galilean," she had written. "I had a most awful dream about him last night. We will suffer if you condemn him."

Pontius Pilate swore in frustration. His wife told him to do one thing; the Jewish leaders told him to do another.

As Jesus, still wearing the purple robe that Herod had draped on him, was brought before Pilate, the Roman governor looked him up and down. Should he crucify the man or not? Pilate had watched many crucified men writhing in agony, and he had never felt the slightest twinge of conscience over them. But those men had deserved crucifixion. Jesus was no criminal. Pilate was certain of this.

There had to be some way out of this dilemma.

Pilate left Jesus and went out to the crowd. "You brought me this man," he said, "and accused him of inciting the people to rebellion. I have questioned him, and so has King Herod. We find no basis for the charges against him. But, in order to satisfy you, I will flog him, then let him go."

"No!" the mob shouted. "Crucify him!"

The blood lust in their voices left Pilate shaken. The situation was far more dangerous than he had realized. He decided to try a different approach. "It is your custom," he said, "for Rome to release one prisoner in honor of your Passover. I shall release this 'King of the Jews.'"

"No!" the people shouted even more loudly. "Release Barabbas to us!"

Barabbas! That murdering terrorist? The idea of releasing Barabbas while crucifying this innocent Galilean made Pilate sick to his stomach.

"I've made my decision," Pilate said. "I'll have the Galilean flogged, and he'll never trouble you again."

"Crucify him! Crucify him!" the mob chanted.

"Why?" Pilate asked. "What crime has he committed?"

"Crucify him! Crucify him! Crucify him!"

Pilate was frightened. He couldn't afford to lose control of this situation. Maybe if the crowd saw Jesus bloodied and suffering, it would appease them.

Pilate sent Jesus out to be flogged by soldiers. The flogging was done with a braided whip with bits of metal and bone woven into each lash. Jesus was stripped, tied to a post and flogged across his shoulders, back and thighs. This method of flogging shredded the victim's flesh and often exposed raw muscle and bone. Profuse bleeding produced severe dehydration and shock, and it was not uncommon for victims to die from the flogging alone.

After Jesus was flogged, the soldiers made a mock crown by braiding a thorn briar into a circlet and pressing it onto his head, drawing rivulets of blood from his scalp. Though he claimed to be a king, that crown of thorns was the only crown he ever wore. The soldiers then placed the purple robe on his back and mocked him, saying, "Hail, King of the Jews!" Then, they beat him until his face was bleeding and swollen. Finally, they brought him back to Pontius Pilate.

Pilate stared in horror at the bloodied, mutilated features of Jesus. Yet the Roman governor considered those tortures merciful compared to the cross. Surely, the blood lust of the mob would be satisfied when they saw Jesus now.

Pilate led Jesus out before the people. There was a gasp from the mob as they saw Jesus, his face so bruised and bloodied that he was almost unrecognizable. The purple robe was sopping wet with wine-dark stains of blood.

"Look!" Pilate said to the crowd. "Look at the man!"

There was a heartbeat of stunned silence from the

crowd. For a moment, Pilate believed his ploy had worked. Any sane human being would have to agree that the Galilean had suffered enough. The crowd would certainly let this man go free.

Then the chief priests and other officials of the Temple began chanting, "Crucify him! Crucify him! Crucify him!"

Pilate couldn't believe his own ears. He had never faced such a bloodthirsty mob in his life. Anger, mingled with disgust and revulsion, welled up inside him. "You want him crucified, do you?" Pilate shouted back over their chants. "Then you take him and crucify him yourselves! As for me, I refuse to murder an innocent man!"

"Our law says he must die for the sin of blasphemy," the priests shouted back, "because he claims to be the Son of God!"

Pilate's heart pounded. He had tried everything to free this man. He had even flogged him within an inch of his life, but nothing worked. Pilate was not a superstitious man, but he was beginning to wonder if some evil spirit wasn't behind the blood lust of the mob, some hateful force with a will of its own.

Pilate ordered the soldiers to bring Jesus inside, and he took his place on the judgment seat. "Where did you come from?" Pilate demanded, struggling to keep the hysteria out of his voice.

Jesus said nothing.

"Why don't you answer me?" Pilate said, his voice rising to a shriek. "Don't you understand that I have the power to set you free—or to crucify you?"

"You have no power over me," Jesus answered, "except the power that was given to you from above. I don't hold any of this against you. The one who turned me over to you bears the greater guilt."

Guilt! Pilate knew that if he crucified this man, there would be a stain of guilt on his soul that could never be erased!

He got up and went back out to the crowd. "I tell you, this man is innocent of any crime! I cannot crucify an innocent man!"

"If you let him go," the mob shouted back, "you are no friend of Caesar! Take him away! Crucify him!"

"Do you really want me to crucify your king?" Pilate asked.

The chief priests answered, "We have no king but Caesar!"

Pilate went back into the house and filled a basin with water from a pitcher. Then he brought the basin out onto the portico and washed his hands in front of the crowd. "Let this man's death be upon all of you!" he said. "I wash my hands of his blood!"

"Let his blood be upon us," the mob answered, "and upon our children."

> *Jesus Christ suffered and died to sanctify death and suffering.*
> Blaise Pascal
> MATHEMATICIAN, SCIENTIST AND PHILOSOPHER

Pilate went back inside and signed two pieces of paper. One was the order releasing Barabbas. The other was the death warrant for Jesus of Nazareth.

It Is Finished

Roman soldiers forced Jesus to carry the horizontal crossbar (the patibulum) through the streets of Jerusalem. Before he reached the city gate, Jesus staggered under the weight of the hundred-pound crossbar. Exhausted by the beating and flogging, the sleeplessness and stress, Jesus collapsed in the street. So the Romans pulled a man from the crowd, Simon of Cyrene, and forced him to carry the crossbar the rest of the way.

They led Jesus out through the city gate to a stone quarry on the outskirts of Jerusalem. The place was called Calvary, the "Place of the Skull." There, the soldiers stretched Jesus out upon the crossbar. Large nails—seven inches long and half an inch in diameter—were pounded through his wrists, damaging the median nerve and shooting bolts of incredible pain through his arms. The crossbar was raised and fastened to the vertical stake of the cross, called a stipes. This formed a T-shaped cross. Then a single nail was driven through both heels of Jesus, fastening his feet to the stipes.

By this time, Jesus had already lost a great deal of blood from the flogging. As the weight of his body pulled against the nails, his shoulders and elbows were dislocated—just as Psalm 22 had predicted: "All my bones are out of joint." Hanging on the cross with his knees bent to the side, it was impossible for him to breathe normally. Because of pressure on his diaphragm, Jesus had to painfully push his body up against the nails in his feet in order to exhale— and in order to speak. The Gospel accounts yield only a few statements of Jesus on the cross, and every word he spoke required unbelievable exertion and pain.

The cross killed its victims in many ways at once. The effort required to breathe caused slow suffocation. Blood loss produced dehydration. Collapsing lungs and heart failure also contributed to a shutdown of the body. The pain of crucifixion was simply beyond human endurance. The word *excruciating* comes from the Latin *ex cruciare,* or "from the cross," a recognition that the cross is the most cruel and painful instrument of execution ever invented.

On orders of Pontius Pilate, a sign was fastened to the top of the cross. The sign read, "Jesus of Nazareth, the King of the Jews." This sign was offensive to the chief priests. They scurried off to the Antonia Fortress and demanded to see Pontius Pilate. "You can't write that he is the King of the Jews!" they shouted. "You should write only that he claimed to be such a king!"

Pilate replied, "What I have written, I have written." Then he turned his back on the priests and went inside to brood over what he had done.

Jesus was crucified between two thieves at about nine o'clock in the morning. The soldiers who had nailed him to the cross gambled for his clothing as they watched him die.

Some people gathered around the cross to mourn and weep. Others gathered to mock him. "You were going to destroy the Temple and rebuild it in three days?" said one man. "Then come down from the cross and save yourself!"

"If he's the Son of God, why doesn't God rescue him?" another man sneered.

"He saved others, but he can't save himself!" said another.

Even while Jesus was being taunted and ridiculed during his agonizing death, he raised his eyes and prayed. "Father, forgive them. They don't know what they are doing." Each word of that prayer was an effort, spoken between labored gasps for breath.

The thieves who were crucified on either side of him also shouted insults at him.

"You claimed to be the Messiah," one of the thieves groaned. "If you are, then save yourself—and us, too!"

"Don't you have any respect for God?" said the other thief. "You and I are dying for our crimes, but this man did nothing wrong! I've never seen a crucified man die this way—blessing instead of cursing." He looked Jesus in the eye. "Jesus," he said, "remember me when you enter your kingdom."

"I tell you the truth," Jesus replied, "you and I will soon be together in the gardens of heaven."

Suffering slows time. The suffering of Jesus was so intense, time seemed to stand still.

Then, through a red haze of pain, Jesus saw familiar faces approaching him. Some of the women who had followed him and helped him in his three-year ministry had heard that their Master was being crucified. They rushed out of the city to find him—and they wept and wailed when they saw his bloodied body nailed to a cross.

One of the women who came to the cross was Mary from the village of Magdala, a woman he had delivered from demon possession. Another was Salome, the mother of two of his closest disciples, James and John.

Then Jesus saw Mary, his mother. She had always believed in him, even before he was born. From the time he was a baby, she had whispered to him the words the angel Gabriel had said to her. "You will give birth to a son, and will call him Jesus. He will be great and will be called the Son of the Most High God."

As Mary stood before the cross, watching her son's agony in death, she remembered another prophecy that was spoken to her by an old man named Simeon when she and Joseph had taken Jesus to the Temple. "A sword will pierce your own soul." Weeping uncontrollably, Mary wished that it was her own body nailed to that cross—not her son, not Jesus!

Then Jesus saw John, one of his three closest disciples. John had been with him since the beginning of his public ministry. He was the only one of the Twelve who had dared to come back and be with Jesus as he died.

Jesus looked at his mother. "Dear woman," he said, "here is my friend, John. From now on, he is your son. And John, from now on, this woman is your mother. Watch over her for me."

At noon, after Jesus had been on the cross for about three hours, a mass of clouds rolled over the sky and darkened the landscape. The cloud cover was like a wall that separated Jesus from his Father in heaven.

"Eloi, Eloi, lama sabachthani?" he cried out, his voice echoing across the darkened quarry. "My God, my God,

why have you abandoned me?" Suspended between heaven and Earth, Jesus was more alone than he had ever been in his life.

Each heartbeat was an eternity. Each breath was a struggle against the inevitable.

"I'm thirsty," Jesus said.

Someone held up a sponge on a stick. There was sour wine in the sponge, wine that had spoiled and turned to vinegar. It was offered to him mockingly and cruelly, one last attempt to increase his suffering. Jesus tasted a little.

"Father," he said, looking heavenward, "I place my spirit in your hands. It is finished."

With that, his chin fell against his chest. After six hours on the cross, his heart stopped. His lungs stopped. His physical pain and men-

> *Christ has not only spoken to us by his life but has also spoken for us by his death.*
> Søren Kierkegaard
> PHILOSOPHER AND THEOLOGIAN

tal anguish ceased. In life, he had preached and healed, commanded demons and opposed corruption, offered love and forgiveness.

Now he was gone. It was truly finished.

A Complete Life

The prospect of death terrifies us all. Even if life is not all we wish it would be, even if life is full of disappointment, pain and sorrow, we cling to life as something precious, and we fear death as a dark and horrible unknown. The reality of death requires us to face the realities of living, including the meaning of life, the value of relationships and our connection with God.

The way a person dies is usually a reflection of the way that person has lived. We see that principle clearly in the life and death of Jesus. In his death, he demonstrated all of the same character qualities he displayed in life, only more so.

He approached his death with prayer and obedience, saying to the Father, "Let it not be as I will, but as you will." He submitted to the humiliating death of a common criminal, demonstrating the humble heart of a true servant. He endured suffering without complaint. During his agony of death, his thoughts were of others. He demonstrated love toward his mother, compassion toward the repentant thief on the cross and forgiveness toward his tormentors.

By exemplifying authentic character to his very last breath, Jesus showed us how we should live and how we should die. His death was as exemplary as his life. He never wasted anything, not even his suffering. He taught us that living a good and righteous life is the only way to prepare for death. In the words of St. Vincent de Paul, the seventeenth-century champion of the poor, "To die like Jesus, it is necessary to live like Jesus."

Those who knew Jesus best tell us we should copy his life and his death. "Jesus the Messiah suffered for you," his disciple Peter wrote to the early Christians. "He left you an example, intending that you should follow in his footsteps." The disciple John wrote, "We know the meaning of love because Jesus loved us and gave his life for us. So we should follow his example and give our lives for each other."

Jesus willingly laid aside his own life in order to accomplish the mission God had given him. He submitted to torture and death in the absolute certainty that he was returning to the Father. Yes, he faced a time of intense loneliness when he cried out to a dark and silent sky, "My God, my God, why have you abandoned me?"

His life, however, didn't end in that loneliness. Sometime later, he offered his final, peaceful prayer. "Father," he said, "I place my spirit in your hands. It is finished."

His suffering was finished. His life was finished. His mission on Earth was successfully concluded.

Though the death of Jesus was horrifying, heartbreaking and unimaginably gruesome, it can truly be said that the death of Jesus was not a tragedy. Though Jesus died young, at age thirty-three, his life wasn't taken away from him. He gave it willingly. His life was not ended. It was completed. His mission was not terminated. It was accomplished.

Most important of all, Jesus knew that death was not the end of his spirit. We can die like Jesus if we have the same confidence of a life beyond this life. We can die like Jesus if we can say, as he did, "Father, I place my spirit in your hands."

When we die, we do not go into a hole in the ground. The body may be buried, but our spirit is in the hands of God. We do not vanish into a dark void. When we die, we fall into the gentle hands of our loving Father.

If we have committed our lives to trusting in Jesus, to being like Jesus and dying like Jesus, then his message to us is the same as his message to the repentant thief on the cross: "I tell you the truth, you and I will soon be together in the gardens of heaven."

CHAPTER EIGHTEEN

HOW TO CONQUER LIKE JESUS

esus was crucified at about nine in the morning and he died at three in the afternoon. The body of Jesus was claimed that evening by two men who had been secret disciples. These two men were wealthy and powerful members of the religious community. While Jesus was alive, they had feared what would happen to them if anyone found out that they were followers of Jesus.

Now Jesus was dead. Somehow, all the things these men once valued—wealth, power, prestige—no longer mattered. They didn't care what people might think of them or say about them. They didn't even care what the religious leaders or the Roman government might do to them.

So these two men came out of hiding and publicly declared that they were followers of Jesus of Nazareth. They went to Pontius Pilate and asked permission to take the body of Jesus and give it a proper burial. It was an unusual request. As a gruesome reminder to other law-breakers, the bodies of crucified criminals were usually left on their crosses to rot. However, Pilate agreed to turn over the body of Jesus to them.

One of these two men was Joseph, from the town of Arimathea. The other was Nicodemus—the same Nicodemus who had once visited Jesus by night and asked him for the secret of eternal life.

Joseph and Nicodemus went outside of Jerusalem and pried the nails out of the wrists and feet of Jesus, then they eased the body to the ground. They wrapped the body in a linen cloth along with a hundred pounds of costly aromatic spices and they placed the body in a tomb. The tomb had been freshly cut out of the solid stone of a hillside, and it was surrounded by a garden. It was a rich man's tomb—the tomb that Joseph of Arimathea had originally purchased for himself.

In life and in death, Jesus owned nothing. When he was born, he slept in a borrowed manger. When he traveled, he stayed in borrowed homes. He rode into Jerusalem on a borrowed donkey. He ate the last supper with his disciples in a borrowed room. When he wanted to make a point about whether or not it was right to pay taxes, he even had to borrow a coin. Now, in death, he was laid in a borrowed tomb.

Should we have expected different? This man who claimed to be the King of the Jews lived and died as a humble servant, owning nothing.

As Joseph and Nicodemus prepared the body of Jesus for burial, a group of women approached the tomb. Standing in the garden, they watched and wept. These were the women who were with Jesus as he hung on the cross.

One of them was Mary, of the village of Magdala, whom Jesus had delivered from demon possession. On this day, Mary's soul was dark with grief and despair. Her Master was dead, and she felt as if her own life

> *Mary Magdalene was the first person to tell the good news that Jesus was alive again. She was a plain, ordinary woman who dared to obey.*
>
> Sandy Smith
> INSPIRATIONAL SPEAKER

was over. How could she know—how could she possibly imagine—the strange and thrilling event that was about to sweep her up and transform her life?

Could It Have Been Jesus?

The day after Jesus was buried, the chief priests and the Pharisees returned to Pontius Pilate and demanded to speak to him. When Pilate came out to meet them, his face was drawn and his eyes were bloodshot. He had not slept well.

"What do you want from me now?" he asked.

"Sir," one of the high priests said, "we have just remembered that this imposter who claimed to be the Messiah had promised he would rise again on the third day. So we ask you to secure the tomb, so his disciples cannot come and steal the body, then claim he has risen from the dead. If such a thing were to happen, this new lie would be more troublesome than all the lies he told when he was alive."

Pilate sighed. "That's your problem, not mine. You have

guards for your Temple, don't you? Send some of them to the tomb and secure the entrance with a large stone, then have the guards stand watch."

With that, Pilate dismissed the priests. The religious leaders went away and had a massive stone rolled over the entrance of the tomb. They placed a Temple guard to make sure that the stone was not tampered with.

At dawn on the first day of the week—the third day after the Crucifixion—Mary of Magdala and several other women came to the tomb. They had brought more sweet spices and perfumed oils, and they wanted to anoint the body again. They arrived at the garden by the tomb expecting to find the entrance sealed and watched by Temple guards.

Instead, they found that the tomb was open and the stone was rolled away. The guards were gone.

With wonder, they crept to the mouth of the tomb and looked inside. On a stone slab where the body of Jesus had lain, they could see linen burial cloths arranged as if the body had simply evaporated out of them!

"Why do you look for the living among the dead?" said a voice.

Startled, the women turned and saw two men in brilliant white clothing.

"Don't be afraid," one of the men said. "You seek Jesus of Nazareth, who was crucified. But, he isn't here."

"Go tell Peter and the disciples that he is risen," said the other.

Trembling and afraid, the women ran from the tomb,

but most of them were too afraid to do as they were told. Only Mary of Magdala did as the man in white clothing told them to do. She went back to the house where Simon Peter and the other disciples were huddled together. "Come and see!" she said. "The Master's body is no longer in the tomb!"

Peter and John dashed to the tomb with Mary. John arrived first and stood at the opening, staring. Peter arrived moments later, out of breath, and went inside the tomb. Everything appeared just as Mary had described it. The body was gone, but so were the two men in white clothing.

The two disciples didn't know what it all meant, but they knew that the rest of the disciples needed to be told. Peter and John returned to the house in the city, leaving Mary of Magdala at the tomb.

As Mary stood outside the tomb, she wondered what had happened. The two men in white clothing had told her that Jesus had risen from the dead. If that was true, where was he?

No. It couldn't be true. Mary had heard his last words, and she had seen him die. She had watched his body being prepared for burial, smothered in spices and perfumed oils, then bound up in yards and yards of burial cloth. She couldn't believe that he was alive again. She refused to get her hopes up.

"Woman," said a nearby voice, "why are you crying so?"

Mary looked at the man who had spoken, but she

> *We live and die. Christ died and lived!*
>
> John Stott
> BIBLE SCHOLAR AND AUTHOR

didn't recognize him through her tears. Assuming he was the caretaker of the garden, she said, "Sir, if you have taken the body of Jesus from here, please tell me where I can find him."

"Mary!" the man said to her.

Her eyes went wide with recognition. "Master!" she gasped.

Standing before her was the last person in the world she expected to see.

Who did Mary see? Could it truly have been Jesus?

The Stranger on the Road

Later that day, two disciples were walking westward from Jerusalem toward the village of Emmaus seven miles away. They were depressed and heavyhearted. They had believed in the Teacher. They had followed him, hung on his words, watched him perform miracles and saw him transform hundreds of lives.

Now it was over. The dream of a coming kingdom had been nailed to a Roman cross. Both the dream and the dreamer were dead.

These two disciples of Jesus talked in low tones as they walked down that road. Sometimes they wept together.

A stranger joined them.

The stranger seemed to catch up to them from behind, though they didn't realize that anyone was following them on the road. The man joined their conversation as they walked. "Who have you been talking about?" he asked.

"Didn't you just come from Jerusalem?" one of the disciples said.

"Don't you know what just happened there?" said the other.

"Tell me about it," the stranger said.

The two disciples exchanged glances. It wasn't safe to be known as a disciple of Jesus. Still, this fellow seemed harmless enough.

"It's about Jesus of Nazareth," said one disciple. "He was a prophet of God who said and did the most amazing things."

"Yes," said the other disciple. "But the chief priests and rulers handed him over to the Gentiles, and they crucified him."

"You believed in this man they crucified?" asked the stranger.

The two disciples hesitated. Dare they admit to a stranger that they had followed Jesus of Nazareth? Finally, one of them boldly answered, "Yes. We were hoping he was the redeemer who would set Israel free. But, they killed him, and that was three days ago."

"I see," the stranger said. "So you no longer believe in this crucified man?"

"We don't know what to believe," one of the pair answered. "Early this morning, a woman who was one of his disciples came from the tomb with an amazing report. She said his body was gone, and she even saw a vision of angels who said that Jesus was alive. Two of the disciples went to see the tomb for themselves, and they found it empty, but they saw no angels and no sign of Jesus himself."

"I'm amazed at your lack of understanding," said the stranger. "Don't you believe what the prophets have told you about the Messiah? Don't you know that it was necessary for the Messiah to suffer and die before entering his place of majesty?"

As they walked together, the stranger explained the prophecies about the Messiah that were written in the Jewish Scriptures. He recited passages from almost every Book of Scripture, from Genesis to Malachi.

He reminded them that the sufferings of the Messiah were predicted as far back as the Garden of Eden. After the Serpent led the human race into sin, God told the Serpent, "I will place hatred between you and the woman, and between your offspring and her offspring. And he— the woman's offspring—will strike you on the head, and you will strike him on his heel."

The stranger explained that the Serpent was Satan, the woman's offspring was the Messiah and Satan succeeded only in wounding Messiah's "heel" when Messiah was crucified. Yet, at the very moment Messiah was wounded on the cross, he conquered Satan, crushing the Serpent's head and destroying the power of sin.

"So, my friends," the stranger concluded, "God himself spoke through the prophets in the Scriptures. Again and again, the prophets told us that Messiah would suffer and die. Why, then, are you dismayed? Why does your faith waver when everything has happened exactly as the prophets foretold?"

It was almost dark when they reached the village of Emmaus. "I must go on," the stranger said to the two disciples. "I have friends in another place, and it's important that I talk to them."

"Please," the two travelers said, "stay with us tonight. The day is spent. You can have a meal with us and get a fresh start in the morning."

The stranger paused to consider, then said, "Thank you. I'll share your table tonight."

That evening, as they sat together at the supper table, the stranger took bread, gave thanks to God for it, broke it and handed a piece to each of the two disciples. At that instant, their eyes were opened, and they suddenly knew that the stranger was no stranger at all. He was the Teacher himself!

In that instant, the Teacher vanished from their sight.

The two disciples looked at each other in amazement. "Didn't our hearts burn inside us," one of them said, "while he talked with us on the road?"

"Yes!" said the other. "And the truth of the Messiah became so clear when he explained it to us from the Scriptures."

Could it truly have been Jesus the two disciples saw on the road to Emmaus?

> *It was only in the light of Easter that the disciples understood Jesus' work and intention; they now realized that the Messiah had to undergo rejection and suffering, that he was to conquer not Rome but death and evil.*
>
> Otto Betz
> PHILOSOPHER AND AUTHOR

Does a Ghost Have Flesh and Bones?

The two disciples immediately got up, left Emmaus and hurried back to Jerusalem. It took a little over two hours of brisk walking to reach the house where the rest of the disciples were staying. The disciples were still reeling from the death of Jesus, still drowning in guilt and shame over having abandoned him in Gethsemane, and still wondering about the meaning of the empty tomb.

When the two disciples arrived and told their story—that they had just seen Jesus alive, and he had talked to them about himself from the Jewish Scriptures—the other disciples didn't know what to think. Could it be true? Or was it just a hallucination?

The disciples had received a similar report from Mary of Magdala. She, too, claimed to have seen Jesus, though she hadn't recognized him at first. If it was true, why didn't Jesus show himself to all of them? As they debated the meaning of these reports—the Teacher himself appeared! He stood among them, smiling broadly, as if he had been with them all along. "Peace to all of you!" he said.

The disciples felt anything but peaceful! Startled and terrified, they thought they saw a ghost!

Observing the fear in their eyes, the Teacher spread his hands before them. The nail wounds were clearly visible. "Why are you frightened?" he asked. "Look at my hands and feet! Look at the wounds of the nails! Touch me. See? Does a ghost have flesh and bones?"

The disciples gathered around him, their eyes and hearts full of wonder.

"Do you have anything to eat?" the Teacher asked. They set a platter of broiled fish before him, and he ate it.

Then he said, "Everything that has happened while I was with you, and everything that is going to happen, is being accomplished to fulfill the Law of Moses, the books of the prophets and the Psalms. Don't you remember that I told you that the Son of Man must suffer and die, then rise again on the third day? And now you are witnesses of all the things I promised, and all that the Scriptures predicted. Soon I will send you out into the world, just as the Father has sent me."

> *Christ stands for Life, and his Resurrection should give convincing proof that God is not satisfied with any "cycle of life" that ends in death. He will go to any extent—he did go to any extent—to break that cycle.*
>
> Philip Yancey
> AUTHOR AND JOURNALIST

Then he was gone! He vanished as suddenly as he had appeared.

Could it truly have been Jesus that these disciples saw?

A Skeptic Convinced

One man who was not present when the Teacher appeared to the disciples was Thomas Didymus (Thomas the Twin). He arrived at the house sometime after the Teacher had left. The disciples all told him, "We have seen the Master! He was here!" Thomas, though, wouldn't—couldn't—believe. "Unless I see the nail wounds with my own eyes," he said, "I'll never believe it's true!"

That statement is why he has come to be known as "Doubting Thomas." But is that fair? After all, the other disciples got to see the nail wounds with their own eyes. They had seen the *proof* that the Master was dead, and that he lived again.

Perhaps the problem Thomas struggled with was not so much doubt as it was pessimism. He was, after all, the melancholy cynic of the group, the one who had once said, "Let's go with Jesus so that we can be martyred with him!" When Jesus was arrested, tried and executed, Thomas probably thought to himself, *I knew this would all end in failure! I just knew it! Didn't I tell everyone that Jesus would be martyred—and us with him?*

I suspect that Thomas was chosen as a disciple precisely because Jesus needed a pessimist in the group—a cynic, a prophet of doom. Jesus probably looked at Thomas and said, "If I can make a believer out of this fellow, I can make a believer out of anyone! If people see that a wet blanket like Thomas can be transformed into a fired-up apostle for the

From my youth onwards I have found in Jesus my great brother. That Christianity has regarded and does regard him as God and Savior has always appeared to me a fact of the highest importance which, for his sake and my own, I must endeavor to understand.

Martin Buber
JEWISH PHILOSOPHER
AND THEOLOGIAN

kingdom, then they will be convinced that my kingdom is for real."

So eight days later, the Teacher appeared again at the house of the disciples, and this time, Thomas was with them. "Peace to all of you!" the Teacher said.

Thomas stared in shock.

"Reach out and touch my wounds," the Teacher said. "Let go of your skepticism and believe!"

Thomas didn't need to touch the wounds. The proof of his eyes convinced him. "My Master," he said, "and my God!"

"Thomas," the Teacher said, "is it because you have seen me that you now trust in me? Those who trust in me without seeing me will be especially blessed."

Could it truly have been Jesus whom Thomas the pessimist met that day?

Follow Me!

When Jesus was with his disciples on the night he was betrayed, he predicted that one would betray him, the rest would desert him and Peter would three times deny him. "But after I have risen," Jesus added, "I will go to Galilee and meet you there."

So, a few days after the Teacher appeared to the disciples in Jerusalem, the disciples journeyed north into Galilee, the region in northern Israel where they had first met him. They went to Capernaum, reasoning that Jesus would probably come to them in his adopted hometown. But days passed, and Jesus did not appear.

Finally, Simon Peter said to the other disciples, "I'm going out to fish on the lake." Some of the others said, "We'll go with you."

Peter had been a fisherman before Jesus came into his life. Now it appeared that Jesus was gone—and perhaps he would never come back. The weight of those three awful denials still weighed heavily on Peter's soul. He had failed miserably as a disciple of Jesus. Perhaps it was time to return to his trade and get on with his life.

So Peter set out in his boat upon the Lake of Galilee. The disciples who went with him were Thomas Didymus, Nathanael, James, John and two others.

They left the shore at dusk and were out all night. When dawn came, they were still on the lake, but their nets were empty—they hadn't caught a single fish. Grim-faced and disheartened, they headed back toward shore.

As they got within a hundred yards of the shore, they saw a man standing on the beach. "Friends," the stranger called out to them, "haven't you caught any fish?"

"No," Simon Peter shouted back. "None at all."

"Drop your net on the right side of the boat," the stranger replied. "You'll catch some fish."

Peter stared in surprise at the stranger on the beach. For a moment, he thought that the man on the shore was— No, it couldn't be.

"Right side of the boat, left side of the boat," Thomas scoffed. "What difference does it make to the fish where we drop our nets? If there are no fish, there are no fish."

"Who is that man?" Nathanael asked. "And what does he think he can teach us about our own business?"

"I'm bone tired," John said. "We've been out all night. Let's go ashore."

Peter stood at the rail, staring toward the shore. "Do what the stranger says."

"Huh?" said several disciples at once.

"Do it," Peter said. "Drop the net on the right side of the boat."

Together, they lifted the net and dropped it over the side. In seconds, the net was filling with fish. Wide-eyed, the men pulled on the net, but it was so full they couldn't lift it into the boat. Hundreds of fish, their silver scales flashing in the early morning sunlight, flopped and wriggled in the net.

As the other disciples tugged at the net, John stood staring toward shore. "It's him!" he said in a hoarse whisper. "It's the Master!"

Peter nodded. "I knew it was him!" he said. "I knew it!" In an instant, Peter shed his outer garment, leaped over the side of the boat and swam toward the shore.

The other disciples followed in the boat, towing the overloaded net behind them. When they reached the shore, Peter ran out to them and helped them beach the boat and drag the net ashore. The disciples stared at the net in amazement. As full as it was, the net was not torn.

Peter led them up the beach to where the Teacher sat beside a fire pit. The Teacher had a few fish skewered on sticks and roasting over the fire, plus some bread wrapped in linen cloth. He said to them, "Bring some of the fish you've just caught."

The disciples added some of their catch to the fish that were already roasting. When the skin of the fish was crackling-crisp and the flesh was tender, Jesus said, "Let's have breakfast."

The Teacher took the bread, broke it and passed it out to the disciples. He then did the same with the fish.

When they had finished their breakfast, the Teacher looked Peter in the eye and called him by his *old* name. "Simon, son of Jonah, do you truly love me more than they do?" The Teacher pointed to the other disciples.

Peter hung his head and hesitated before answering. The Teacher had used a powerful word: *love*. Peter wanted to say that he loved Jesus, but how could he? He remembered the boast he had made in front of all the other disciples. "Even if all the rest desert you, I never will." Yet, just hours after making that boast, he had denied Jesus three times. How do you say "I love you" to someone you have abandoned and denied?

"Master," he said, "you know that I—I *care* about you very much."

Jesus looked away. He seemed to think about Peter's answer for a long time. Finally, he said, "Feed my lambs."

Peter nodded silently.

Several minutes passed.

"Simon, son of Jonah," the Teacher said again, "do you truly love me?"

Peter winced. The Teacher had said that word *love* again. It was a word that was used to speak of love for God—a love that is perfect, flawless, unfailing, devoted. That word was like a hot needle in Peter's conscience.

"Master," Peter answered haltingly, the words catching in his throat, "you know that I—I am your friend."

The Teacher sighed. "Shepherd my sheep," he said.

Peter nodded sadly.

Several more minutes passed.

"Simon, son of Jonah," the Teacher said again, "do you truly care about me? Are you truly my friend?"

This question stung Peter more than the first two. This time, the Teacher hadn't even used the word *love,* and it hurt Peter to know that the Teacher saw him as the failure he was. Peter talked big, but he folded under pressure. He had even denied Jesus with an oath, with a horrible curse!

Maybe he was cursed. Maybe he had truly proven himself unworthy of calling himself a follower of Jesus. Finally, with his third question, the Teacher had grasped the truth about Peter: The rugged fisherman could not be trusted. His love didn't stand up under pressure. The name Peter—the Rock—was a lie, a cruel joke.

"Do you care about me, Simon? Are you truly my friend?" The Teacher was waiting for an answer.

"Master," Peter replied, "you know everything about me. You see right through me. You know how weak I am. You know how many times I've failed you. But you also know that I care about you. I am your friend."

The Teacher smiled. "Feed my sheep," he said.

Peter nodded.

"Peter," the Teacher said, "you failed me, but that is in the past. You are still Peter. You are still my rock. As a young man, you dress yourself as you please, and you come and go as you please. But a day will come when you will put out your hands, and someone will place manacles on them. You'll be made to wear the clothing of a prisoner, and you'll be forced to go where you do not wish to go— but you will go for my sake. Peter, you do love me. I know you do. Next time, Peter, you will not deny me, you will not desert me. You will be my rock when it truly counts."

Peter's emotions were a swirl of fear and wonder. The Teacher had just given him a glimpse of a future that frightened him, but also comforted him. Yes, it was a prophecy of persecution and imprisonment and possibly even execution, but it was also a prophecy in which Peter would stand firm for his Master's sake. The next time, there would be no denial, no desertion.

> *Based on overwhelming historical evidence, Christians believe that Jesus was bodily resurrected in time and space by the supernatural power of God. The difficulties of belief may be great, but the problems inherent in unbelief present even greater difficulties.*
>
> Josh McDowell
> SPEAKER AND AUTHOR

As Peter was thinking about everything he had just heard, the Teacher said to him the same words he'd said the first time they met. "Follow me!"

Could it truly have been the crucified and risen Jesus who repeated his call, "Follow me"?

Could a dead man live again? Could it be possible?

Jesus Conquered Death

Thomas Jefferson was offended by the idea of the Resurrection of Jesus. The author of the Declaration of Independence believed that Jesus was a good teacher and a great man. Jefferson, however, did not believe that miracles, such as the Resurrection, were possible. So he took a pair of scissors and physically cut all the miracles, including the Resurrection, out of his Bible.

In the writing of this book, one fact has impressed itself upon me again and again: You cannot separate the miraculous from the life of Jesus. You cannot understand Jesus unless you believe in miracles. If you tried, like Jefferson, to grasp the personality of Jesus while editing out his miracles, you are left with a distorted and disfigured picture of Jesus.

We cannot be like Jesus unless we know what Jesus was really like, so we cannot be like Jesus if our image of him is based on a distorted and incomplete picture of his life and personality. The miracles of Jesus are not just add-ons that can be neatly lifted out of his life with his personality and his teachings intact. His miracles, his teachings and his personality are a seamless whole.

It's not hard for me to believe in miracles. I've seen things take place in my own life and the lives of people around me that can only be attributed to the power of God. In fact, the existence of our universe is nothing short of miraculous. No one can explain how everything that exists could spontaneously appear out of nothing, a completely uncaused event. Yet, miraculously, our universe does exist, and no one can explain it. So I believe that the universe itself is one of God's miracles—and so is the Resurrection.

I can't explain the Resurrection, but the evidence forces me to believe that the Resurrection actually did take place at a particular moment in time in a particular geographical location outside of Jerusalem.

What evidence?

1. *The Gospels.* I believe that the Gospels of Matthew, Mark, Luke and John are a reliable account of the life of Jesus. They were written within two to five decades of the Crucifixion. Matthew, Mark and Luke are dated at between A.D. 50 and 65, while John's Gospel was written at around A.D. 80 to 95. In the past, some critics have claimed that John's Gospel was a forgery written around A.D. 190, and that it was not the eyewitness account of the apostle John. They based their belief on the "fact" that the author had certain details wrong and had invented locations in Jerusalem that didn't exist.

Recent archaeological discoveries, however, uncovered the actual ruins of such sites as Jacob's Well (where Jesus met the Samaritan woman; see chapter 5) and the Pool of Bethesda (where Jesus healed a disabled man; see chapter 11). Jerusalem was destroyed by the Romans in A.D. 70, so a later writer could not have known about the Pool of

Bethesda and other sites John mentions. Only a contemporary of Jesus could have known. In addition, the discovery of the Rylands Fragment, a papyrus fragment of the Gospel of John that was found in Egypt, has been reliably dated at around A.D. 115 to 130, so John's gospel clearly couldn't have been written as late as A.D. 190.

The four Gospels have been shown to be reliable and historically accurate, and they tell us the story of an actual historical person known as Jesus of Nazareth.

2. *The empty tomb.* The religious leaders, recalling that Jesus had predicted his own Resurrection, had guards placed at the tomb to prevent any tampering. Despite these precautions, the women who went to the tomb found the stone rolled away and the tomb empty. All four Gospels clearly state this to be so.

One of the most moving experiences I have ever had was a trip I took to Israel. During that journey, I saw the places where Jesus walked and talked, and the places where he died and rose again. I looked up from the Jerusalem bus terminal and saw the place of the skull, the hill called Calvary, and it is just as the Gospel accounts describe it. I have visited the empty tomb—at least, it is a tomb that many historians think was the actual tomb of Jesus.

The story of the empty tomb is also found in secular accounts. Jewish historian Flavius Josephus wrote one account in his *Antiquities* (book 18, chapter 3):

> At this time there was a wise man who was called Jesus. And his conduct was good, and [he] was known to be virtuous. And many people from among the Jews and the other nations became his disciples. Pilate condemned him to be crucified and to die. And those who had become his disciples did not abandon their discipleship. They reported that he had appeared to them three days after his crucifixion and that he was alive; accordingly, he was perhaps the Messiah, concerning whom the prophets have recounted wonders.[1]

The Roman historian Tacitus wrote in his *Annals* (book XV) that the Roman emperor Nero blamed the great fire of Rome in A.D. 64 on a group called "Christians"—followers of the crucified Jesus of Nazareth. Tacitus recorded the following account of the Resurrection:

> Nero fastened the guilt and inflicted the most exquisite tortures on a class hated for their abominations, called Christians by the populace. Christus [Jesus of Nazareth], from whom the name had its origin, suffered the extreme penalty [crucifixion] during the reign of Tiberius at the hands of one of our procurators, Pontius Pilatus, and a most mischievous superstition [the story of the Resurrection], thus checked for the moment, again broke out not only in

---

[1] From the tenth-century Arabic translation into English by Shlomo Pines, *An Arabic Version of the Testimonium Flavianum and Its Implications* (Jerusalem: Israel Academy of Sciences and Humanities, 1971), 69.

Judaea, the first source of the evil, but even in Rome.[2]

The Christian religion began in the city of Jerusalem, in the very city where Jesus was crucified and buried. The burial tomb belonged to a prominent and influential member of the Sanhedrin, Joseph of Arimathea. His tomb would have been easy for any citizen of first-century Jerusalem to locate and inspect. Without question, many people did visit the tomb and found it empty. The evidence of the empty tomb was powerful and convincing proof.

3. *The rapid spread of first-century Christianity.* Just a few years after the Crucifixion, Christianity had spread far beyond Judea and far beyond Palestine. It spread like a flood of love and hope, moving north into Asia Minor, Greece, Italy and Spain. It spread south into Egypt, Ethiopia and across North Africa. Before the end of the first century, it had even spread as far east as India.

Why did Christianity spread so rapidly? In part because the fact of the Resurrection was so convincingly validated. There were literally thousands of people who had seen and heard Jesus during his three-year ministry, and hundreds who claimed to have seen him alive after his Resurrection. There was an empty

---

[2] *The Annals of Publius Cornelius Tacitus,* translated by Alfred John Church and William Jackson Brodribb, Modern Library edition of Church and Brodribb's text, published as *The Complete Works of Tacitus,* electronically retrieved at *classics.mit.edu/Tacitus/annals.11.xv.html.*

tomb just outside the walls of Jerusalem. The eyewitness evidence was overwhelming.

4. *Transformed lives.* How do you explain the transformation of the disciples? Immediately after the Crucifixion, they were disillusioned, depressed, hiding behind locked doors, afraid of their own shadows. They were convinced that their cause was lost, their Master dead. Then, three days after the Crucifixion, those same disciples came roaring out of hiding, preaching with joy and excitement that their Master had risen from the dead! There is no other explanation for the dramatic transformation of these lives. They believed that what they saw and experienced was real, that Jesus was alive, and that he was, therefore, the Messiah.

5. *Courage under persecution.* The Christian movement grew exponentially in those early years despite intense opposition, ridicule, persecution and torture. The religious rulers persecuted the early Christians with the same hatred and vindictiveness they had shown Jesus himself. The persecution that came from Rome was even worse. Tacitus recorded some of the tortures Nero inflicted on the Christians in Rome. Some were torn apart by wild animals. Others were crucified. Still others were covered with tar, then the tar was ignited and the Christians were burned alive as human torches to illuminate Nero's gardens at night.

History records that all of the apostles died martyrs' deaths except John, who was exiled to the Mediterranean island of Patmos. Most underwent torture. They all claimed to have seen Jesus alive after the Crucifixion. Certainly, they must have believed their own claim, because who would risk torture and execution for the sake of a hoax? They took that risk because they were absolutely convinced of the Resurrection. In fact, they were *eyewitnesses* to the Resurrection.

I have looked at the evidence, and I am convinced that the Resurrection of Jesus Christ is a historical fact. I am convinced that Jesus conquered death.

> *The unbelieving mind would not be convinced by any proof, and the worshiping heart needs none.*
> A. W. Tozer
> PASTOR AND AUTHOR

If Jesus conquered death, then you and I can conquer death as well.

In fact, we can conquer a lot *more* than death.

How to Conquer Like Jesus

Look at some of the other conquerors in the story of Jesus.

Mary of Magdala watched Jesus suffer and die. She heard the awful loneliness in his voice when he cried out, "My God, my God, why have you abandoned me?" She heard him speak his last words, "Father, I place my spirit in your hands. It is finished." She saw him draw his last tortured breath, and then she saw his body hang limp and still in death.

Mary of Magdala was also one of the women who went to the tomb to anoint his linen-wrapped body with costly spices and perfumes. She was given a special privilege: Of all the disciples and followers of Jesus, she was the first to actually see and speak with the risen Jesus.

Who was Mary of Magdala? There is a tradition that she was a prostitute before she met Jesus, but I doubt that this is so. There is no mention anywhere in the four Gospels that she was ever a prostitute. All we really know about her is that she came from the village of Magdala, near the Lake of Galilee, and that Jesus commanded seven demons out of her. This fact is actually mentioned only in passing in the Gospels, with the story of her deliverance from evil spirits never actually told.

So how did Mary of Magdala conquer like Jesus?

Through Jesus, she conquered her inner demons. We often hear people use that metaphor—"he's wrestling with his inner demons." Those inner demons might be an addiction, an obsession, a compulsion, a sense of guilt or inadequacy, or a sense of meaninglessness or hopelessness. A person who is driven by inner demons is a person whose emotional and spiritual life is out of control.

In the case of Mary of Magdala, her inner demons were not a metaphor. They were *real*, and they were evil spirits! She was powerless to control them. Instead, they controlled her. They drove her to do what she didn't want to do.

You may be having the same sense of powerlessness over something in your life: alcohol, drugs, smoking, gambling, pornography, illicit sex, shame, guilty memories, fear of death, a sense of worthlessness. Whatever your inner demons may be, you can conquer them through Jesus, just as Mary of Magdala did. You can't command those demons out of yourself, but if you go to Jesus as Mary did, he can command those demons out of your life.

Next, there was Thomas Didymus. He wrestled with pessimism, cynicism, skepticism and doubt. He had to see in order to believe. How was he able to conquer like Jesus?

After the Resurrection, Jesus appeared to all the other disciples except Thomas. Why was Thomas the only one who wasn't there? I suspect it's because Jesus knew that Thomas needed a little extra attention. He had a problem with pessimism and doubt, and he needed an extra measure of convincing. The testimony of eyewitnesses didn't satisfy him. He wanted to see Jesus with his own eyes. He wanted to touch the nail wounds with his own hands.

So Jesus made a point of showing up when Thomas wasn't there! Of all the people to be absent on that occasion, it had to be Thomas Didymus, the noted skeptic. When did Jesus finally return and reveal himself to Thomas? Eight days later! For a whole week and a day, Jesus let Thomas stew in his own juices. Thomas had to listen to the excited stories of the other disciples while he sat in a corner thinking his pessimistic thoughts. Everyone else was happy about the Resurrection of Jesus. All

Thomas could do was grumble, "Why wasn't I here? How could I have missed it?"

After eight days alone with his gloomy thoughts, Thomas got the surprise of his life: Jesus appeared to him! In fact, Jesus went out of his way to reveal himself specifically to Thomas.

Are you doubtful about the Resurrection? Are you pessimistic about life? Do you feel you are the odd person out, that you have missed out on the life that everyone around you seems so excited about? Well, you're not alone. Thomas Didymus is right there with you.

I have a feeling that, when the time is right, Jesus is going to come calling on you, just as he called on Thomas. When you least expect it, he'll surprise you and say, "Here I am! Reach out to me! Let go of your skepticism and believe!"

Of course, he won't come to you visibly. You won't be able to actually see him with your eyes or touch him with your hands, but you won't need to. He'll be real to you nonetheless, and he has a special word of commendation for you that even Thomas could not receive: "Those who trust in me without seeing me will be especially blessed."

The fact that Jesus made a special trip to convince Thomas tells me that he has a special place in his heart for doubters. He knows how hard it is for some people to believe. He's patient and kind to those who struggle with faith. He knows it isn't easy to believe in what you can't see. With his help, however, you'll conquer even your doubts and questions.

Thomas conquered like Jesus. Through the Resurrection of Jesus, he was able to conquer his doubts, his pessimism and his skepticism. So will you.

Finally, there was Peter. He wrestled with his own impetuous and unstable nature. He was up one moment and down the next. He tended to speak and act without thinking, and his neurotic impulsiveness repeatedly got him into trouble.

In the Garden of Gethsemane, after Jesus was arrested, all of Peter's impetuous boasts dissolved away, his spine turned to jelly, his heart shriveled up inside him. He ran away and left Jesus to face his enemies alone. Later, he denied Jesus, and not because he was being questioned by a big Roman soldier with a sword in his hand. The person who questioned him was a mere servant girl! She was no more than a teenager, yet her questions terrorized him!

After the Crucifixion, Peter was filled with shame, guilt and self-loathing. He could hardly stand living in his own skin. The memory of his failure was always on his mind. When Jesus asked him, "Simon, do you truly love me?" Peter couldn't face him, couldn't answer the question, couldn't use the word *love.*

But the Bible records, and history confirms, that after Jesus reinstated Peter on that morning beside the Lake of Galilee, Peter was *transformed.* He ultimately became the rock that Jesus had always envisioned him to be. After that time, Peter became a bold and effective messenger for the story of Jesus. Thousands of lives were changed by Peter's message, and the course of history was changed as well. In the end, as Jesus predicted, Peter was martyred for his faith. He stood firm, like a rock. Through his faith in Jesus, Peter overcame his guilt, fears, failures, impetuousness and neurotic instability.

We all wrestle with character flaws, weaknesses, failures, bitter memories, guilt and shame. We all have episodes in our lives we wish we could go back and change. We all remember things we've said and done that continue to haunt us for years, making us feel inadequate and unworthy.

We can conquer all of those self-inflicted emotional wounds the same way Peter did. Jesus knows the times we've let him down, just as Peter let him down. Jesus is patient. He's kind. He wants to heal our bitter memories, mend our character flaws, release us from our guilt and shame. He believes in us more than we believe in ourselves.

Just as Jesus forgave Peter, reinstated him and gave him a job to do— "Feed my sheep" —he has a mission for you and me. He wants to use us to help others, meet the needs of others and reach others with his love. Jesus wants us to be like him, to do his work and spread his message of the kingdom of heaven.

If we want to be like Jesus, then we have to conquer like Jesus. The good news is that we *can* conquer like Jesus. We can even conquer death as he did.

How?

By answering the same call Jesus gave Peter: "Follow me."

A PERSONAL EPILOGUE

I answered the call to follow Jesus on Thursday, February 22, 1968.

Until that day, the only religion I knew was sports, especially baseball. One of my dad's best friends when I was growing up was Bob Carpenter, the then-owner of the Philadelphia Phillies. So, I grew up around a Major League ballpark, and I lived and breathed baseball.

After a brief career as a catcher in the minor leagues, I moved to Spartanburg, South Carolina, to be the general manager of a minor league baseball team, the Spartanburg Phillies. I was twenty-four years old, and my goal was to succeed as a minor league executive and move up and conquer the world of Major League Baseball.

I worked hard and experienced some early successes. I won acclaim from my boss and from the community. I turned a shabby, rundown ballpark into a sparkling showplace, and I turned a struggling franchise into a winning team. I won awards. I drove a nice car and had all the money I wanted. What's more, my early successes were catching the eye of the Phillies' front office and the national media, and I knew that it was just a matter of time before I started moving up the ladder to even greater successes.

So with everything I had going for me, I was surprised that I didn't feel satisfied. Instead, I felt restless and empty. All my life, I had assumed that happiness came from achieving your goals and succeeding in life. Yet with each new triumph, each new award, I discovered that my sense of satisfaction faded long before the newspaper clippings turned yellow. I was in constant pursuit of happiness, but I never seemed to catch up to it.

My boss, the owner of the Spartanburg ball club, was a man named R. E. Littlejohn. Everyone called him "Mr. R. E." He was a wealthy, successful businessman and, unlike me, he seemed completely content and happy. Yet, the serenity and contentment I saw in him

> *A man who was merely a man and said the sort of things Jesus said would not be a great moral teacher. He would either be a lunatic—on a level with the man who says he is a poached egg—or else he would be the Devil of Hell. You must make your choice. Either this man was, and is, the Son of God; or else a madman or something worse. You can shut him up for a fool, you can spit at him and kill him as a demon; or you can fall at his feet and call him Lord and God. But let us not come with any patronizing nonsense about his being a great human teacher. He has not left that open to us. He did not intend to.*
>
> C. S. Lewis
> SCHOLAR, NOVELIST AND
> LAY THEOLOGIAN

seemed to have nothing to do with his wealth. He was the most impressive person I've ever known, and he was also the most humble and self-effacing.

Mr. R. E. was a follower of Jesus of Nazareth. He often talked about Jesus—not in a preachy or pushy way, but simply as if he was talking about his best friend. I could see that Mr. R. E. was as much like Jesus as any person I had ever known. His integrity, his leadership ability, his commitment to prayer, his loving and forgiving nature, and above all, his servanthood, generosity and humility reminded me so much of Jesus.

I knew that Mr. R. E.'s number-one goal in life was to be like Jesus. One day I told him, "You know, it seems that Jesus must have been a lot like you." I meant it as a compliment, but to his ears, I was speaking sacrilege! I could see that the comparison to Jesus embarrassed him. To my surprise, he rebuked my compliment.

"Don't ever say that about me," he said. "No man has a right to be compared to Jesus."

A Big, Empty Hole Inside

While I was managing the Spartanburg team, I met many other people whose goal in life was to be like Jesus. We brought in Bobby Malkmus, a former big-league infielder, as a player-coach. Bobby was a terrific guy, and he reminded me a lot of Mr. R. E. He didn't chew tobacco or drink or cuss. Though a genuine leader, he was humble and self-effacing. He didn't buttonhole you or preach to you, but he had a soft-spoken, gentle way of telling you about this friend of his named Jesus. I saw the same indefinable *something* in Bobby that I had seen in Mr. R. E. I didn't know what that *something* was, but I wanted it.

For one of our pregame promotions, I brought in Olympic gold medalist Paul Anderson. He was a champion weight lifter, and he accomplished amazing feats of strength: He'd drive a big nail through two wooden planks with his bare hand. He'd lift eighty-five pound dumbbells with his pinkie fingers. He lifted a wooden platform on his back and shoulders while eight of our heaviest ballplayers sat on it. This immense man (5' 9" and 375 pounds) then told the crowd, "I've lifted more weight than anyone in the history of mankind! I once lifted over six thousand pounds in a back lift, and I'm listed in the *Guinness Book of World Records*. I've been declared a wonder of nature from the United States to Russia. They call me the strongest man in the world."

Listening to these boasts, I thought, *Man, this guy's really got an ego!*

"But, I want you to know," he continued, "that I can't get through one minute of my life without Jesus Christ."

In an instant, he went from sounding like an egomaniac to sounding like one of the most humble souls I had ever met.

"The goal of my life," he continued, "is to know Jesus and to become as much like him as I possibly can. Now, if I can't make it through life without Jesus, how can you?"

Amazingly, Paul Anderson didn't say a word about religion. Instead, he talked as if this man Jesus just happened to be his best friend, and he wanted to introduce everybody to him. Like Mr. R. E. and Bobby Malkmus, Paul Anderson had that same indefinable *something,* and I wanted it—but I didn't know what it was or where to find it.

There were so many people who came into my life at that time—people who were committed to becoming like Jesus, and I wanted what they had, I wanted to be like they were. All this Jesus talk I was hearing was getting into my head and under my skin. I was thinking about Jesus all the time. At night, I couldn't sleep because I was thinking about Jesus.

Finally, I decided I had to talk to Mr. R. E. and find out what Jesus was all about and how I could get to know Jesus the way he and Bobby Malkmus and Paul Anderson did. When I arrived at the office, I was surprised to see my roommate, John Gordon, there. John was the radio announcer for our games. I was stunned to find out that John had gone to talk to Mr. R. E. for the same reason I had—to find out how you get to know Jesus! In his own mind and heart, John had heard Jesus saying to him, "Follow me," and he had made a decision to do just that.

I knew that it was my turn, and I wanted to follow Jesus, too. I felt as if the carpenter from Galilee was looking me right in the eye and saying to me, just as he had said to Peter, "Follow me!"

For a moment, I experienced a sense of reluctance. Something inside me was saying, *No, don't surrender control of your life to Jesus! You don't need Jesus. You're okay just the way you are. You don't drink or smoke. You're honest and hardworking. You're doing fine without Jesus.*

In the next instant, however, I knew that I wasn't doing fine. Despite my successes and my awards, my money and my nice car, I was empty inside. I didn't want to go through the rest of my life with that big empty hole inside of me.

> *My one purpose in life is to help people find a personal relationship with God, which, I believe, comes through knowing Jesus.*
> BILLY GRAHAM
> EVANGELIST AND AUTHOR

I knew what I had to do: I had to let go and allow Jesus to set the direction of my life. So I asked Mr. R. E. to pray with me, and he did. I prayed, and I asked Jesus to take control of my life.

At that moment, my struggle for satisfaction in life was over. Jesus had won that battle. I had been conquered by his love and forgiveness, and I have followed him ever since.

Pardon, Peace, Power and Purpose

That was thirty-five years ago as I write these words. Since that day, I have known successes and failures, triumphs and disappointments. I can identify with impulsive, unstable Peter, because I've had many ups and downs in my walk as a follower of Jesus. I won't lie to you—I've failed the Master many times.

Through it all, though, I have experienced a powerful and exciting way of living that I never imagined before I answered that call to follow him. I can summarize my life since that day in four words: *pardon, peace, power and purpose.*

I have experienced God's *pardon* for every wrong I've ever done. I know the freedom of being forgiven, of having my guilt taken away. Like the paralyzed man who was lowered to Jesus from the rooftop (chapter 8), I have heard Jesus say to me, "My son, your sins are forgiven." There are no sweeter words that anyone could hear.

I know the *peace* that God brings even in the most unpleasant and anxious circumstances. It is a peace that transcends human understanding. I have gone through some painful struggles, through periods of uncertainty and testing. However, I never felt I was going through it alone. I never experienced panic or despair. I had peace, because I felt the presence of Jesus alongside me. I had the peace of knowing that, though he was not going to take me *out* of my trials, he would always carry me *through* them.

I know the *power* that comes from following Jesus. He commanded evil spirits with power and authority. He healed with power and authority. He spoke with power and authority. He sent out his disciples with power and authority. I have that same power flowing through me as a twenty-first-century disciple of Jesus. In the years since I answered his call, I have often felt his power in me, enabling me to do things I didn't think possible. His strength works through my weakness, and that is true power.

I have a *purpose* in life. I no longer have to wrestle with such questions as, "What does life mean? Does my life count for anything? Where do I fit in? Where do I come from and where am I going?" I have the peace of knowing that God has a plan for my life. Jesus once said, "I have come so that people may have life, and have it more abundantly." That is what my life is like as his follower—abundant and overflowing. Whatever my triumphs and failures, my joys and sorrows, I am having a wonderful life, a life that overflows with direction and purpose. I know that my life is part of an amazing eternal plan. Yours is, too.

> *You either accept Jesus or reject him. You can analyze Mohammed and Buddha, but don't try it with him. You either accept or you reject.*
>
> Sholem Asch
> YIDDISH NOVELIST AND DRAMATIST

Jesus says, "Follow me!" If you choose to answer that call, you won't necessarily win fame and fortune. You won't be guaranteed a life of ease and luxury. Following Jesus won't lower your cholesterol level or prevent you from getting cancer. When you follow Jesus, you will still have problems to solve and crises to face—but you won't face them alone.

Conquer with Jesus

There was a time when I thought that the years before I answered the call of Jesus were "wasted" years. Then, I made a profound discovery. When you answer the call to follow Jesus, God takes your talents and interests, plus everything you've learned and experienced up to that time. He even takes your trials, mistakes and failures, and he uses them to produce good things in your life. Everything you've gone through is preparation for the day when you make that connection with God. Nothing from your previous life is wasted. It is all valuable. You can conquer the blame and shame of the past if you choose to trust Jesus, follow him and allow his spirit to work through your life.

Another discovery I made is that from the moment I decided to follow Jesus, God planted within my heart a supernatural love. Suddenly, I had love for everyone—for people I had never met before, and even for people I didn't like! I'm convinced that what I have experienced is a supernatural love that mirrors the love of Jesus himself. His love doesn't just flow *to* us, but *through* us, touching the lives of everyone around us. Because Jesus loves and accepts us unconditionally, we can accept others—and ourselves!—the same way.

The all-accepting, unconditional love of Jesus enables us to approach him exactly as we are: flawed, failed and unclean. We don't have to fix ourselves up and clean ourselves out before coming to Jesus. We come to him on an "as-is, where-is" basis, and leave all the fixing, changing and cleansing to him. All we have to do is trust him and follow him.

Near the end of his life, Karl Barth, the famous theologian, was asked what was the most profound theological truth he had discovered in his years of study. He answered, "'Jesus loves me, this I know, for the Bible tells me so.'" I completely agree. There is no more profound truth than that expressed in the children's hymn, "Jesus Loves Me." The love of Jesus is the deepest and most profound truth of my own life and of all human existence. As Jesus hung on that cross, he was calling to us down through the ages, "I love you! I love you! I love you!" Later, after he came out of that tomb, he called to us again, "Follow me!"

Jesus of Nazareth is the conqueror. He has conquered death, and now he is ready to conquer whatever enemies you and I face: our inner demons, our addictions and destructive habits, our obsessions and compulsions, our guilt and shame, our meaninglessness and hopelessness, our pessimism and doubt, our character flaws and failures, our bitter memories of the past, our fear of the future.

You can conquer life and death with Jesus if you choose to be like him and if you respond to his call. Jesus says to you, "Follow me!"

Say yes, my friend, and live forever.

You can contact Pat Williams at:

Pat Williams
c/o Orlando Magic
8701 Maitland Summit Blvd.
Orlando, FL 32810
(407) 916-2404
pwilliams@orlandomagic.com

If you would like to set up a speaking engagement for Pat Williams, please call or write his assistant, Melinda Ethington, at the above address or call her at (407) 916-2454. Requests can also be faxed to (407) 916-2986 or e-mailed to *methington@orlandomagic.com.*

We would love to hear from you. Please send your comments about this book to Pat Williams at the above address.

ACKNOWLEDGMENTS

With deep appreciation, I acknowledge the support and guidance of the following people who helped make this book possible.

Special thanks to Bob Vander Weide and John Weisbrod of the Orlando Magic.

I owe deep gratitude to my assistant, Melinda Ethington, for all she does and continues to do for my family and me.

Hats off to three dependable associates—my adviser, Ken Hussar; Hank Martens of the Orlando Magic mail/copy room; and my ace typist, Fran Thomas.

Hearty thanks are also due to Peter Vegso and his fine staff at Health Communications, Inc., and to my partner in writing this book, Jim Denney. Thank you all for believing that I had something important to share and for providing the support and the forum to say it.

I am also grateful to the following friends who took the time to proofread the final manuscript: John Adams, Mark Atteberry, Dwight Bain, Bill Gothard, Tim Grosshans, Ken Hussar, Dr. Bill Jones, Dr. Wendell Kempton, Dr. Al

Mahwinney, Peg Matthews-Rose, Dr. James Merritt, Don Otis, Robert Spicer, Dr. Jay Strack, Janet Thoma, Dr. Will Varner, Ruth Williams and Dr. Charles Zimmerman.

And, special thanks and appreciation go to my family and my wife, Ruth. They are truly the backbone of my life.

I would like to sincerely thank the people listed below who responded to my request for advice and suggestions as we started this enormous project. I can't thank these people enough for all of the help they offered us. I apologize if we have omitted any names.

John Adams
David D. Allen
Mark Atteberry
Ron Blue
Darrell Bock
Bill Bright
Pete Briscoe
Stuart Briscoe
Mark Brister
Steve Brown
Paul Bubar
Wendell and Joan Calder
Bryan Chapell
Ron Cline
Ray H. Crawford
Mike Cromartie
Dennis J. DeHaan
Jay Dennis

Charlie Duke
Roger Dutromble
Charlie Dyer
Thomas D. Elliff
Tim Ferguson
John Frame
Tom Fries
Bill Gaither
Norm Geisler
Bill Gillham
Bill Glass
Bull Gothard
Franklin Graham
Chuck Green
Wayne Grudem
Steve Harper
O. S. Hawkins
Ken Hemphill

Howard Hendricks
Jim Henry
Kent Hughes
Johnny Hunt
Joel Hunter
Ken Hussar
Jimmy E. Jackson
Roland Jarrard
Jerry B. Jenkins
Dennis E. Johnson
Joe Jordan
Chuck Kelley
Pat Kelly
Wendell Kempton
D. James Kennedy
Karen Kingsbury
Simon Kistemaker
Jimmy Knott
Larry Krieder
Woodrow Kroll
Nate Krupp
Knute Larson
Mike Lawyer
Richard Lee
Duane Litfin
Anne Graham Lotz
Erwin W. Lutzer
John MacArthur
Paul L. Maier

Charlie Martin
Al Mawhinney
John Maxwell
David McCasland
Fred McCormick
Josh McDowell
Larry McFadden
Robertson McQuilkin
Gordon D. Miller
R. Albert Mohler Jr.
Ray A. Naugle
John Ortberg
Luis Palau
Bob Pecord
Roy L. Peterson
Richard A. Powell
Cecil R. Price
Ray Pritchard
Bob Pyne
Pat Robertson
Haddon Robinson
Adrian Rogers
Phil Rolsing
Doug Ross
Jeff Ryan
Skip Ryan
David Sandford
Robert H. Schuller
Robert Schuller Jr.

Renald E. Showers

Dean Smith (Geneva College)

Robert Spicer

R. C. Sproul

Joseph Stowell

Jay Strack

Steve Strope

David Talley

Erik Thoennes

Stanley Toussaint

Ted Traylor

Will Varner

Jerry Vines

Tommy Vinson

Alan Weathers

Douglas Weiss

Richard Wells

Hayes Wicker

Jud Wilhite

Doug Wilson

Danny Wood

Zig Ziglar

Charles Zimmerman

Also from the
How to Be Like series

Code #9551, paper back $12.95

In this extraordinary book you will learn, through Michael's example, how to attain star status in your own life and succeed at any endeavor you set your mind to.

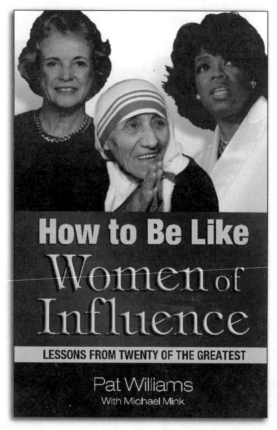